PROFESSOR MICHAEL S NEIBERG

WORLD WAR I

ILLUSTRATED ATLAS

CAMPAIGNS, BATTLES & WEAPONS FROM 1914–1918

PROFESSOR MICHAEL S NEIBERG

WORLD WAR I

ILLUSTRATED ATLAS

CAMPAIGNS, BATTLES & WEAPONS FROM 1914–1918

amber
BOOKS

This Amber edition published in 2023

Reprinted in 2024

First published in 2021

Copyright © 2023 Amber Books Ltd

ISBN: 978-1-83886-354-8

Published by
Amber Books Ltd
United House
North Road
London N7 9DP
United Kingdom

www.amberbooks.co.uk
Facebook: amberbooks
YouTube: amberbooksltd
Instagram: amberbooksltd
X(Twitter): @amberbooks

Editor: Sarah Uttridge
Design: Brian Rust
Cartographer: Malcolm Swanston

Printed in China

All map artworks ©Amber Books Ltd.

CONTENTS

Symbol Guide

XXXXX ▢	Army Group	XX ⊠	Army Division	X ▢	Brigade
XXXX ▢	Army	◩	Cavalry/Mounted	III ▢	Regiment
XXX ⊠	Corps	◖	Armoured	II ▢	Company
II ▣	Artillery	II ⊠	Communication	⚓	Naval
II ⊓	Engineer				

Franz Ferdinand (1863–1914), Archduke of Austria.

BACKGROUND TO WAR

Scholars and historians will likely never agree on what caused World War I to begin in the summer of 1914. Some blame an overly aggressive response to a relatively minor Balkan crisis by German and Austro-Hungarian statesmen. Others argue that the relatively recent unification of Germany and the resurgence of Russia after the revolution of 1905 unbalanced the geopolitics of the continent. Still others argue that the war resulted from simple misperception and poor decision making by key leaders across the continent.

All observers, however, agree that the war utterly shattered the world of 1914 and ushered in massive changes, some of which we are still feeling today. Because the belligerents were empires, the war impacted the entire world, even states that attempted to remain technically neutral.

'Entente Cordiale'
Great Britain's King Edward VII and French President Emile Loubet promoted the 'Entente Cordiale' between their countries in 1903. The Entente buried long-standing grievances and reset the politics of Europe.

Franco-Prussian War
The Franco-Prussian War of 1870–71 made Germany a dominant power in the heart of Europe. Great Britain, France and Russia all sought to balance it by signing collective security pacts.

Assassins of Sarajevo in court, 1914
Gavrilo Princip (front row, centre) and accomplices on trial in a Sarajevo court. By the time he was sentenced in October, the war was about much more than the causes for which he had assassinated Archduke Franz Ferdinand.

Volunteers sign up
Foreign volunteers parading in Paris in July 1914. Leaders in all countries promoted their actions as essentially defensive. In the first few months, most of their subjects and citizens agreed.

Kaiser Wilhelm II
Although not the monster he is sometimes portrayed, Kaiser Wilhelm II certainly lacked a clear understanding of the military and political situation in 1914. His recklessness helped lead to war.

British Territorials march to war
Unlike its continental counterparts, the British Army relied on a small force of regulars. They were supplemented by Territorials like these men answering the call to arms in the first weeks of the conflict, here on 5th August in Croydon, Surrey.

The World 1914

Outside of areas like the Balkans, the map of the world had remained reasonably stable in the years leading up to World War I. Treaties between the great powers had resolved most imperial issues. East Asia, not Europe, seemed to most contemporaries the least stable region.

The world of 1914 was, in modern parlance, fully globalized. Connected by communications and transportation technologies of the Industrial age, goods and people moved relatively freely. Most areas of global tension did not impact the core interests of the great European powers. Thus they found compromises to deal with flashpoints such as Morocco and sub-Saharan Africa. In 1898 the British and French clashed over the oasis of Fashoda in modern-day Sudan. Similarly, the French and Germans clashed over access to the raw materials of Morocco. But these crises were solved peacefully because the great powers saw nothing worth fighting for in them.

The imperial borders of Africa were also set as a result of the Berlin Conference in 1878. The new borders bequeathed a legacy of problems for the Africans affected, but they solved the issue of imperial rivalry. Indeed, the European colonies of the various states depended upon one another for trade and mutual security.

In Asia, the growth of Japan and the decline of China worried many contemporaries. Since opening to the west in the 1860s Japan had grown powerful by selectively imitating European models. China, however, had undergone a revolution in 1911 that left it disorganized and without strong leadership. In part because of Western interference in its affairs, China did not industrialize or modernize.

In 1894–95 Japan proved the superiority of its system by defeating China in the Sino-Japanese War. Just ten years later they defeated Russia leaving them the dominant power in the western Pacific. The British signed a naval alliance with Japan, hoping to harness Japanese power to their interests and protect British colonies in the region from Japanese avarice.

The U.S. seemed a reasonably satisfied power after taking the Philippines from Spain and emerging as the most powerful influence over the Caribbean. The Americans were therefore happy to support the status quo and contribute to the security of global trade networks. They also sent troops as part of the international effort to put down the anti-Western Boxer movement in China in 1900.

Imperialism

In the event of a large war, the imperial system created both strengths and vulnerabilities. France and Britain could rely on the manpower and raw materials of a worldwide empire, but also had to devote resources to protect the sea lanes on which they depended.

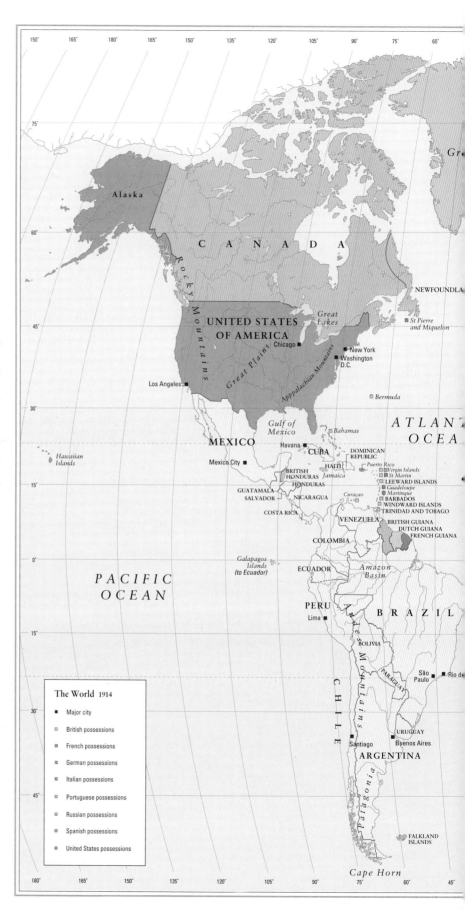

The World 1914

- ■ Major city
- British possessions
- French possessions
- German possessions
- Italian possessions
- Portuguese possessions
- Russian possessions
- Spanish possessions
- United States possessions

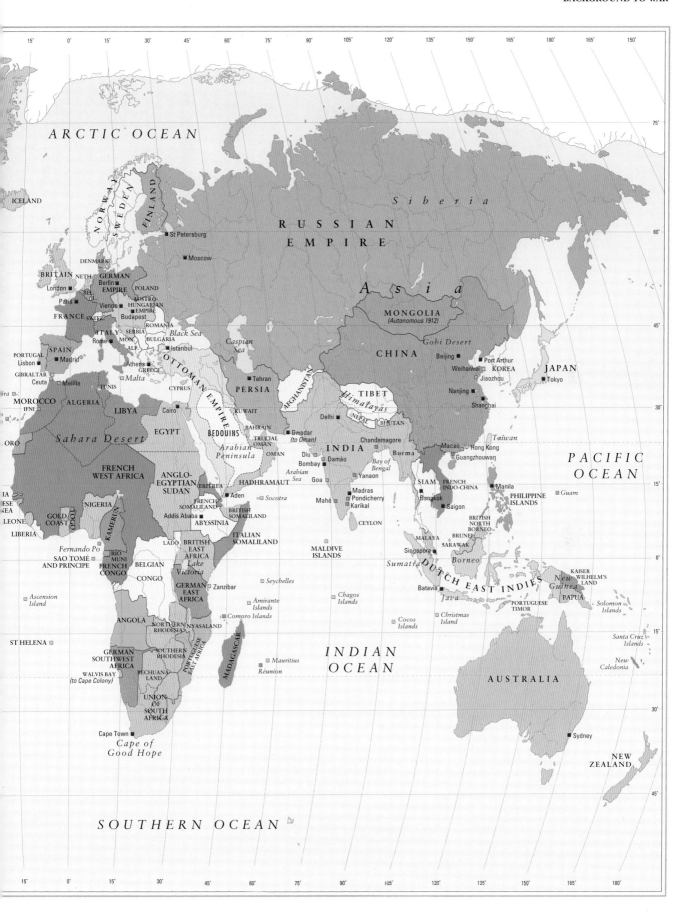

15° 0° 15° 30° 45° 60° 75° 90° 105° 120° 135° 150° 165° 180° 165° 150°

ARCTIC OCEAN

ICELAND

Siberia

RUSSIAN
EMPIRE

NORWAY SWEDEN FINLAND

■ St Petersburg

A s i a

DENMARK
■ Moscow

BRITAIN NETH. GERMAN
Berlin ■ EMPIRE
London ■ BEL. POLAND
Paris ■ Vienna AUSTRO-
HUNGARIAN
EMPIRE
SWITZ. Budapest
FRANCE
ROMANIA
ITALY SERBIA *Black Sea*
Rome ■ MON. BULGARIA
ALB. Istanbul ■
PORTUGAL SPAIN Athens
Lisbon ■ ■ Madrid GREECE
Malta
GIBRALTAR OTTOMAN EMPIRE
Ceuta ■ Melilla CYPRUS
TUNIS
MOROCCO ALGERIA
IFNI LIBYA Cairo ■
ORO *Sahara Desert* EGYPT
BEDOUINS

MONGOLIA
(Autonomous 1912)

Gobi Desert

CHINA
Beijing ■ ■ Port Arthur
Weihaiwei ■ KOREA JAPAN
Jiaozhou
Nanjing ■ ■ Tokyo
Shanghai ■

Caspian Sea

PERSIA
Tehran ■

AFGHANISTAN
TIBET
Himalayas
Delhi ■ NEPAL BHUTAN

KUWAIT
BAHRAIN
TRUCIAL Gwadar
OMAN *(to Oman)* Chandemagore
Arabian Peninsula OMAN INDIA
Diu
Arabian Damão
Sea Bombay ■ *Bay of*
Goa *Bengal*

Taiwan

Macao ■ ■ Hong Kong
■ Guangzhouwan

PACIFIC
OCEAN

ANGLO-
EGYPTIAN
SUDAN ERITREA
FRENCH
SOMALILAND
HADHRAMAUT
Aden ■
BRITISH
SOMALILAND
Addis Ababa ■
ABYSSINIA

Burma
Yanaon
Madras ■
Pondicherry ■
Karikal
Mahé ■

SIAM
Bangkok ■
FRENCH
INDO-CHINA
Saigon ■

■ Manila

PHILIPPINE
ISLANDS

■ *Guam*

NIGERIA
GOLD
COAST
LIBERIA
TOGO
KAMERUN

Socotra

CEYLON

BRITISH
NORTH
BORNEO
BRUNEI
SARAWAK
MALAYA
Singapore ■ *Borneo*

Fernando Po
SAO TOMÉ
AND PRINCIPE RIO
MUNI
FRENCH
CONGO BELGIAN
CONGO

LADO BRITISH
EAST
AFRICA

ITALIAN
SOMALILAND

MALDIVE
ISLANDS

SUMATRA

DUTCH EAST INDIES

*Lake
Victoria*

GERMAN
EAST
AFRICA ■ Zanzibar

Seychelles

Batavia ■
Java

KAISER
WILHELM'S
LAND
New
Guinea
PAPUA

*Solomon
Islands*

*Ascension
Island*

*Chagos
Islands*

*Amirante
Islands*
Comoro Islands

*Cocos
Islands*

*Christmas
Island*

PORTUGUESE
TIMOR

ST HELENA ■

ANGOLA

NORTHERN
RHODESIA NYASALAND

PORTUGUESE EAST AFRICA

MADAGASCAR

Mauritius
Réunion

INDIAN
OCEAN

*Santa Cruz
Islands*

New
Caledonia

GERMAN
SOUTHWEST
AFRICA SOUTHERN
RHODESIA
WALVIS BAY BECHUANA-
(to Cape Colony) LAND
UNION
OF
SOUTH
AFRICA

Cape Town ■
*Cape of
Good Hope*

AUSTRALIA

■ Sydney

NEW
ZEALAND

SOUTHERN OCEAN

15° 0° 15° 30° 45° 60° 75° 90° 105° 120° 135° 150° 165° 180°

75°

60°

45°

30°

15°

0°

15°

30°

45°

Franco-Prussian War 1870–71

The wars that Europeans had recently fought brought with them important changes, but they were relatively short and contained. This led some to think that future wars would follow the same pattern. Today, historians disagree about their importance in causing World War I.

In 1870, France declared war on Prussia over a relatively minor diplomatic crisis. Prussia not only won the war, known as the Franco-Prussian War, but it used the occasion to unify the German states under Prussian leadership. As a result, a new, powerful country appeared on the map. Germany imposed an indemnity on France, forcing it to pay for Germany's war expenses. The Germans also took two French provinces, Alsace and Lorraine. To add insult to injury, the Germans held the first coronation ceremony for their new emperor in Versailles, the traditional home of French kings.

Although the loss stung France, by 1914 it had long ceased to be a reason for Frenchmen to want a war of revenge. France's allies had no desire to support France in an offensive war of conquest. While nationalists continued to blame the republic for its loss of the two provinces, virtually no one in France in the years before 1914 argued for war as the solution.

Nevertheless, the creation of Germany created some instability in Europe. The occasionally bellicose behavior of Kaiser Wilhelm II did not help matters, but he did prove to be a voice for moderation in the diplomatic crises in Morocco. He himself often said that he had no intention of disturbing the peace of Europe.

His cousin, Czar Nicholas II of Russia, said much the same. His nation's humiliation at the hands of a rising Japan in the 1904–05 Russo-Japanese War forced Russia to reduce its influence in Asia. As a result, Russia began to pay more attention to Europe, especially the Balkans. Russia's alliance with France was designed both to deter Germany and to free Russia to get more involved in southeastern Europe. It also gave Russia access to French finance and industry to expand its transportation infrastructure and buy new weapons.

Still, Nicholas knew that Russia needed time to recover from the Russo-Japanese War and to make some critical domestic reforms. His regime therefore tried to walk a careful tightrope in the Balkans, pledging support for the Orthodox Christians of the region but discouraging them from doing anything that would disturb the peace of Europe.

The Legacy of War

Although important historical events, neither of these wars caused World War I. By 1914 Franco-German relations seemed better than they had been for decades. For its part, Russia still needed to wait a few years to recover and rebuild.

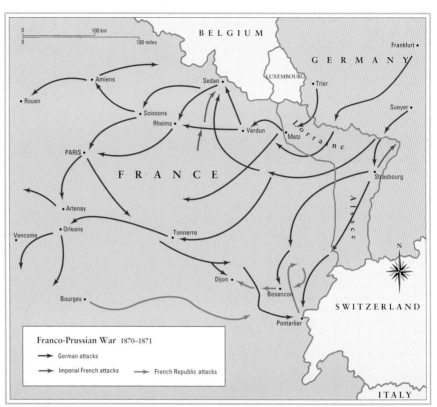

Franco-Prussian War 1870–1871

→ German attacks

→ Imperial French attacks

→ French Republic attacks

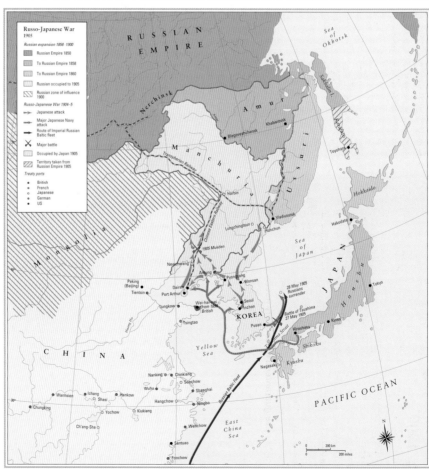

Russo-Japanese War 1905

Russian expansion 1858–1900

Russian Empire 1850

To Russian Empire 1858

To Russian Empire 1860

Russian occupied to 1905

Russian zone of influence 1900

Russo-Japanese War 1904–5

→ Japanese attack

→ Major Japanese Navy attack

→ Route of Imperial Russian Baltic fleet

✕ Major battle

Occupied by Japan 1905

Territory taken from Russian Empire 1905

Treaty ports

● British

● French

● Japanese

● German

● US

Austro-Hungarian Empire c. 1900

The Austro-Hungarian Empire faced daunting problems. It had two parliaments, one based in Vienna and one in Budapest, which dealt with almost all issues outside of military and diplomatic policy. It also had a variety of ethnic groups, many of whom had little loyalty to it. Despite its many problems, in 1914 the states of Europe considered it a great power. It had a large army, modern arms industries and a strategic location. It also had an alliance with Germany that might have guaranteed its security needs.

The relationship between Austria-Hungary and Germany deteriorated just before the war. In 1913, the Germans had uncovered a massive spy scandal involving a senior Austrian intelligence official who had been selling military secrets to the Russians. The man, Col. Alfred Redl, committed suicide rather than face a trial. After the scandal, the Germans essentially broke off joint staff talks. They had never had much respect for their Austro-Hungarian allies, whom they derided in private and even in public.

Austria-Hungary's Army Chief of Staff, Franz Conrad von Hötzendorf, tried to use the army as the glue that could hold together the fissiparous Empire. He had a hatred for Serbia and argued repeatedly for a preventive war that would destroy it. For years, the moderates in the Empire had resisted him. The assassination of the Archduke Franz Ferdinand and his wife in Sarajevo, however, allowed him to renew his calls for war against the Serbs that he and many others held responsible.

War Plans

Not knowing what he would face, Conrad divided his army into three groups. One would head south to fight Serbia, another north to cover the Carpathian Mountain passes against the Russians and a third would stay in reserve. The plan soon fell apart. Conrad sent his reserves south against Serbia at the war's outset only to learn that Germany had sent most of its army west against France. As a result, neither the German nor the Austro-Hungarian army was ready for war in the east against the Russian forces.

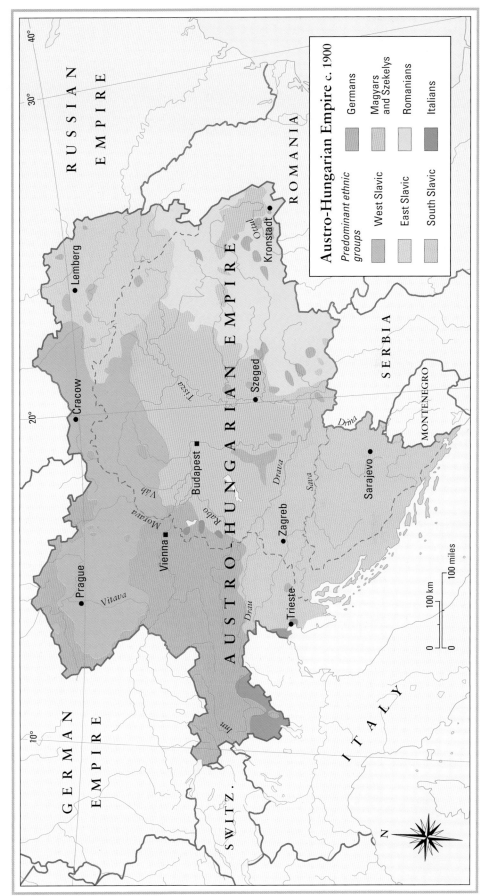

Austro-Hungarian Empire c. 1900

Predominant ethnic groups

- Germans
- Magyars and Szekelys
- Romanians
- Italians
- West Slavic
- East Slavic
- South Slavic

The Balkans, Crete and Cyprus 1878–1913

German Chancellor Otto von Bismarck once said that 'some damn foolish thing in the Balkans' would one day cause a major war. From 1878 to 1913 the region was wracked by war and conflict as the Ottoman Empire's European presence declined. Shifting combinations of small and large powers then vied to fill in the power vacuums in a region already beset by ethnic and religious tensions.

The most important conflicts in the region were the two Balkan Wars of 1912 and 1913. In the first, Montenegro, Greece, Bulgaria and Serbia created the Balkan League to expel Ottoman forces from Europe. They succeeded, pushing the Ottomans off the continent except for a small corner of eastern Thrace around the city of Adrianople. Serbia emerged powerful and confident from the First Balkan War, nearly doubling its territory, but still denied access to the sea. In the Second Balkan War, the victors squabbled over the pieces of the map that remained. Most of the Balkan states allied against the most aggressive state, Bulgaria. Even the Ottoman Empire joined the alliance in the hopes of recovering some of what it had lost.

As a result of the Balkan Wars, Serbia became a major player in the Balkans, terrifying Austro-Hungarian officials who worried that Serbian nationalists might stir up anti-Austrian feelings among the Empire's many Slavs. Bulgaria and Romania were unsatisfied with their share of the spoils. Romania sought the Transylvania region of Hungary where many ethnic Romanians lived. The Ottoman Empire's poor performance in the wars seemed to underscore its role as the 'sick man of Europe,' although future events were to show that the West had underestimated the strength that the Ottomans retained.

The Balkans, Crete and Cyprus 1878–1912

1878 Date of independence from Ottoman rule

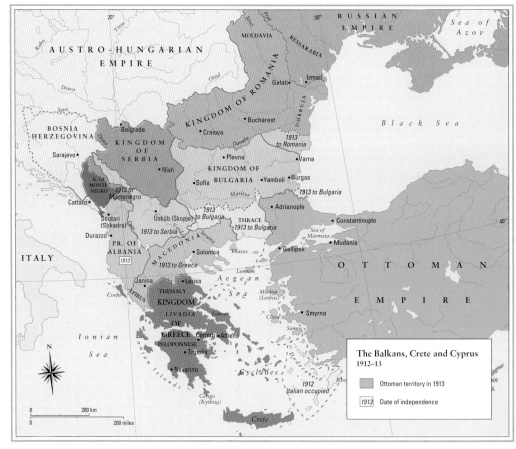

The Balkans, Crete and Cyprus 1912–13

Ottoman territory in 1913

1913 Date of independence

Bulgaria 1878–1915

Bulgaria emerged as a great victor of the First Balkan War, but its success led its erstwhile allies to fight against it in the Second.

Because it had received no help from Russia or the western allies, the Bulgarians turned to the Germans for help in the months between the Balkan Wars and the outbreak of World War I. The Bulgarians hoped to recover territory in Macedonia and Thrace lost to Serbia and Greece. They also sought territory on the Black Sea coast lost to the Romanians. They therefore abandoned territorial claims against the Ottoman Empire to facilitate better relations with Germany and Austria-Hungary.

The Balkans – Ethnic Groups 1914

No part of Europe contained as many mutually antagonistic ethnic groups as the Balkans.

Often called 'the powder keg of Europe,' the Balkans contained large numbers of Orthodox Christians, Catholics, Muslims and Jews. State and ethnic borders rarely matched. Strategic problems also existed, such as Serbia's desire for access to the Adriatic. Nationalists in the Balkan states wanted to expand their borders to encompass their fellow nationalists in other states. This problem of irredentism kept the region in a near permanent state of crisis that increased great power tensions.

The Balkans – Ethnic Groups 1914

Teutonic
- German

Romanic or Latin
- Italian
- Romanian
- Vlach

Slavonic
- Little Russian (Ruthenian)
- Bulgarian
- Croatian
- Macedonian Slav
- Pomak
- Serbian

Greek

Albanian

Finno-Ugrian
- Magyar

Turko-Tatar
- Turkish
- Tatar

European Alliances and War Plans July 1914

Austro-German Alliance, 1879–1918

▶ Triple Alliance, 1882–1915

▶ Franco-Russian Alliance, 1894–1917

Triple Entente, 1907–17

Neutral

War Plans

➡ Central Powers

➡ Allied Powers

Germany

① Main effort in the west to surround the French army presumably concentrating in the north-east

② Second-line units holding the Russians in the east

Russia

③ To support Serbia by concentrating part of the army along the border

④ Attacking the exposed German provinces of East Prussia in support of France

Austria-Hungary

⑤ The major portions of the army concentrating on the border with Russia

⑥ A significant portion of the army to mount a punitive campaign against Serbia

Serbia

⑦ To hold out against Austria

France

⑧ To attack in the north-east; to recover Alsace and Lorraine

Britain

⑨ Send a expeditionary force to the Continent in support of Belgian neutrality and France. Institute a naval blockade of the Central Powers

European Military Strengths 1914

Two major European alliance systems were intended to deter an outbreak of war.

The Triple Entente of Great Britain, France and Russia had the advantages of British naval control, the size of the Russian Army and the sophistication of the French Army. The Central Powers of Germany, Austria-Hungary and the Ottoman Empire had the advantage of 'interior position,' theoretically allowing them to move men and supplies easily between theatres. Both alliances, however, suffered from abiding suspicions and differing strategic aims among the partners.

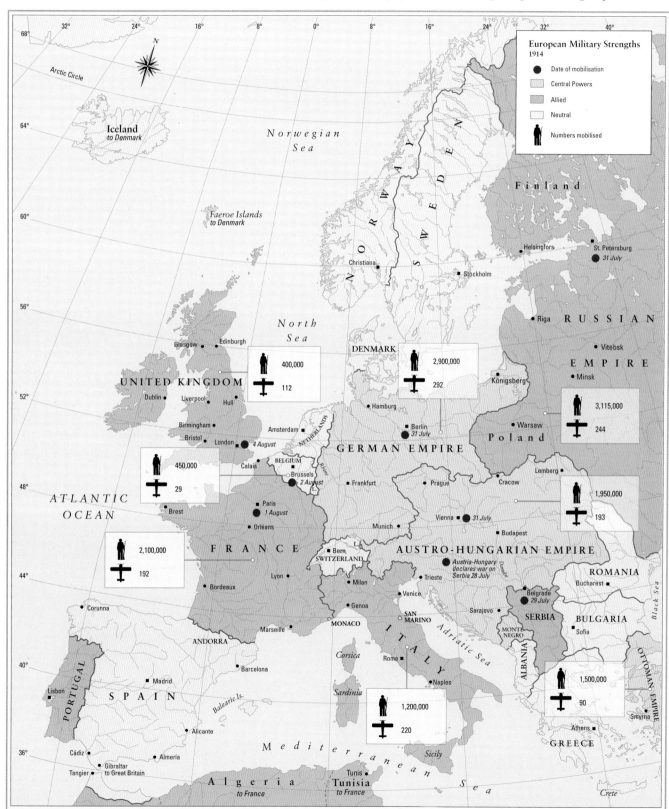

The Eastern Front
July 1914

Russia mobilized its army quickly, upsetting the plans of Germany and Austria-Hungary.

Russia mobilized in stages, allowing it to send units to the front as they became ready. This plan gave them enough men to pressure both the Galician front against Austria-Hungary and the East Prussian front against Germany. Both the Germans and the Austro-Hungarians wanted to send the bulk of their forces to other regions, but the early Russian movements forced them to reconsider. Germany recovered from the false assumptions in their war plan, but Austria-Hungary stumbled badly in 1914.

The Eastern Front
July 1914

- Austro-German Alliance, 1879–1918
- Triple Entente, 1907–17
- Neutral
- Fortified towns
- Other forts

1. Two Russian armies concentrate on East Prussia's border
2. Russian forces move eastward to meet reinforcements
3. Russian armies concentrate on Austro-Hungarian's border
4. Prittwitz prepares to abandon East Prussia
5. German forces stay to defend and prepare an attack into Poland
6. Austrian armies concentrate on the Polish-Russian border
7. Austrian forces prepare to attack Serbia
8. Austrian Second Army is re-directed to the Galician front

Albanian soldiers keep watch.

THE BALKANS

The chronic instability in the multi-ethnic Balkans had worried diplomats for years. Two wars there in 1912–13 saw tensions rise, but until the summer of 1914, the violence remained localized. When a Serbian teenager assassinated the heir to the throne of Austria-Hungary that June, however, senior leaders in Vienna decided to use the incident as a pretext to start a war against Serbia.

The Austrians hoped that they could diplomatically isolate the other great powers or move so quickly that the other states of Europe could not react quickly enough to stop them.

Their German allies issued a now infamous 'blank check' of support. But both the Germans and Austro-Hungarians had badly miscalculated the attitude of their opponents, and soon all of the major powers of Europe (and their empires) suddenly found themselves at war.

French troops in Salonika
Allied forces (like the French troops seen here) established a front in Salonika, Greece, that they hoped would pressure the Ottoman Empire. It failed and turned into yet another frustrating stalemate.

Ottoman artillery
Sometimes underestimated by their opponents, the Ottoman Empire's soldiers managed to fight battles on multiple fronts for years despite not having the latest equipment or a modern logistical network.

Montenegrin infantry attack an Ottoman fort at Decic, Montenegro
The Balkan front in many ways represented a continuation of the two Balkan Wars of 1912–13. Longstanding historic rivalries continued amid the changing nature of global power dynamics.

A prince on a firing range
The Balkans also showed two other World War I patterns: the conflict of ethnic versus national loyalties and the decline of kings like the Montenegrin King Nikola I.

Turkish soldiers
Turkish soldiers fought from Suez to Mesopotamia to the Caucusus mountains. By the end of the war their loyalties had begun to shift from the Ottoman Empire to the new Republic of Turkey.

First Invasion of Serbia August 1914

Austria-Hungary sent three armies against Serbia as part of a disjointed war plan. One of those armies had to reorient north to deal with the mobilizing Russians in the Carpathians.

Austria-Hungary had the advantage of numbers over Serbia, but the terrain favoured the defenders and Serbian commanders had recent experience in the Balkan Wars. Belgrade, the Serbian capital, was shelled in advance of a major offensive. The Austro-Hungarian commander, Oskar von Potiorek, had been in charge of security for Archduke Franz Ferdinand's fateful visit to Sarajevo a few

long weeks earlier. His Serbian opposite, Radomir Putnik, was in poor health but he had internalized the lessons of the Balkan Wars and led his men with confidence. The confusion of the Austro-Hungarian war plan handicapped the attackers and gave Serbia a chance to respond. Using mountains and rivers, Serbian forces drove the Austro-Hungarians back in a series of battles west of Belgrade.

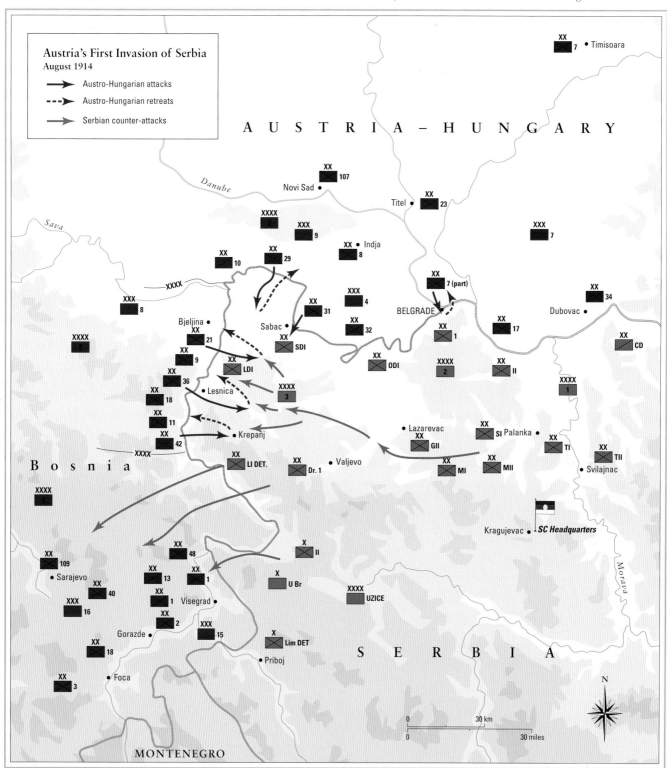

Austria's First Invasion of Serbia
August 1914

→ Austro-Hungarian attacks

--→ Austro-Hungarian retreats

→ Serbian counter-attacks

Second Invasion of Serbia November–December 1914

Rough Serbian terrain and a need to deal with the deteriorating situation in the Carpathians sowed confusion in the Austro-Hungarian ranks, thus opening a chance for Serbia to respond.

The Serbs tried to attack, both to secure Belgrade and in support of the Russians in the Carpathians. A successful Serbian offensive in the Balkans might prevent Austro-Hungarian Second Army from redeploying to the Carpathians, giving Russia a chance to win the war. The plan did create confusion for the Second Army, but they still had enough men to launch a two-pronged offensive.

The Serbians used the rivers to their advantage but found themselves outflanked. On 2 December, the Austro-Hungarians entered Belgrade from the south after having outflanked the city's defenders and expected to stay there indefinitely. The Serbian Army, however, had other plans and began to design another counter-attack aimed at liberating their capital and taking the war into Austria-Hungary.

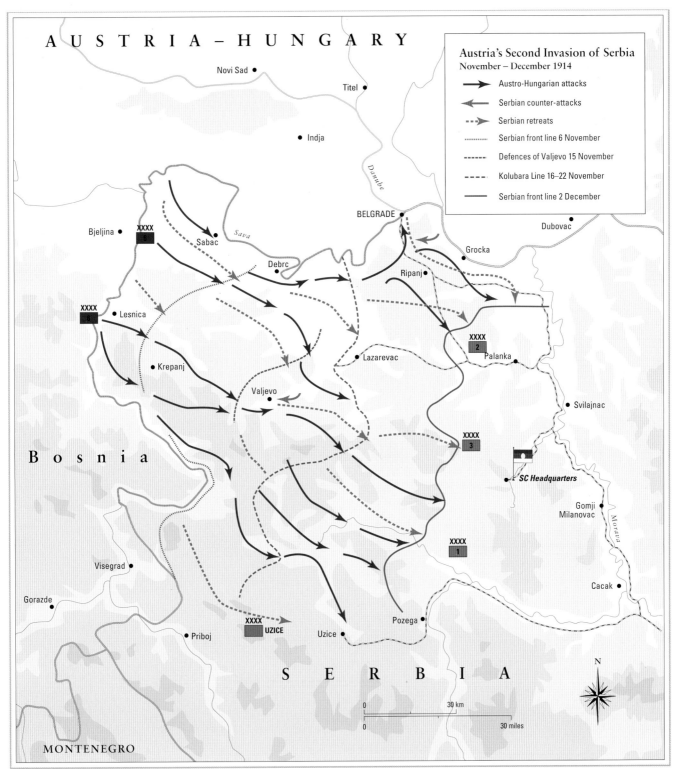

Serbian Counter-offensive 3–15 December 1914

Supplies of artillery pieces and shells arrived in Serbia, mostly from France and Greece. Serbian forces used them in a winter counteroffensive to liberate their capital from enemy occupation.

Serbian commander Radomir Putnik attacked as the rivers in Serbia began to swell from winter rains. Artillery barrages and costly infantry attacks drove Austro-Hungarian soldiers from their positions. As they retreated, they were often trapped by fast flowing rivers. Casualties on both sides rose from combat and from disease amid the approaching winter. Austro-Hungarian commanders abandoned Belgrade on 15 December, having occupied it for just two weeks. By the end of 1914 both sides had lost thousands of men and the lines had returned almost to where they had been when the war started. Serbian casualties approached 175,000 and Austro-Hungarian exceeded 210,000. Both sides sought help from their allies for a 1915 campaign that was expected to be brutal and prolonged.

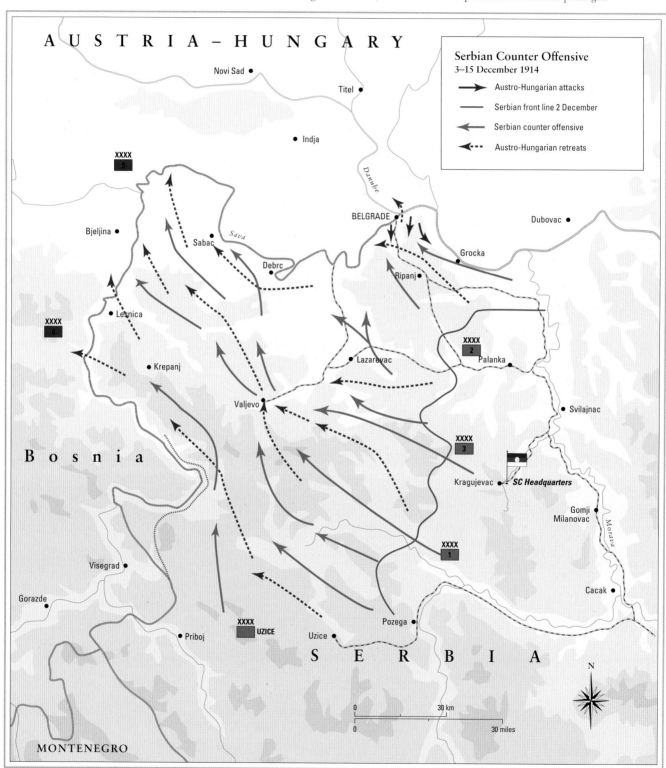

Serbian Counter Offensive
3–15 December 1914

→ Austro-Hungarian attacks
— Serbian front line 2 December
← Serbian counter offensive
◄--- Austro-Hungarian retreats

Invasion of Serbia
October–November 1915

The Ottoman Empire's war entry made Serbian conquest important for the Central Powers.

Bulgaria's entry into the conflict meant that Serbia now had to face a two-front war. The Bulgarians invaded from the east and Austria-Hungary from the north. Belgrade fell again and the Serbs began a difficult retreat in terrible weather. The retreat did not end until Serbian troops had passed through Montenegro and into Albania. Britain and France tried to help, but it was too little too late. By the end of 1915, almost all of Serbia lay in enemy hands and 175,000 Serbians were prisoners of war.

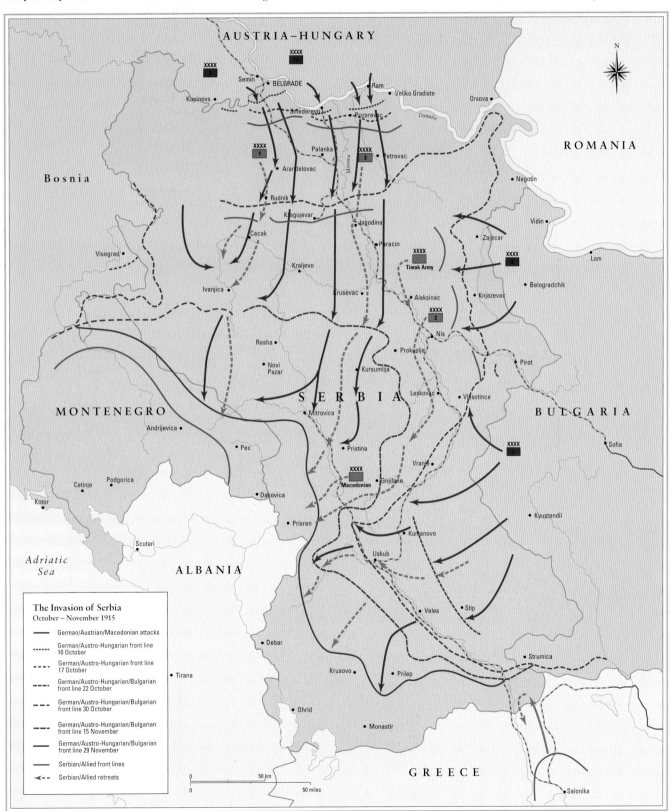

The Invasion of Serbia
October – November 1915

- German/Austrian/Macedonian attacks
- German/Austro-Hungarian front line 10 October
- German/Austro-Hungarian front line 17 October
- German/Austro-Hungarian/Bulgarian front line 22 October
- German/Austro-Hungarian/Bulgarian front line 30 October
- German/Austro-Hungarian/Bulgarian front line 15 November
- German/Austro-Hungarian/Bulgarian front line 29 November
- Serbian/Allied front lines
- Serbian/Allied retreats

Serbian Exodus 1916

The remnants of the Serbian Army fled in disarray to the Adriatic coast, riddled with disease, low on morale and having abandoned most of their heavy equipment.

The Allied navies evacuated hundreds of thousands of Serbian soldiers to camps in remote locations like Sardinia and Corfu. More than 150,000 Serbian soldiers went to Corfu alone, which soon became a virtual Serbia in exile. The soldiers and the civilians who fled with the soldiers needed massive supplies of food, clothing and medicine. The civilians included government officials who hoped to establish a Serbian state in exile. They also included children and the elderly. Britain, France, Greece, Russia and even private groups in the United States worked to alleviate their suffering as best they could, but the first few days on Corfu coincided with wet winter weather. The misery of the Serbian refugees and the inability of the great powers to help them became a symbol of the suffering of the war.

The Germans divided Serbia and its ally Montenegro between themselves and their Bulgarian allies. In this sense, the war in the Balkans seemed like only the final act in the three-act drama of the Balkan Wars. On the strategic level, the collapse of Serbia opened up a land bridge from Germany to the Ottoman Empire. The rail lines from Belgrade to Sofia to Constantinople now sat safely in the hands of the Central Powers. Together with the failure of the Anglo-French offensive in Gallipoli, Serbia's collapse seemed to confirm allied failure in the Balkan theatre. Failure in Serbia also exposed the tenuous Allied position in Greece, where the prime minister and the government favoured an alliance with Britain and France, but the king preferred Germany – in part because his wife was Kaiser Wilhelm's sister.

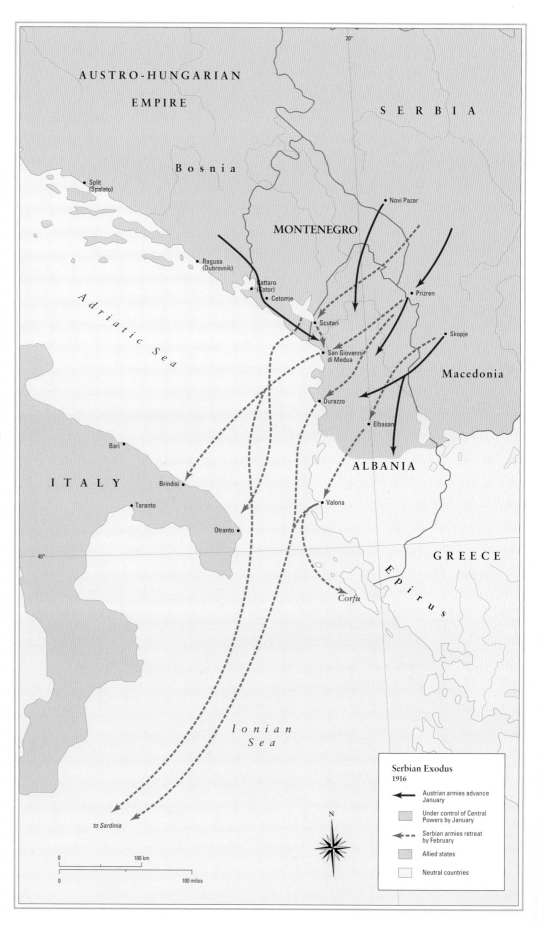

Serbian Exodus 1916

→ Austrian armies advance January

▨ Under control of Central Powers by January

◄- - - Serbian armies retreat by February

▨ Allied states

☐ Neutral countries

The Balkans 1916

The Allies chose to set up another front based at Salonica, Greece. They hoped to give the Serbs a place to fight and to help the Russians.

The Salonica Operation began with one French and one British division, but soon grew to 150,000 men. Commanded by Maurice Sarrail, a French general who had grown unpopular with the high command, they spent months training. Sarrail's superiors in Paris and London thought that the expedition was a political idea with little military utility. Anything sent to Salonica, they argued, weakened the Western Front. They refused to send men and supplies except when ordered. Enemy resistance, composed largely of Bulgarians, was light but had the advantage of excellent high ground to defend. Without supplies and reinforcements, Sarrail opted for caution. Perhaps creating a distraction alone could help the Russians and Romanians. But the longer the Salonica garrison sat without moving the lower its morale fell and the higher its disease rate climbed. Sarrail also had to face the ambivalence of the Greek government, large sections of which did not favour the Allied presence in their country despite their desire to gain territory at the expense of the Ottoman Empire.

In August 1916 Bulgarian forces attacked the Salonica garrison. Their aim was to pin the Allied soldiers in order to cover the German offensive into Romania. They had no intention, and probably no capability, to destroy the garrison. Sarrail counter-attacked and regained parts of Albania and Serbia but the offensive soon stalled – the problems of morale, supply and difficult terrain remained. The Allies in Salonica soon came to be known by derisive nicknames such as the Gardeners of Salonica and the Largest Internment Camp in Europe.

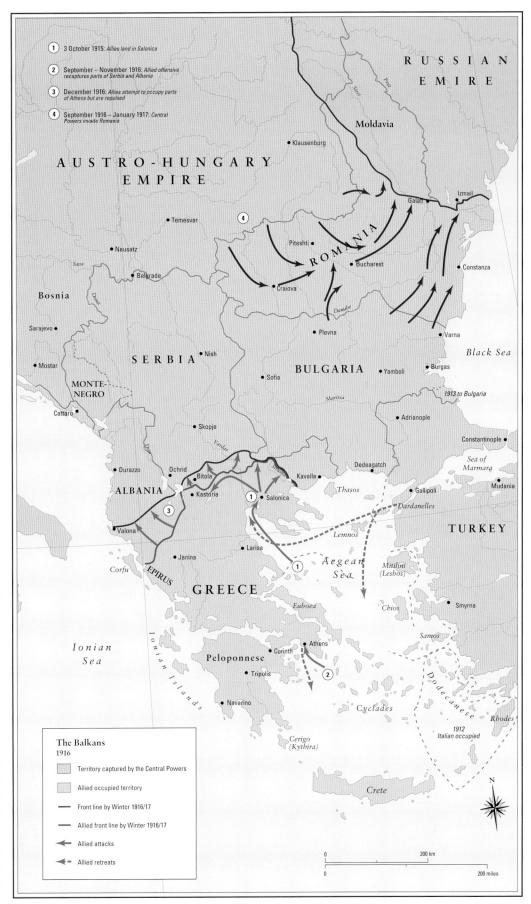

1   3 October 1915: *Allies land in Salonica*

2   September – November 1916: *Allied offensive recaptures parts of Serbia and Albania*

3   December 1916: *Allies attempt to occupy parts of Athens but are repulsed*

4   September 1916 – January 1917: *Central Powers invade Romania*

The Balkans
1916

▨ Territory captured by the Central Powers

▨ Allied occupied territory

— Front line by Winter 1916/17

— Allied front line by Winter 1916/17

← Allied attacks

◄-- Allied retreats

0   200 km

0   200 miles

Salonica: The Spring Offensive April–May 1917

By 1917, fresh supplies reached Allied forces on the Salonica front. Sarrail opted for another offensive to break the stalemate in the Balkans.

Eventually, the British sent seven divisions to Salonica to join six French divisions. Enough Serbian forces came from Corfu and Sardinia to form six more. The Greek government added three divisions, despite the firm opposition to the scheme from many its countrymen. The Allies took this polyglot force on the offensive against Bulgarian positions. It failed to break through despite numerical superiority, and the French opted for a change of commanders. They turned to the more aggressive Louis Franchet d'Esperey.

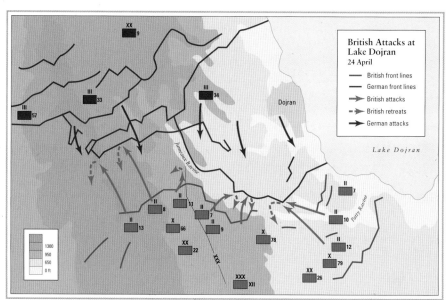

British Attacks at Lake Dojran
24 April

—— British front lines
—— German front lines
⟶ British attacks
⇢ British retreats
⟶ German attacks

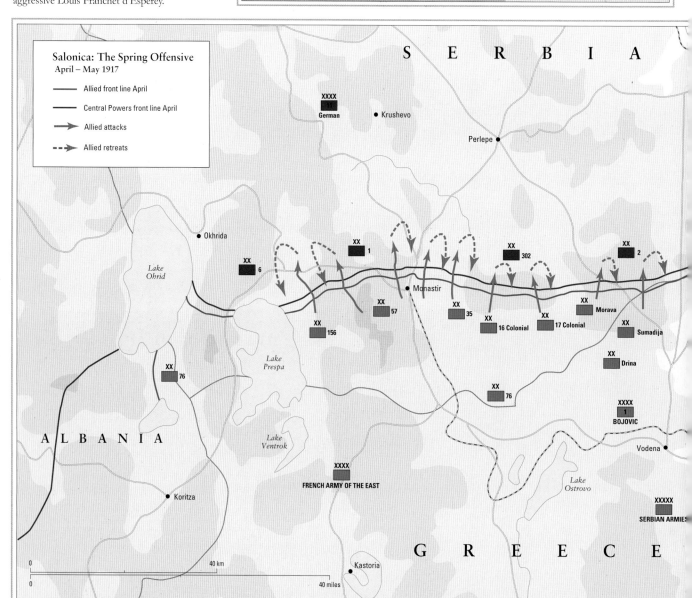

Salonica: The Spring Offensive
April – May 1917

—— Allied front line April
—— Central Powers front line April
⟶ Allied attacks
⇢ Allied retreats

British Attacks at Lake Dojran 24 April–8 May 1917

The Battle of Lake Dojran was the British and Greek part of a larger Allied offensive at Salonica. The Allies hoped to take advantage of the weakening Bulgarian positions.

The British plan proposed to compensate for the difficult terrain with artillery. A heavy bombardment would clear Bulgarian forces out of their positions and gas would chase the remaining opposition away from the front. But the plan did not go to form and much of the artillery was inaccurate. British and Greek forces enjoyed some local success, but not enough to force the Bulgarians out of their defences. The battle did, however, badly shake the morale of the Bulgarian Army.

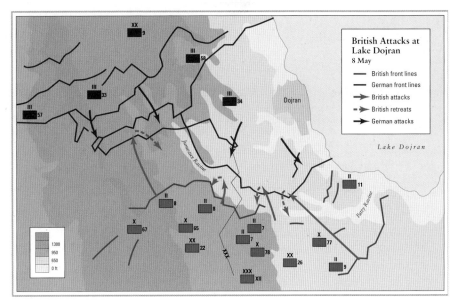

British Attacks at Lake Dojran
8 May

— British front lines
— German front lines
→ British attacks
⇢ British retreats
→ German attacks

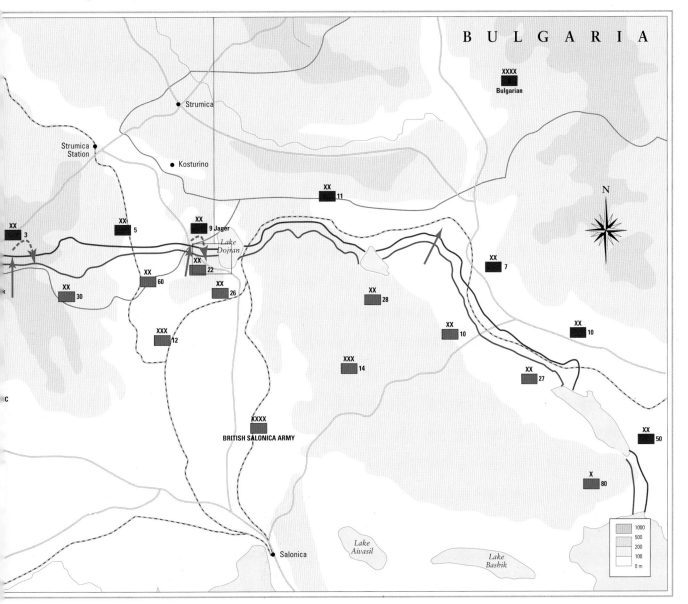

The Balkans
September–November 1918

By 1918, the Bulgarians on the Salonica front were showing signs of fatigue. Their morale was low and they lacked much of the basic equipment they needed, included artillery, food, medicine and even shoes.

Although the departure of the Russians from the war removed one of the strategic reasons for creating the Salonica front in the first place, the Allies decided to reinforce it. They hoped to take advantage of the decline of both the Bulgarian Army and its principal allies in the region, the Ottoman and Austro-Hungarian Empires. The Allies got a morale boost when the 6000-man Czech Legion arrived at Salonica eager to resume the offensive. By September, it was obvious to the Bulgarians that the Germans would lose in the west. Bulgarian morale, already low, plummeted further. Few Bulgarian soldiers wanted to fight another long, hard winter campaign in the mountains for a cause that looked increasingly lost.

The Allies attacked at Dobro Pole in what is today Macedonia. They led with a powerful and accurate artillery barrage that unhinged the Bulgarian defenders. Then two waves of French and Serbian infantry advanced. Bulgarian commanders refused to authorize a retreat and in some places, notably against the British in a second engagement at Lake Dojran, the Bulgarians fought well enough to repulse Allied attacks. But in other places, they were surrounded and soon surrendered. In still other locations Bulgarian troops fled or deserted. Some went to the capital, Sofia, to demand that the government order a general surrender. They were instead met with troops and violence.

Allies Take Macedonia

The Allies advanced into this confusion, seizing most of Macedonia and pressuring the critical city of Skopje. A front that had remained stationary for two years was suddenly mobile, and the Allies took maximum advantage. Franchet d'Esperey urged his men on, believing that the capture of Skopje would likely force Bulgaria out of the war. Once Skopje fell, the Allies would be able to control the supply routes into Bulgaria itself from the lightly defended western approaches. The dismal state of the German, Austro-Hungarian and Ottoman armies meant that Bulgaria could expect no help from the outside. It might even face renewed pressure from Russia if the Bolsheviks sought to take advantage of a situation that now looked beneficial to them.

The Bulgarians thus asked for an armistice as soon as the fall of Skopje seemed inevitable. Franchet d'Esperey granted it, requiring the Bulgarians to demobilize and evacuate all non-Bulgarian territory pending a final peace treaty. The region remained unstable and violent, however, as people in the Balkans looked forward to an uncertain future.

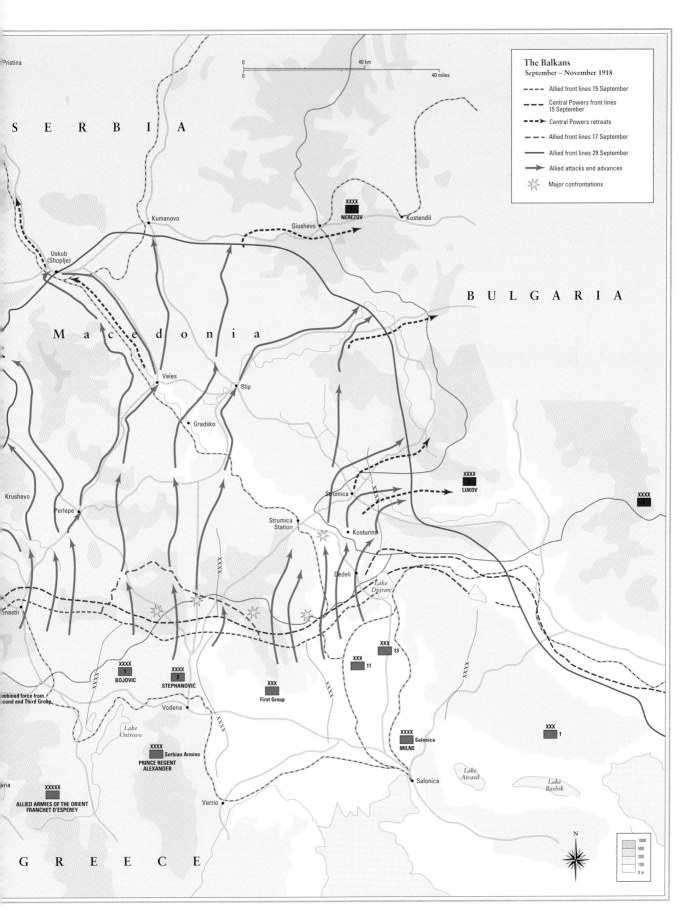

The Balkans
September – November 1918

- - - - Allied front lines 15 September
— — Central Powers front lines 15 September
▶▶▶ Central Powers retreats
- - - Allied front lines 17 September
——— Allied front lines 29 September
➤ Allied attacks and advances
✦ Major confrontations

SERBIA

Pristina

0   40 km
0   40 miles

Kumanovo

Giushevo

XXXX
NEREZOV

Kustendil

Uskub
(Shoplje)

BULGARIA

Macedonia

Veles

Stip

Gradsko

Krushevo

Perlepe

Strumica

XXXX
LUKOV

XXXX

Strumica
Station

Kosturino

Dedeli

Lake
Dojran

Monastir

XXX
13

XXX
11

XXXX
1
BOJOVIC

XXXX
2
STEPHANOVIC

XXX
First Group

Combined force from
Second and Third Group

Vodena

Lake
Ostrovo

XXXX
Salonica
MILNE

XXX
1

XXXX
Serbian Armies
PRINCE REGENT
ALEXANDER

Lake
Aivasil

Lake
Bashik

Salonica

aria

XXXXX
ALLIED ARMIES OF THE ORIENT
FRANCHET D'ESPEREY

Verrio

GREECE

N

1000
500
200
100
0 m

Russian troops occupy Austro-Hungarian trenches following the Brusilov Offensive, September 1916.

THE EASTERN FRONT

Unlike the relatively cramped spaces in the west, Eastern Europe had too much open territory to allow soldiers to entrench comprehensively. Combat in the east was therefore much more fluid and aimed at control of rail junctures, roads, river crossings, and major fortified towns like Lemberg (modern-day Lviv) and Przemysl.

In the early days of the war, the Russians achieved large successes against the Austro-Hungarians in the Carpathian Mountains, but simultaneously lost huge battles to the Germans. Civilians suffered terribly as the war moved back and forth across their homelands. The war placed enormous stresses on the Russian and Austro-Hungarian states, which were both unprepared for modern war. By 1918 both had collapsed, leaving revolution and devastation in their wake.

Przemysl fortress is captured
Announcement posted during the taking of Przemysl fortress in Poland by the Russians in 1915. Russia's hold on the city proved short lived as the eastern front moved back and forth.

Gas attack
Russian soldiers seen here suffering the effects of poison gas and being cared for by members of the Russian Red Cross during their disastrous Gorlice-Tarnow retreat in 1915.

A road in the Prussian city of Tannenberg
Tannenberg (present Olsztyn, in Poland) was the scene of a massive victory by the German army in 1914. It convinced German leaders that they could defeat the much larger Russian army.

'Charge!'
A cavalry attack led by Russia's best general of the war, Aleksei Brusilov. Even Brusilov, however, could not save the corrupt and ineffective Russian political system from disintegrating in 1917.

Austrian artillery in Romania
Austrian and German troops led by Germany's Erich von Falkenhayn invaded and devastated Romania in 1916, forcing the Romanians to sign the one-sided Treaty of Bucharest in 1918.

Lenin speaks to a crowd
Unable to knock the Russians out of the war by military means, the Germans smuggled bolshevik leader V.I. Lenin into St. Petersburg in 1917. He soon began a revolution against Tsar Nicholas II.

The Eastern Front August 1914

The causes of the war lay in the east. The first military actions involved the Austro-Hungarian army mobilizing against Serbia. Russia soon followed with its own mobilization.

Unlike the bitter conflict on the Western Front, the Eastern Front battles involved wide open spaces. As a result, the armies could not entrench as fully as they had done in France and Belgium, although trenches did exist in many places. Instead, Eastern Front armies attempted to win large battles of enemy encirclement or they tried to capture strategic places such as fortresses or key railroad junctures. The large Polish salient in the centre of the eastern front tended to divide the 1914 region into a northern front based around East Prussia and a southern front based around the fortified passes in the Carpathian Mountains, such as Lemberg and Przemysl.

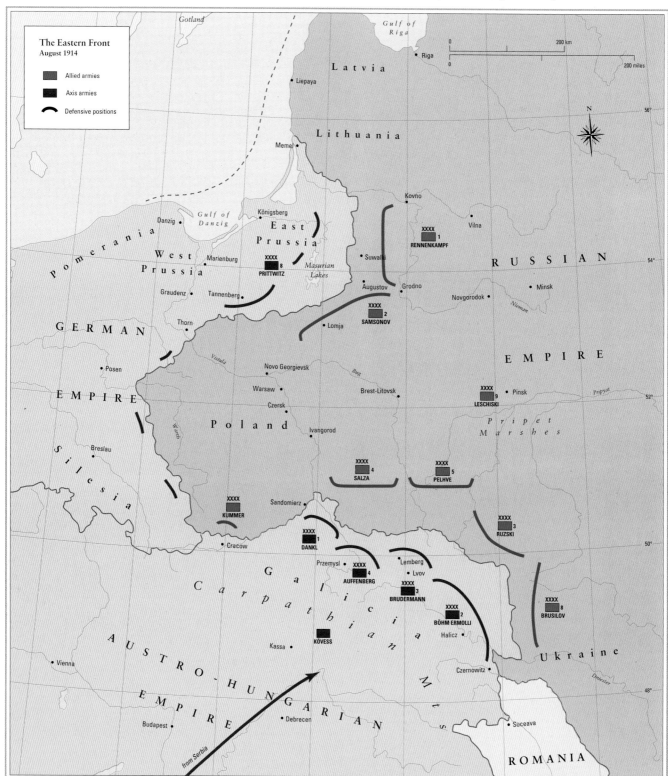

The Eastern Front
August 1914

- Allied armies
- Axis armies
- Defensive positions

Tannenberg
26–31 August 1914

Austria-Hungary's war plan called for most
of its forces to head south against Serbia,
while Germany's war plan sent seven-eighths
of its manpower west against France and
Belgium. As a result, neither country was
prepared to engage the Russian forces. Both
of them expected the Russians to mobilize
slowly, but their mobilization plan proved
to be more efficient than almost anyone
expected. As a result, the German Eighth
Army found itself alone against two Russian
field armies, the First and the Second.
The Eighth Army commander proposed a
massive withdrawal behind the safety of
the Vistula River, but that plan would have
required giving East Prussia to the advancing
Russians. The German high command thus
decided to change commanders in the east
and take a gamble.

The new German Eighth Army command
team included Gen. Paul von Hindenburg,
recently recalled from retirement, and Gen. Erich
Ludendorff, a hard-driving professional. They read
the map in the same general way as the Eighth
Army's chief of operations, Lt. Col. Max Hoffman.
Instead of retreating and surrendering East Prussia,
they saw an opportunity to take the offensive and
change the character of the war in the east in a
dramatic way. Together they devised a plan that
sought to take advantage of the series of lakes and
swamps known collectively as the Masurian Lakes.

The Russian First Army had to move north of the
lakes, while the Second Army moved to their south,
producing a gap of almost 64km (40 miles) between
their flanks. As a result, the two Russian armies
would not be in a position to support one another.
Thus the Germans opted to place a token screening
force opposite the slow-moving Russian First Army
and concentrate the bulk of their strength against
the Russian Second Army. By moving quickly and
taking advantage of poor Russian communications,

the Eighth Army was able to encircle most of the
Russian Second Army and cut off its avenues of
retreat before the Russian leaders could respond.

The Germans created a Kesselschlacht, or 'killing
cauldron'. By doing so, they hoped to win the battle
by movement more than by combat, thus saving
their men from a major engagement. The plan
worked almost to perfection. Unable to reinforce or
retreat, the Russians panicked. Their commander,
Gen. Alexander Samsonov, disappeared into the
woods and shot himself, leaving his men with no
leadership. The Germans blocked the main roads in
the region and began to strangle the pocket. Only
10,000 Russians from the 135,000-man Second
Army managed to find a route out of the pocket.
More than 100,000 were captured and 25,000 killed.
The lopsided victory convinced the Germans that
they could win battles against the Russians even
if they were outnumbered. Russian headquarters
expected the Germans to be satisfied with their
win and move into defensive positions in northern
Poland. The Germans, however, had other plans.

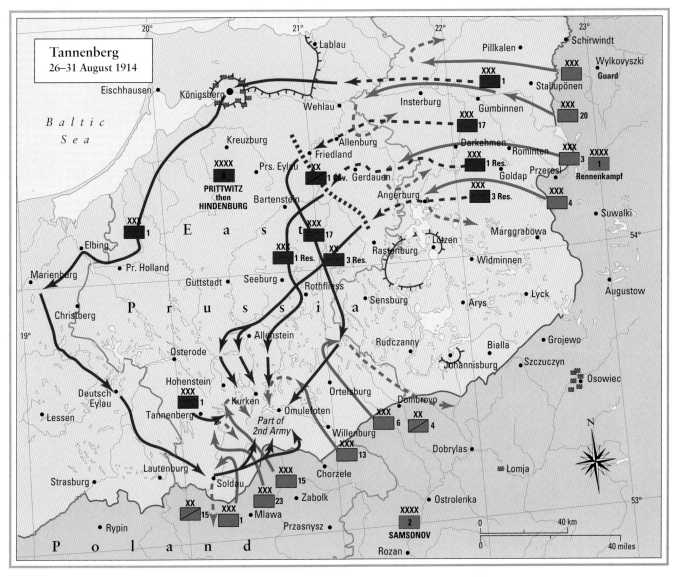

Masurian Lakes
September 1914

Expecting the German Forces to move toward Warsaw after their giant victory at Tannenberg at the end of the previous month, Russian First Army Commander General Pavel Rennenkampf moved cautiously toward East Prussia. Believing there to be only light German forces in front of him, he hoped to pressure the German heartland and force the German Army to stop their movements in Poland. But Russian manoeuvres put the First Army in a dangerously exposed position with potentially vulnerable flanks. It was therefore decided that the German Eighth Army would take yet another calculated gamble.

General Hermann von François commanded the German corps closest to the Russian First Army positioned to the north of the Masurian Lakes. His aggression and audacity had been one of the keys to the German victory at Tannenberg. Now he marched his men more than 113km (70 miles) in four days and attacked the exposed Russian left flank. He hoped to roll the Russian left back into the main body of Russian troops, then move other German units behind the lines to cut off any Russian retreat. Eighth Army headquarters was so confident of another massive victory that it invited the Kaiser to come east and see the battle for himself.

Quick Response

The Russians did not expect the German attack. Rennekampf knew, however, that the Germans had not moved on Warsaw. He was thus more awake to the danger that the Germans posed than Samsonov had been. Rennekampf responded quickly to the report of von François's sudden appearance on his flank. He dispatched two of his best divisions to hold off the advancing Germans while the rest of his army escaped. In that way, he hoped to avoid being surrounded and cut off as Samsonov had been at Tannenberg.

Russian soldiers abandoned most of their heavy equipment, but avoided the mass confusion that had caused panic at Tannenberg. Moving 80km (50 miles) to the east, the Russians fell back on their supply lines and set up a better defensive position. Heavy rains also slowed the German pursuit. Russian losses, never fully calculated, were undoubtedly enormous although smaller than at Tannenberg.

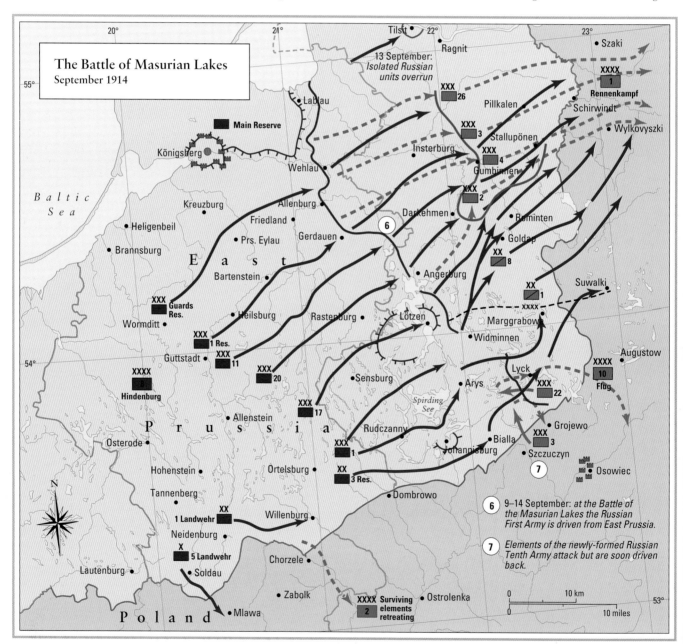

The Battle of Masurian Lakes
September 1914

13 September: Isolated Russian units overrun

6 *9–14 September: at the Battle of the Masurian Lakes the Russian First Army is driven from East Prussia.*

7 *Elements of the newly-formed Russian Tenth Army attack but are soon driven back.*

The Galician Campaign, 1–26 September 1914

The key to Galicia lay in the fortress cities that guarded the mountain passes into Hungary. The ultimate Russian objective was to move west along the line Lemberg–Przemysl–Tarnow–Cracow, laying siege to them instead of fighting battles in open terrain. If the Russians could reach Cracow, they had the option of moving southwest into the agricultural heartland of the Austro-Hungarian Empire or moving northwest into Germany itself. Capturing those cities would also give Russia control of the main Galician rail junctures on which the Austro-Hungarian relied to move men, supplies and crops. The Austro-Hungarians had for these reasons heavily fortified the line.

In contrast to their failures in the north, the Russians enjoyed great success against the Austro-Hungarians in Galicia. In part, they benefited from a confused and disorganized Austro-Hungarian war plan. By sending the bulk of their forces south against Serbia, the Austro-Hungarians left far too few men in Galicia. The Russians, for their part, mobilized relatively smoothly, giving them an early advantage.

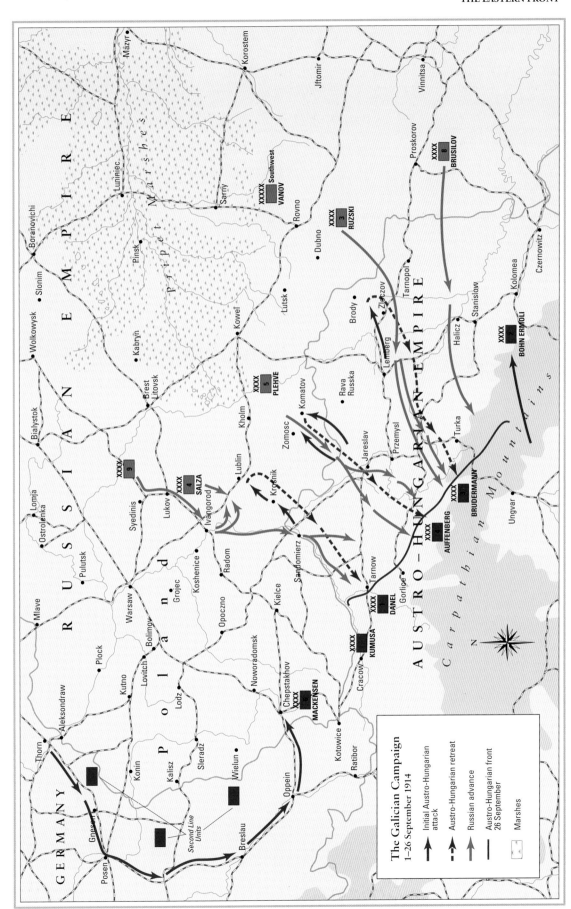

The Galician Campaign
1–26 September 1914

↑ Initial Austro-Hungarian attack
⇡ Austro-Hungarian retreat
↑ Russian advance
| Austro-Hungarian front 26 September
☐ Marshes

43

Przemysl 19–27 March 1915

Almost 100,000 soldiers garrisoned in 44 fortresses defended Przemysl, making it one of the strongest fortified positions in the world. After Lemberg surrendered in early September 1914, the Austro-Hungarians prepared to defend the city at all costs.

Russian battlefield success in Galicia led Austro-Hungarian forces to retreat past Przemysl in south-east Poland, but they left the garrison with enough food and supplies to last for several months. The Russians surrounded Przemysl but lacked the strength to take it throughout the autumn and winter. As the garrison at Przemysl went through its food and ammunition, it grew weaker and weaker. Finally in March 1915 Przemysl surrendered along with 120,000 of its terribly beleaguered defenders.

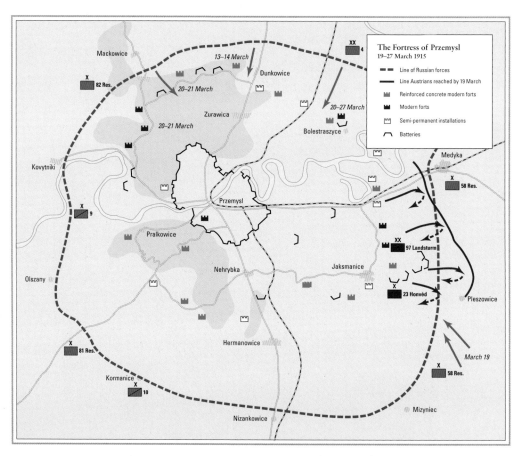

Lodz 11–17 November 1914

A reorganized German Army made one more push for a decisive victory against the Russians in November when they targeted the supply and rail centre of Lodz. The battle devolved into an indecisive slugfest, leaving both sides near exhaustion.

In what they hoped would be a replay of the early battles of 1914, a new and revitalized German Ninth Army moved to encircle an exposed and seemingly unprepared Russian army. This time, however, the German forces were spread out too thinly and the Russians reacted with speed. At one point it looked as though the Russians might turn the tables and encircle the German forces, but quick thinking and a fortuitous snowstorm combined to save the German position. Warsaw stayed in Russian hands.

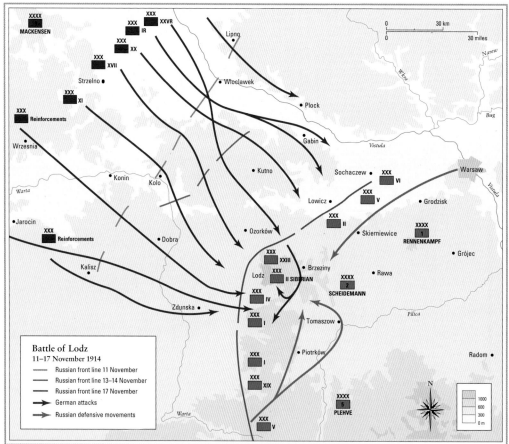

Eastern Front Late 1914

The first year of fighting on the Eastern Front saw the Germans inflict massive casualties on the Russians, but still not enough to force them to sue for the separate peace that Germany wanted.

Germany's Austro-Hunga-rian ally did not fare as well in 1914. The Austro-Hungarians had taken enormous casualties in the war's first few months and they had botched their initial mobilization so badly that not even their capture of Belgrade could help them to recover. The fissures in the Austro-Hungarian system began to reveal themselves, forcing the Germans to devote more and more energy to helping them. That help came at a price, as German officers made more and more of the key decisions for the Austro-Hungarians.

Trading Space for Time

For their part, the Russians had survived, but they too had shown weaknesses. Many senior leaders in Paris and London worried that the Russians would not survive 1915 if they did not get some help. The size of the Russian Army, and the traditional Russian strategy of trading space for time, gave the Russians options. Their success in the Carpathians, moreover, helped the Russians to have faith that 1915 might be a better year than 1914 had been.

German strategists did not intend to fight a prolonged two-front war. They had to decide whether the bulk of their efforts for 1915 should be spent on the Western Front or the Eastern. The so-called 'easterners' argued that Russia was closer to defeat than France and Britain, and that a string of victories in 1915 would force them out of the war. Critics contended that the Russians could replace their manpower losses and could also retreat as they had done against Napoleon a century earlier, denying Germany a true victory.

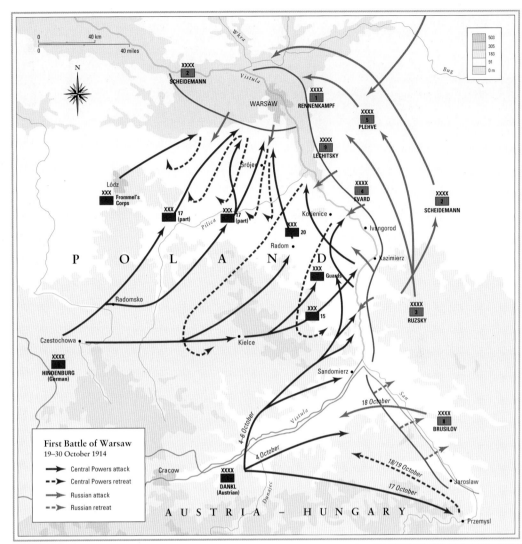

First Battle of Warsaw
19–30 October 1914

The Eastern Front to December 1914

45

Winter Battle in Masuria
7–18 February 1915

As had happened in the 1914 First Battle of
Masurian Lakes, the Germans moved quickly
and threatened to encircle the Russians. The
Eighth Army launched a surprise attack in a
snowstorm to prove that the Russians were
close to collapse. They also hoped to convince
their leaders to focus on the east in 1915.

In the confusion of the attack the entire Russian
corps surrendered in a forest, and the lines
moved about 113km (70 miles) in Germany's
favour. Tens of thousands of Russians surrendered
and many thousands more were killed. Supporters
argued that the battle proved the superiority of the
German Army to the Russian. Critics countered
that the territory the Germans gained held no real
strategic value and only made Germany's logistical
and supply problems worse.

The battle occurred at the same time that the
Austro-Hungarian garrison at Przemysl was faltering
and the surrender of the fortress became inevitable.
German strategists thus had to decide whether to
reinforce the operational success they had enjoyed
at the Masurian Lakes or dedicate themselves
to helping their faltering ally in the Carpathians.
The Masurian Lakes also failed to resolve the
fundamental debate inside Germany about whether
to seek victory in the east or the west.

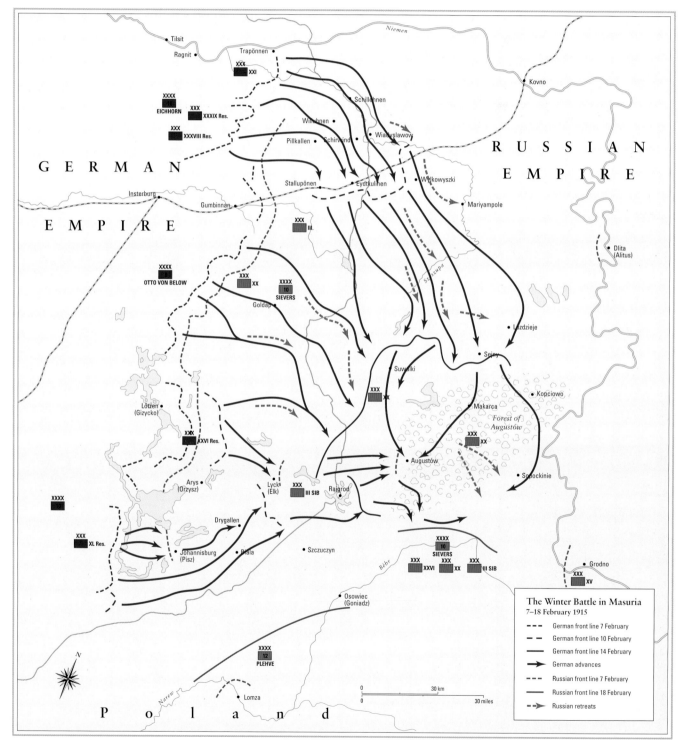

Central Powers Advance
May–September 1915

The massive Russian defeat at Gorlice-Tarnow quickly led to what became known as the Great Retreat from Poland. As Russian units in the direct path of the German advance in Galicia fell back, others also withdrew to protect their flanks. What should have been an orderly retreat soon degenerated into a rout from the Baltics to the Carpathians.

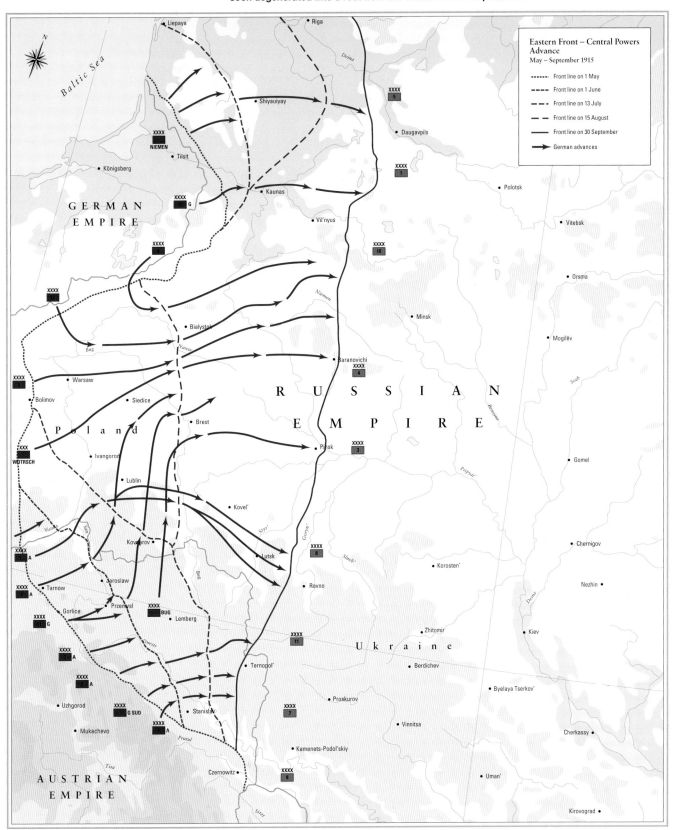

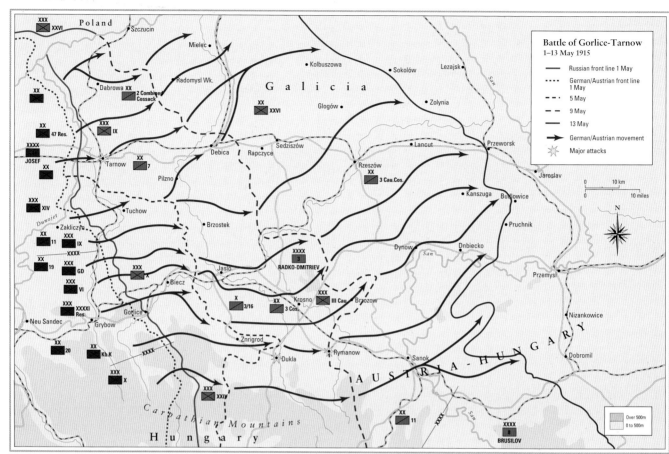

Central Powers Advance May–August 1915

Germany placed their main spring 1915 effort in the Carpathians. In the west they launched a diversionary attack in the Ypres salient.

German officers led a joint offensive with their Austro-Hungarian allies that stunned the Russian forces. Between the towns of Gorlice and Tarnow the Russians collapsed in the face of the offensive. As they began to retreat they exposed the flanks of their neighbouring units, forcing them to retreat also. By the time it ended, Russia had yielded all of Poland and suffered a massive defeat. Tsar Nicholas II fired his top commanders and took control of the armies, even though he was manifestly unqualified to do so. Despite the defeat the army managed to regroup and Russia stayed in the war. Criticism inside Russia, however, was growing.

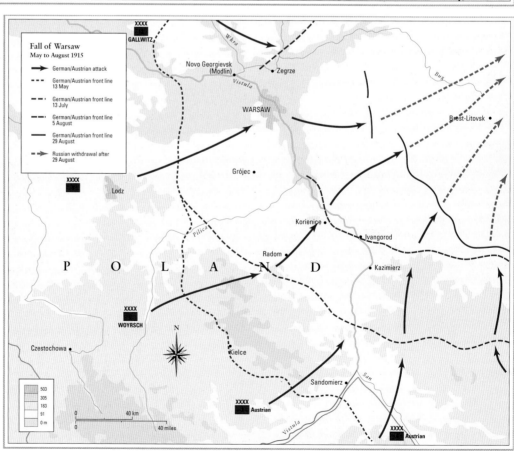

Bolimov – the First Use of Gas 3 January 1915

Looking for a decisive weapon, the Germans first introduced poison gas on the battlefield on a large scale at Bolimov in January 1915.

The Germans hoped to find a way to win a major battle in Poland in order to allow them to focus most of their efforts in the Carpathians, where their Austro-Hungarian ally needed them. At the Battle of Bolimov they faced a far larger Russian Army, but they hoped to even the odds by introducing a new weapon. They fired 18,000 shells containing xylyl bromide, a tear gas still used by police forces today. It failed to react as the Germans had hoped, in part because the cold Russian weather kept it in a solid state for too long. Circling winds also blew gas back into German lines. The gas did cause momentary panic in Russian lines, but the Germans were unable to take advantage. German commanders also realized that the gas scared their own men as much as it frightened the Russians.

Artillery Targets

Hoping to disrupt the confused Germans, the Russians counter-attacked with 11 divisions. But the command arrangements for the attack were put together too hurriedly and haphazardly. Russian forces proved too hard to control and the attack, although quite large, failed to have its desired effect. Tactically, the Russians concentrated their troops too tightly, giving German artillerists easy targets. Russia lost 40,000 men in three days, many of them young recruits recently called to the colours. No significant territory changed hands and the battle therefore proved to be inconclusive, although it led generals on all sides to begin to look more closely at using gas weapons, their limitations notwithstanding.

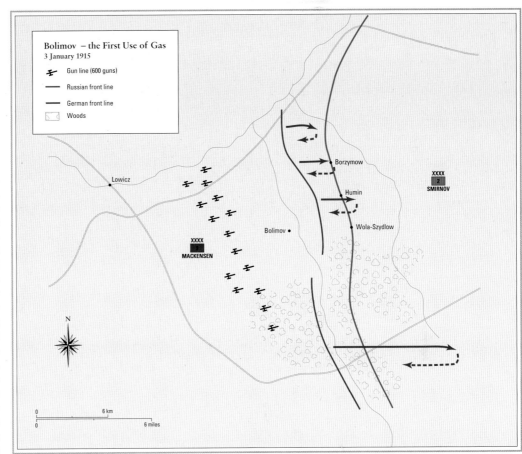

Bolimov – the First Use of Gas
3 January 1915

Gun line (600 guns)
Russian front line
German front line
Woods

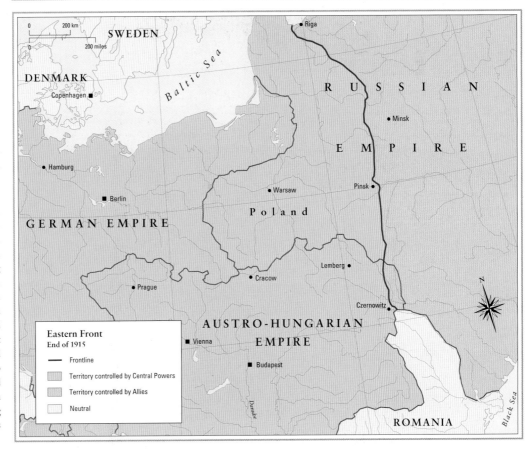

Eastern Front
End of 1915

Frontline
Territory controlled by Central Powers
Territory controlled by Allies
Neutral

Lake Naroch
17–24 March 1916

In December 1915 the Allies agreed to launch simultaneous offensives against the Central Powers in 1916. The Russian part of the plan became the Lake Naroch offensive.

The French put pressure on the Russians to launch an early offensive because of the German attack on Verdun. Tsar Nicholas responded by focusing 350,000 Russian troops against 75,000 Germans near Lake Naroch in present-day Belarus. Two days of artillery fire preceded the infantry assault. Nevertheless, much of the artillery failed to find its targets in poor weather, and Russian infantry tactics were too predictable. The Germans gave ground, but did not break, then counter-attacked, recovering much of their lost ground. The Russians lost more than 100,000 men while the Germans lost fewer than 20,000. As a result, Russian morale took another serious hit.

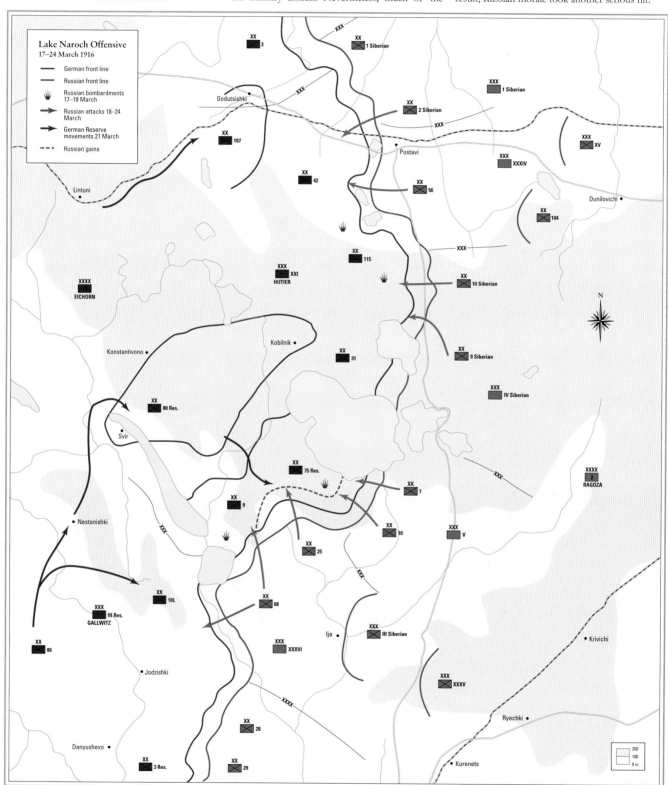

Brusilov Offensive 4 June–15 September 1916

This infamous Russian offensive temporarily changed the momentum of the war. Alexei Brusilov prepared his soldiers for the attack, mostly aimed at Austro-Hungarian forces.

rusilov used short but intense artillery barrages called 'hurricane bombardments' to strike units in the Austro-Hungarian front lines. With a reasonably accurate intelligence picture, Brusilov exploited his enemy's weaknesses and opened up an enormous hole in the Austro-Hungarian line. Stunned by the Russian movements, the Austro-

Hungarians responded poorly, allowing Brusilov to maintain his momentum. The Germans soon took over, directing nine German and four Austro-Hungarian divisions to the threatened sectors. At the same time, Russian commanders to the north and south of Brusilov moved slowly. As a result, Brusilov's offensive lost steam despite its good start.

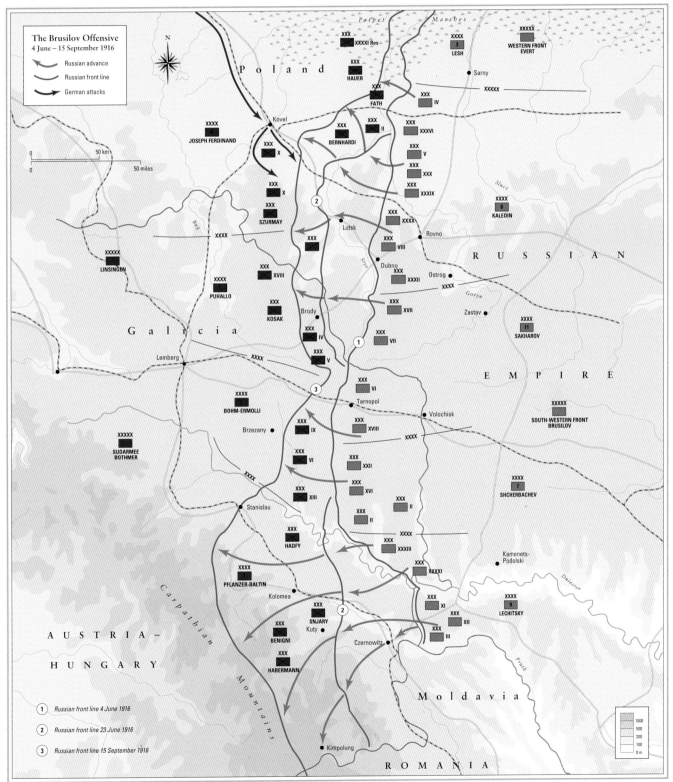

The Brusilov Offensive
4 June – 15 September 1916

→ Russian advance
⌒ Russian front line
➤ German attacks

1 Russian front line 4 June 1916
2 Russian front line 23 June 1916
3 Russian front line 15 September 1916

Romanian Invasion of Transylvania

27 August–18 September 1916

Afraid that Brusilov's success might mean they would lose their chance to seize Transylvania, the Romanians entered the war. They invaded Austria-Hungary hoping to keep the Russians from capturing Transylvania.

Transylvania contained large numbers of ethnic Romanians, most of whom greeted the invading Romanians as liberators. The Romanians declared war on Austria-Hungary only, and sent a 700,000-man army into Transylvania. Although large, the Romanian Army was short of heavy equipment and inexperienced in the methods of war developed since 1914. Romania had fought inconsistently in the Balkan Wars but the British and French had wooed them anyway. The Russians, however, had hoped they would remain neutral. Angry at Romanian expansion, the Russians refused to lend support. Nevertheless, the Romanian Army fought well against Austro-Hungarian forces already deeply engaged in other theatres. They pushed 80km (50 miles) into Transylvania, threatening the agricultural heartland of the empire. Germany responded by declaring war on the Romanians. Kaiser Wilhelm felt betrayed by the Romanian royal family, which had promised its neutrality. The Ottoman Empire and Bulgaria soon followed suit.

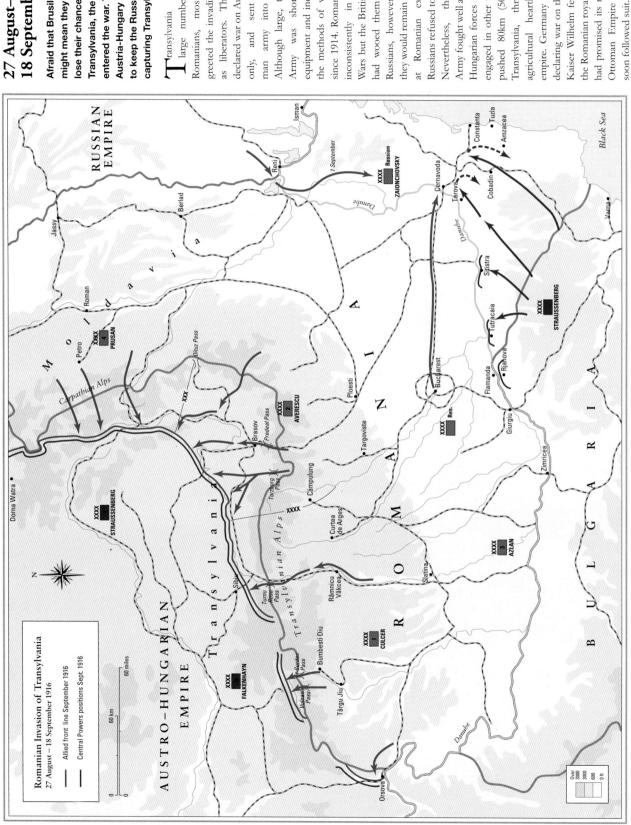

Romanian Invasion of Transylvania
27 August – 18 September 1916
— Allied front line September 1916
— Central Powers positions Sept. 1916

Invasion of Romania
September 1916–January 1917

Within just a few weeks of entering a war they hoped they could keep contained to Austria-Hungary alone, the under-equipped and inexperienced Romanian Army faced the full fury of a Central Powers offensive. Romanian forces found themselves terribly outmatched in every way. The ruthless German General Erich von Falkenhayn, who had just been relieved of command at the murderous Battle of Verdun, took command of the Central Powers forces. Falkenhayn designed a campaign of annihilation for the Romanians both to avenge their betrayal to the Kaiser and to send a warning to any remaining neutral states that might want to join the Allies.

Falkenhayn commanded two field armies made up of soldiers from Germany, Austria-Hungary, Bulgaria and the Ottoman Empire. They were led by veteran officers with experience of successful offensives. The Central Powers invaded Romania from two directions, setting up a giant pincer movement aimed at the Romanian lines of communication. The Romanians tried to disrupt this plan with a counteroffensive of their own but failed. The southern arm of the Central Powers pincer headed for the Black Sea coast and the critical port town of Constanta. The northern pincer smashed through makeshift Romanian defences in Transylvania then moved into the plains around Ploesti before turning northeast in an effort to trap the fleeing Romanian soldiers against the mountains.

The Romanian forces crumbled before the lightning movements of the Central Powers. The Germans captured Bucharest in early December, sealing Romania's fate. In less than four months the Romanians lost more than 300,000 men – killed, wounded, captured or missing. Central Powers forces moved at will, seizing territory, grain and animals. Terrified of having their enemies on yet another front, the Russians agreed to provide support to Romanian forces in Moldavia, but it was too little too late.

Having won the campaign, the Central Powers wrote a harsh peace. They divided Romania between them, and took out favourable 90-year leases on the valuable oil deposits in and around Ploesti. The Central Powers also took as much food as they could, hoping to use the Romanian breadbasket to compensate for the food lost to the British blockade. The brutal Treaty of Bucharest confirmed Romania's devastation, although after the war the Romanians not only recovered what they had lost, the Treaty of Versailles gave them most of Transylvania, which had been their war aim in the first place.

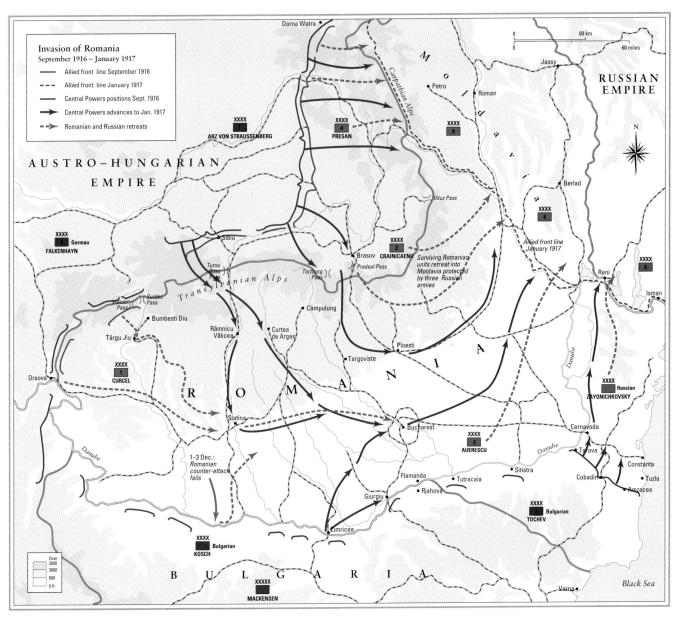

Eastern Front
December 1916–March 1917

Despite all of the killing and bloodshed, the Eastern Front remained active and the Germans still faced a two-front dilemma. Easterners in the Germany Army high command continued to argue that the east offered the best prospect of victory against a Russian Army whose morale must be declining. They also argued that further efforts in the east would provide help to the Austro-Hungarians – and possibly the Ottomans as well. The Germans had plans to raise enough food on the captured land to sustain Germany through the end of the war.

The Eastern Front posed nearly infinite problems for the German forces. The dizzying number of ethnicities presented enormous challenges for an army of occupation. Moreover, the further east the Germans pushed, the longer and more exposed their various supply lines became. Although the Germans delivered a series of seeming knockout blows to the Russians, Russia always seemed able to bounce back and replace its considerable losses. The east appeared to absorb every German thrust, no matter how powerful. Germany's Austro-Hungarian allies, moreover, seemed almost as close to collapse as the Russians.

The front line in the east was enormous, running from the Baltic coastline to the Black Sea. The Russian retreat that followed the Gorlice-Tarnow Campaign and the defeat of Romania straightened the Russian line and left few exposed salients for the Germans to attack. The huge spaces of the east also contained few critical nodes such as rail junctures or major cities. Thus the Germans had no obvious place on the map to target. Russian forces also still had plenty of space they could trade for time, parrying German blows while complicating their supply problems.

The Germans recognized these complications, but hoped that the Russians would collapse under persistent military pressure in 1917. They knew that dissatisfaction was rising against the Tsar and his system. They also knew that a revolution had occurred during the Russo-Japanese War in 1905 when the Russian people had grown disenchanted with that war.

Success to Build Upon

For their part, Russian generals argued that they had had success during the Brusilov Offensive upon which they could build in the coming year. At the very least, they claimed that they had fared no worse than the British at the Somme or the French at Verdun. Russian leaders promised their allies that with some help they could make a difference on the battlefield in 1917. The outcome of the war on the eastern front thus remained in doubt as the New Year dawned.

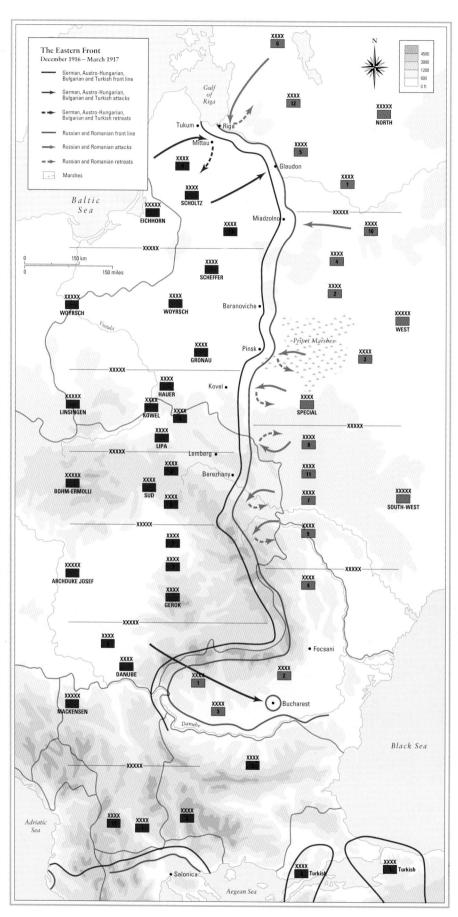

Russian Revolution 1917

Russia's defeat came from within, albeit with help from the Germans. As in 1905 a revolution (more accurately two revolutions) rocked Russia and destroyed the political basis of Russia's war.

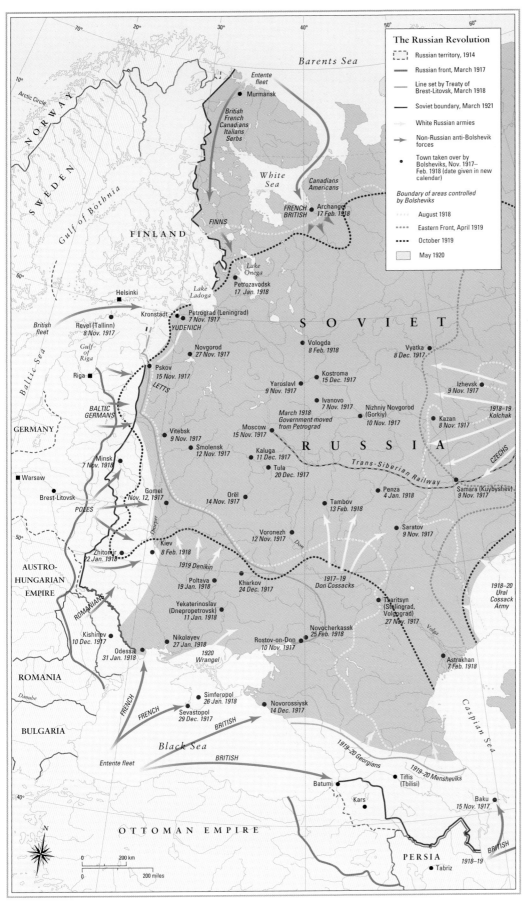

The first Russian revolution led to the abdication of the Tsar on 2 March. The Tsar's brother, Grand Duke Michael, refused to follow Nicholas on the throne, thus ending the Romanov dynasty's time in power. In its place came a provisional government under the moderate politician Alexander Kerensky, who pledged to keep Russia in the war. This time, Russians would fight for their own future rather than for the goals of the Tsar and the aristocracy. Kerensky had the support of the British and French governments, which hoped that he could keep the Germans tied down in the east. They were also happy to get rid of the autocratic Tsar and claim that the new Russian government was at least more representative. Most of Russia's senior military leaders pledged their support for the new government, lending it a further air of legitimacy.

Rise of the Bolsheviks

The second revolution came in November when Vladimir Lenin's Bolsheviks seized power. The Germans had secretly brought Lenin and other radicals into Russia from exile in Switzerland in the hopes that they would foment trouble. They certainly did, although the Germans soon worried that they might not be able to contain the forces they had unleashed. The Bolsheviks pledged to bring Russia bread, peace and land reform. They had the support of many former soldiers who brought their weapons with them when they had deserted. Unlike Kerensky, the Bolsheviks had neither the support of the western Allies nor a desire to remain in the war.

The Russian Revolution

- - - - Russian territory, 1914
- ———— Russian front, March 1917
- ———— Line set by Treaty of Brest-Litovsk, March 1918
- ———— Soviet boundary, March 1921
- ⟶ White Russian armies
- ⟶ Non-Russian anti-Bolshevik forces
- ● Town taken over by Bolsheviks, Nov. 1917– Feb. 1918 (date given in new calendar)

Boundary of areas controlled by Bolsheviks
- ·········· August 1918
- ·········· Eastern Front, April 1919
- ·········· October 1919
- ▨ May 1920

Kerensky Offensive
1 July–4 August 1917

Kerensky vainly hoped that a successful offensive would both prove the new government's value to the allies and its own legitimacy to the Russian people.

Alexei Brusilov commanded the new Russian offensive, hoping to repeat his success of the year before. But the Russian army had deteriorated significantly in one year, with supply and morale problems having worsened significantly. Brusilov also found that some of his 1916 methods did not work as well in 1917.

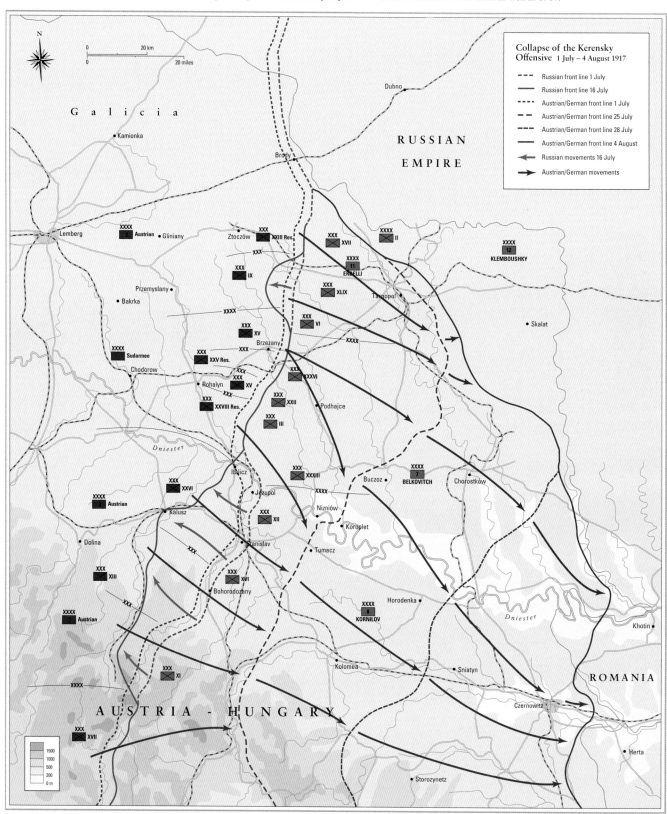

Collapse of the Kerensky
Offensive 1 July – 4 August 1917

- - - Russian front line 1 July
——— Russian front line 16 July
· · · · Austrian/German front line 1 July
– – – Austrian/German front line 25 July
- - - Austrian/German front line 28 July
——— Austrian/German front line 4 August
← Russian movements 16 July
→ Austrian/German movements

German Baltic Operations
1 September–20 October 1917

The Germans introduced new methods in a series of Baltic offensives that proved to be the beginning of the end for Kerensky's provisional government.

The Germans used amphibious warfare to capture islands, but the real innovations came on land. Under General Oskar von Hutier, the Germans developed so-called 'stormtroop' tactics. All armies had been working on something similar, but at Riga the Germans successfully put all the pieces together for the first time.

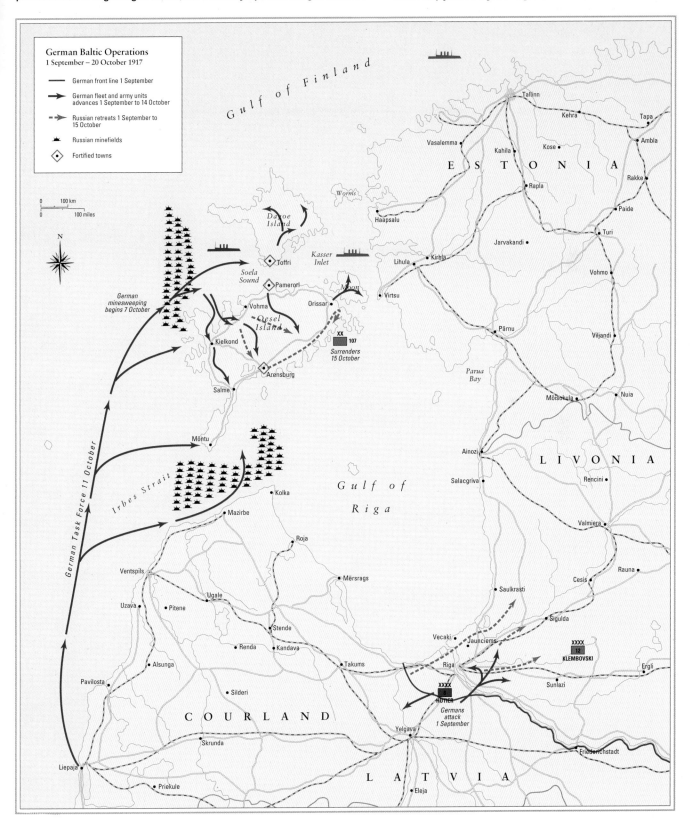

German Baltic Operations
1 September – 20 October 1917

German front line 1 September

German fleet and army units advances 1 September to 14 October

Russian retreats 1 September to 15 October

Russian minefields

Fortified towns

Treaty of Brest-Litovsk
3 March 1918

The Bolsheviks aimed to extract Russia from the war as quickly as possible. Despite being shocked at the excessive demands made by the Germans for Russian territory and resources, they reluctantly agreed to the terms and conditions – they had no other options. However, in Paris and London the terms of the treaty reinforced in Allied minds the need to win the war at all costs or face the same dismal fate the Germans had imposed on Romania and Russia in successive treaties as a consequence.

Germany seized more than 1.6 million km² (620,000 miles²) of formerly Russian territory, as well as all the minerals and food contained therein. Poland, the Baltic states and Finland all went to the German Empire. The Germans were now free to move troops west in the hopes that greater numbers and new Hutier tactics could win the war in France. Still, they had to leave thousands of troops in the east to enforce their new demands, contain the Bolsheviks and control a brewing civil war in the Ukraine. Even with the war in the east over, the Germans still faced problems. Russia exited one war and entered almost immediately into a civil conflict.

The Treaty of Brest-Litovsk
3 March 1918

- Central powers
- Allied powers
- Front line, mid-1917
- Central Powers occupation of Russia, Feb.–May 1918 and occupation of Georgia by Ottoman Empire, May 1918
- Movement of combat divisions from Eastern Front to Western, Italian and Balkan Fronts March – May 1918
- Front line, Nov. 1918

The New States of Eastern Europe, 1919

The war shattered the four empires that had dominated Eastern Europe. With the Germans, Austro-Hungarians, Russians and Ottomans gone, eastern Europe was remade. The new borders solved few problems, however, and often planted the seeds of future conflict.

The statesmen who tried to redraw the borders of eastern Europe faced conflicting pressures. On the one hand, leaders like American President Woodrow Wilson argued for national self-determination. If the ethnic and political borders were made more consistent, they contended, then the causes of war in the region would go away. Still, finding borders that met this criteria in a region of tremendous diversity proved to be nearly impossible.

Even if they could find such borders, the statesmen still had to create states with defensible borders and enough economic resources to make the new states viable. Poland, for example, could not claim the port city of Danzig (Gdansk) based on ethnicity, but to form Poland without it would place the state at an immediate disadvantage.

The final agreements that emerged from the Paris Peace Conference therefore represented a series of compromises. Romania doubled in size, less because of any argument based on ethnicity, but because it had been on the winning side. It therefore had a claim to Transylvania, which had a divided Romanian and Hungarian population.

The great powers also created a Kingdom of Serbs, Croats and Slovenes (later called Yugoslavia), based on the theory that a larger state would be more viable in the long run. The new state nevertheless contained a number of mutually antagonistic ethnic groups within its borders.

The Bastard of Versailles

The most important change on the map of Europe came in the recreation of the state of Poland. Wiped off the map in 1795, the new Poland took territory from Germany, Austria-Hungary and Russia. Both the Germans and the Russians resented losing land to the new state. The Russians called it 'the bastard of Versailles' and normally referred to it as 'western Ukraine' to demonstrate their opposition.

The new Poland and the Soviet Union fought a short, sharp war to decide the exact border between them. France and Britain sent supplies and advisors to the Poles in the hopes that they would stop the Bolsheviks from spreading Communism west. The Polish Army won the dramatic Battle of Warsaw in 1920. Hailed as the 'Miracle on the Vistula,' it preserved Polish independence and set the Polish-Soviet border on terms favourable to the Poles. But both the German and Soviet governments sought to revise those borders or destroy the Polish state once and for all.

The New States of Eastern
Europe c.1919

- Territory lost by Germany
- Territory lost by Russia (Soviet Union after 1917)
- Territory lost by Bulgaria
- States and territories created from the former Austro-Hungarian Empire
- Battles and campaigns fought by emerging states
- Borders recognized by 1920–22

6 December 1917 Date of Independence or state formation

Australian infantry grab what rest they can, while their Vickers machine guns remain at the ready.

THE WESTERN FRONT

The war on the Western Front began as a war of movement, but after the 1914 Battle of the Marne, both sides very quickly entrenched. Generals looked for solutions to the stasis of trench warfare, including massive use of artillery to open holes in the enemy's defences, new technologies like tanks and poison gas, and, finally, grinding attrition.

Soldiers on all sides struggled to adapt to this new form of war, which involved long periods of inactivity, enormous battles of a size previously unheard of, and a constant small war of trench raids and snipers. Poor food, limited health care, and infrequent contact with home added to the burdens of frontline soldiers.

The term 'shell shock' emerged as a way to describe the psychological damage that such war had on combatants.

Flanders fields
English and Belgian soldiers meet near Ypres in Flanders, the site of three massive battles. The Belgians desperately wanted to keep control over some small slice of their country, most of it having been occupied by the Germans.

Australian gunners walk through Chateau Wood
The environmental devastation of industrial warfare can be seen here in what was once a forest called Chateau Wood near Hoodge in the Ypres sector, ca. October 1917. Duckboards became essential in navigating such a landscape.

Artillery barrage
German soldiers prepare to advance while facing an artillery barrage near Ypres, Belgium, 1915. The Germans introduced the first systemic use of poison gas on the Western Front at the same battle.

'Landships' at the Somme
The British first used tanks at the Battle of the Somme, when 49 Mark I types were deployed. Although they often broke down, they pointed the way toward a mechanized style of war that benefitted the Allies.

Machine gun crew
Allied soldiers wearing gas masks operate a Vickers machine gun on the Western Front. Gas warfare was a constant cat-and-mouse game between the quality of masks and the new gases designed to penetrate them.

Voie Sacrée
French soldiers rest near Fort Vaux, Verdun, before moving up the battle line. In the background vehicles are moving along *La Voie Sacrée* ('The Sacred Way'), the only road artery connecting Verdun to the outside world.

Schlieffen Plan 1905 and 1914

Germany's war plan assumed that any diplomatic crisis in Europe would lead to war with both Russia and France. It then presumed that only a rapid movement through Belgium and France toward Paris would defeat the French in time for Germany to reorient east and face the Russians. The plan was always understood as a long-odds gamble. If it failed, Germany would need to improvise a way around the two-front dilemma its leaders most feared.

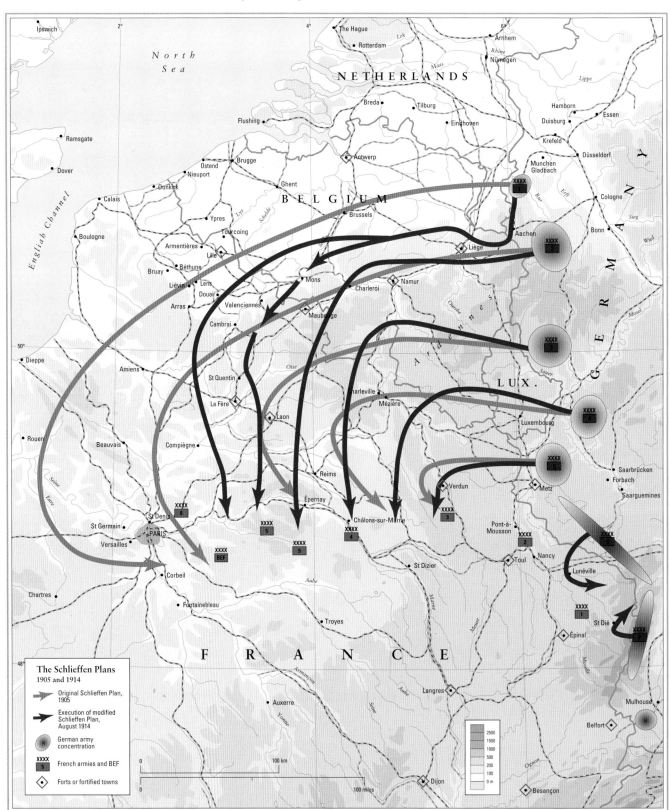

The Schlieffen Plans
1905 and 1914

- Original Schlieffen Plan, 1905
- Execution of modified Schlieffen Plan, August 1914
- German army concentration
- French armies and BEF
- Forts or fortified towns

Plan XVII 1914

The French war plan, Plan XVII, was in reality a plan to concentrate the armies in the critical sectors of the expected front lines. Although it was more offensive than its predecessors, it had no single operational goal like its German counterpart's focus on Paris.

French strategists had guessed that the Germans would attack through Belgium rather than challenge France's impressive chain of fortifications on the Franco–German border. Plan XVII concentrated the French armies to the south of the expected German line of advance. Once there, French troops could either smash in the southern flank of the German attack or attack into Alsace and Lorraine, depending upon which option the French commander thought more likely to produce victory.

In August 1914, French General Joseph Joffre misread German intentions. He did not correctly gauge the number of soldiers the Germans were dedicating to the right wing of the attack. He was thus slow to react to German movements. He ordered attacks into Alsace and Lorraine on the flawed assumption that such attacks could derail the German advance.

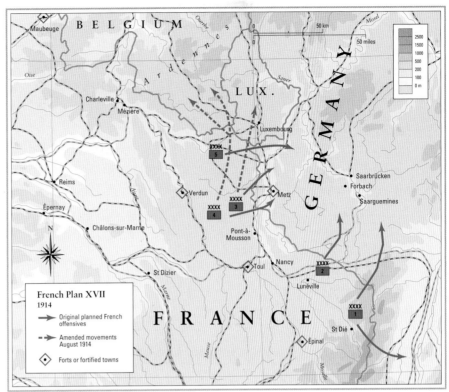

French Plan XVII
1914

→ Original planned French offensives

⇢ Amended movements August 1914

◇ Forts or fortified towns

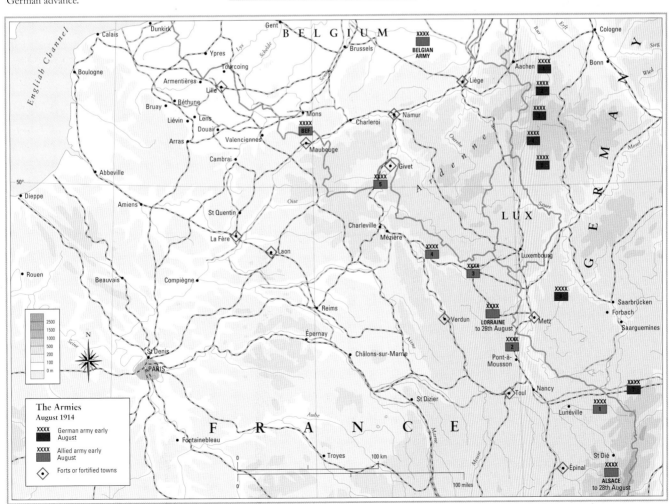

The Armies
August 1914

■ German army early August

■ Allied army early August

◇ Forts or fortified towns

Conquest
of Belgium 1914

Neutral Belgium had
invested heavily in modern
fortifications, most notably
around Liège and Antwerp.
German artillery was designed
to defeat these fortifications
but they still managed to
hold up the German armies.
Belgian partisans known as
franc-tireurs also engaged
in a guerrilla operations that
caused havoc to Germany's
careful timetables. These
frustrations contributed to the
atrocities that the Germans
committed in Belgium.

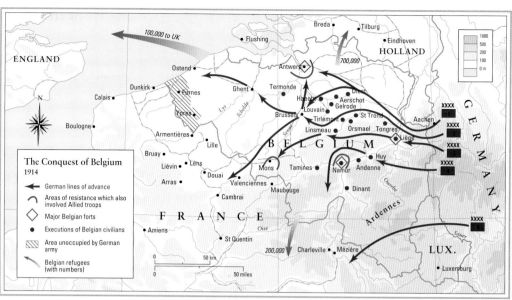

The Conquest of Belgium
1914

⟵ German lines of advance

⌒ Areas of resistance which also
   involved Allied troops

◇ Major Belgian forts

• Executions of Belgian civilians

▨ Area unoccupied by German
   army

⟶ Belgian refugees
   (with numbers)

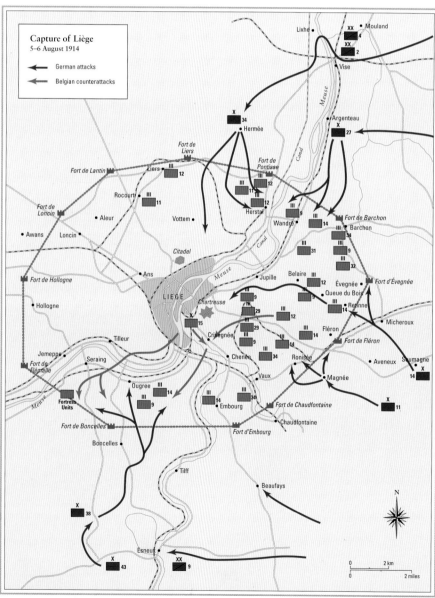

Capture of Liège
5–6 August 1914

⟵ German attacks

⟵ Belgian counterattacks

German military plans depended upon a rapid
movement through Belgium, a nation that
had invested heavily in fortifications around its
most important cities and rail junctures. Liège in
particular was one of Europe's most powerful
fortifications. Redesigned periodically in the years
before the war, it received its latest upgrade from
1880 to 1891. In 1914 Liège boasted 12 separate
forts that guarded the approaches to the town. Each
of the forts was designed to withstand artillery fire
from guns as large as 21cm (8.2in), the largest in the
Belgian inventory. The forts were also designed to
be protected by succeeding lines of advanced field
works defended by infantry as well as interlocking
fire from Belgian artillery.

By 1914 the forts looked more powerful than
they really were. The Germans designed 28cm (11in)
guns to reduce the fortresses of Liège, rendering
many of their defences irrelevant. The Belgians
saw the problem but lacked the time or money
to redesign the forts once again. They therefore
changed the mission of the forts from an indefinite
defence to a defence of one month's time in order
to give the Belgian army time to mobilize. Even that
goal seemed far-fetched given the limited facilities
in the forts for the daily needs of the garrisons.

Erich Ludendorff and Liège

Prescient military leaders understood that the
Belgian forts might well hold the key to victory
or defeat. British General Sir Henry Wilson and
German General Erich Ludendorff both took
prewar holidays in Belgium, making sketches of
the forts and learning what they could about the
local terrain. In 1914, General Ludendorff led one
of the German columns that descended on Liège.
He oversaw the reduction of the town's forts with
German artillery then, in an episode that made him
famous across Germany, he demanded the fort's
surrender by banging on the citadel door with the
hilt of his sword.

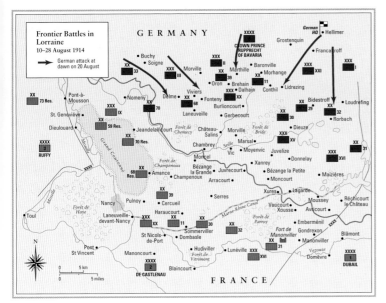

Frontier Battles in
Lorraine
10–28 August 1914

→ German attack at
dawn on 20 August

Battles of the Frontiers 1914

French attacks into the heavily forested and well defended border area with Germany failed miserably. French troops advanced courageously, but they learned the lesson that so many more soldiers would learn during the war: defence was now the stronger form of warfare.

The Battles of the Frontiers were the bloodiest of the war for France in terms of percentages of men lost. Infantry attacks went forward with insufficient artillery support and staff work. German forces, expecting to defend in the sector, allowed the French to advance into Alsace and Lorraine until they reached German positions, almost always sited on high ground. Then machineguns opened fire and decimated the attackers. French medics were overwhelmed by the fighting, and many attacks dissolved due to the deaths of so many officers. Troops suffered serious reversals just as their generals were divining the true strength of the German advance through Belgium. Attacks that had begun with high hopes of returning Alsace and Lorraine to French control melted away with the unprecedented losses.

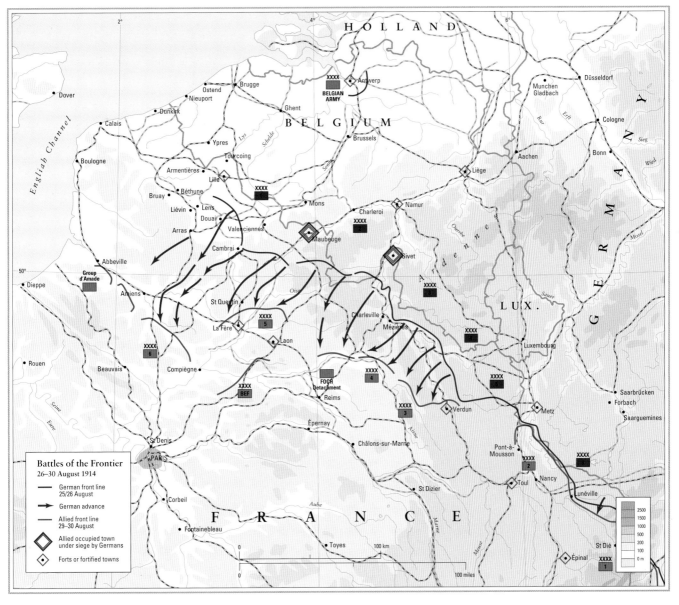

Battles of the Frontier
26–30 August 1914

— German front line
25/26 August

→ German advance

— Allied front line
29–30 August

◆ Allied occupied town
under siege by Germans

◇ Forts or fortified towns

Battle of Mons
22–24 August 1914

The first large-scale action between the British and German armies in the war, Mons pitted almost the entire British Expeditionary Force against the larger and better-equipped German First Army. The BEF set up a defensive line along the Mons canal.

The British commander, Sir John French, set up his two corps in a defensive position and waited for the anticipated German attack. British soldiers were long-service professionals who knew how to do their job, and do it well. Despite being outnumbered, they held the line and delivered their rifle fire both quickly and accurately. However, Sir John knew that he could not hold the Mons position indefinitely given the superiority of German numbers and the withdrawal of the French Army on his flank. Another German attack almost divided the two British corps from one another, a circumstance that might have resulted in both being destroyed. The British Expeditionary Force thus began a retreat from the Mons position, albeit with the knowledge that they had fought well against a larger foe.

The Retreat from Mons

The British II Corps, although bloodied at the Battle of Mons, fought a successful rearguard action at Le Cateau close to Mons in the far north of France. The largest British battle since Waterloo, it slowed the German advance into France but could not stop the British retreat toward Paris. The two battles had inflicted irreparable damage on Britain's small volunteer army. Sir John knew he had to preserve that army. He wanted to retire his men to the west of Paris to give them a much-needed rest, but the French urged them to deploy between the Germans and Paris as part of a planned counteroffensive on the Marne River.

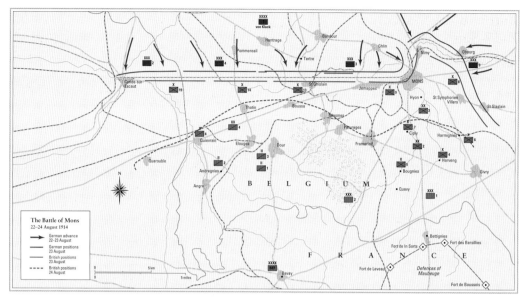

The Battle of Mons
22–24 August 1914
- German advance 22–23 August
- German positions 23 August
- British positions 23 August
- British positions 24 August

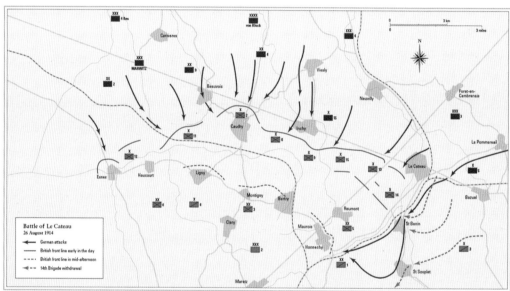

Battle of Le Cateau
26 August 1914
- German attacks
- British front line early in the day
- British front line in mid-afternoon
- 14th Brigade withdrawal

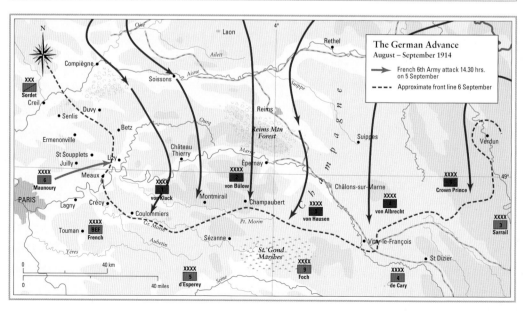

The German Advance
August – September 1914
- French 6th Army attack 14.30 hrs. on 5 September
- Approximate front line 6 September

Battle of the Marne
7–13 September 1914

The First Battle of the Marne involved more than one million men on each side. It was then the largest battle ever fought. It stopped the German advance and put an end to the Schlieffen Plan's hope for the capture of Paris.

The tired German Army, operating at the end of a long supply line, gave up on the idea of taking Paris. Instead, Germany decided to form a pincer movement from Verdun to Paris and trap the British and French armies inside. French aviators detected the change of direction, allowing the Allies to attack the flanks and the centre of the German advance. The key to this enormous battle lay near the Marne River, where French armies and the exhausted BEF attacked, separating two German armies from each other and exposing their flanks. The Germans reluctantly decided to retreat in order to maintain their line. They moved to high ground behind the Aisne River and began to dig-in. The allies pursued but could not dislodge them from their new positions.

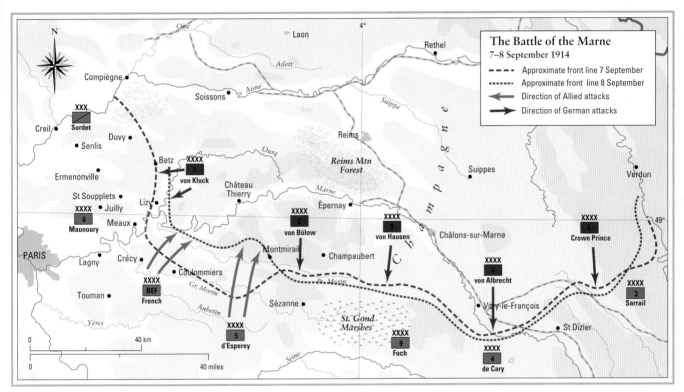

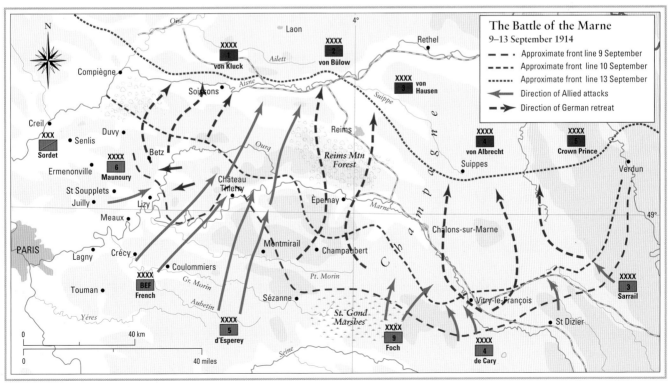

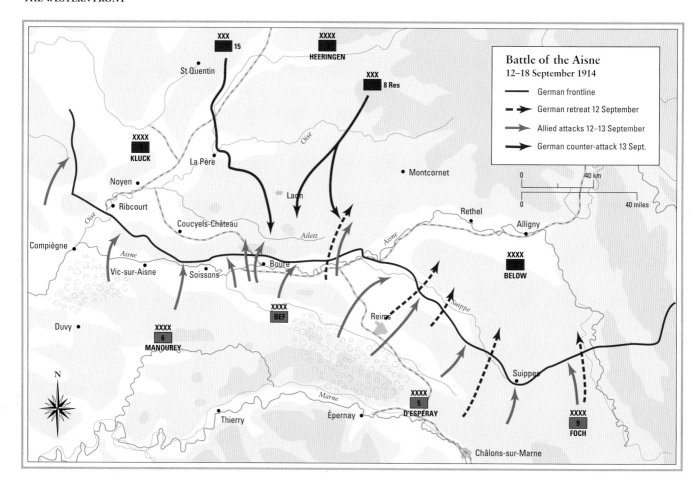

Battle of the Aisne
12–18 September 1914

——— German frontline

━ ━ ▶ German retreat 12 September

——▶ Allied attacks 12–13 September

——▶ German counter-attack 13 Sept.

0   40 km

0   40 miles

The Race to the Sea September– October 1914

With the Marne battle over, each side tried to manoeuvre around the other's flanks in the hopes of winning a great battle. They continued unsuccessfully to do so until they reached the North Sea.

As the contending armies moved further to the north, the Germans generally had the luxury of selectively giving ground in order to choose the best defensive terrain for their objectives. They could therefore choose to dig-in on high ground or in front of important rail and road links. These German strategic choices determined the geography of the next four years of the war. The Allies, desperate to recover as much ground as possible, did not have the same options.

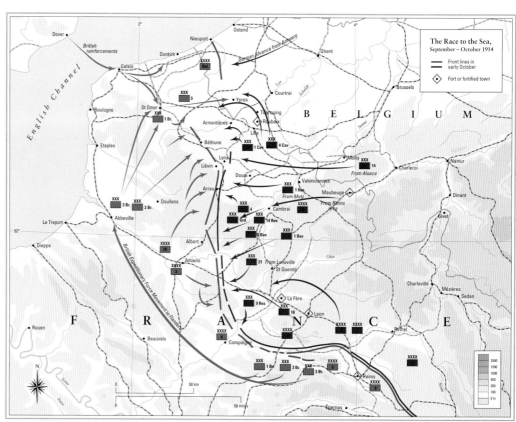

The Race to the Sea,
September – October 1914

━━ Front lines in early October

◈ Fort or fortified town

Yser and Ypres October–November 1914

The Race to the Sea ended at the Belgian town of Ypres and the Yser River. As it was the last strip of Belgian territory not occupied by the Germans, it took on a tremendous symbolic value to both sides.

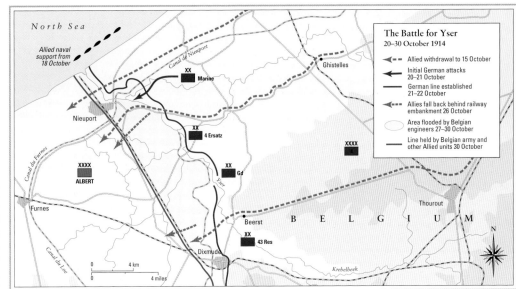

The Ypres salient held the key to the defence of the critical supply bases on the French side of the English Channel, including Dunkirk, Calais and Boulogne. Without those ports, the BEF could not easily resupply itself. Thus Ypres had to be held even if it was difficult terrain to defend. It sat below sea level in many places, making entrenchments difficult to dig. Therefore the battle in the Ypres salient relied on bloody frontal attacks, most famously the Kindermord, a vicious assault by young German volunteers at Langemarck. The battle swung back and forth for almost a month in increasingly deteriorating weather, causing misery for both sides.

Stalemate at Ypres

The Allies managed to hold on at Ypres due to two decisions. The first involved sending the aggressive and optimistic French General Ferdinand Foch to oversee coalition operations in the region. Foch organized the units in the sector and brought confidence to the Allied officers fighting at Ypres. The Allies also opened the sluice gates that kept the North Sea out of the Yser basin. This action sent water rushing all over the sector, destroying agriculture but creating a barrier behind which the Allies could refit and reorganize their troops. The first battle of Ypres ended when snow and freezing weather, as well as the mutual exhaustion of both sides, made further operations impossible. The region was so strategically located and already so symbolic that both sides knew it would again be the scene of heavy fighting.

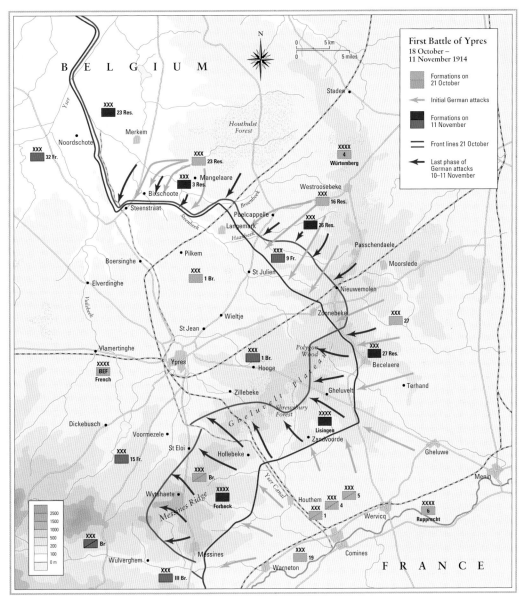

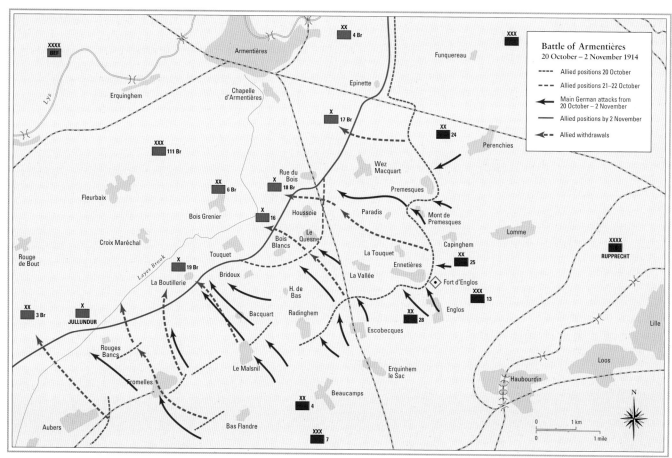

Battle of Armentières
20 October – 2 November 1914

- - - - - Allied positions 20 October
– – – – Allied positions 21–22 October
← Main German attacks from 20 October – 2 November
――― Allied positions by 2 November
←- - Allied withdrawals

XXXX BEF

Armentières

4 Br XX

XXX

Funquereau

Erquinghem

Chapelle d'Armentières

Lys

Epinette

X 17 Br

XX 24

Perenchies

XXX 111 Br

Wez Macquart

Rue du Bois

X 18 Br

Premesques

Fleurbaix

XX 6 Br

X

Houssoie

Paradis

Mont de Premesques

Lomme

Bois Grenier

X 16

Le Quesne

Bois Blancs

La Touquet

Capinghem

XX 25

XXXX RUPPRECHT

Croix Maréchal

Touquet

Ennetières

La Vallée

Rouge de Bout

Layes Brook

X 19 Br

Bridoux

H. de Bas

Fort d'Englos

XXX 13

XX 28

Englos

Lille

La Boutillerie

Radinghem

XX 3 Br   X JULLUNDUR

Bacquart

Escobecques

Loos

Rouges Bancs

Le Malsnil

Erquinhem le Sac

Haubourdin

N

Fromelles

Beaucamps

XX 4

Aubers

Bas Flandre

XXX 7

0   1 km
0   1 mile

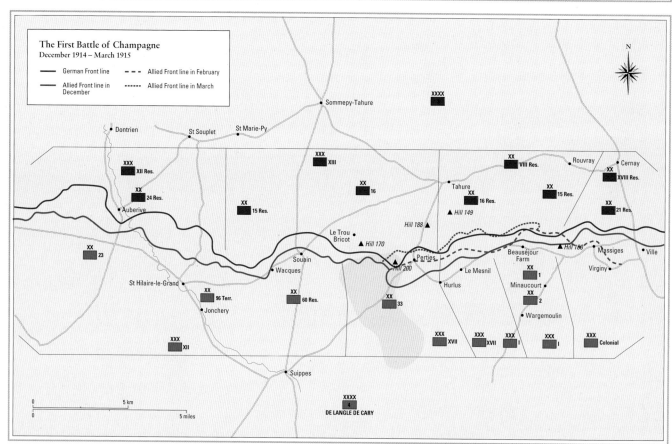

The First Battle of Champagne
December 1914 – March 1915

――― German Front line
――― Allied Front line in December
– – – – Allied Front line in February
· · · · · Allied Front line in March

N

Sommepy-Tahure

XXXX

Dontrien

St Souplet

St Marie-Py

Rouvray

Cernay

XXX XIII

XX VIII Res.

XX XVIII Res.

XXX XII Res.

XX 16

Tahure

XX 16 Res.

XX 15 Res.

XX 21 Res.

XX 24 Res.

Auberive

XX 15 Res.

▲ Hill 149

▲ Hill 188

Le Trou Bricot

Beauséjour Farm

▲ Hill 180

Massiges

Ville

XX 23

▲ Hill 170

▲ Hill 200

Perthes

Virginy

Souain

Wacques

Le Mesnil

XX 1

St Hilaire-le-Grand

Hurlus

Minaucourt

XX 2

XX 96 Terr.

XX 60 Res.

XX 33

Jonchery

Wargemoulin

XXX XVII

XXX XVII

XXX I

XXX I

XXX Colonial

XXX XII

Suippes

0   5 km
0   5 miles

XXXX 4 DE LANGLE DE CARY

The Western Front
October–December 1914

Soldiers began to dig in, both to protect themselves from the enemy and to provide some protection from the weather. Not all strategists thought that the entrenchments would become a near-permanent condition of the war. Many believed that in the Spring they could break through the enemy lines with a combination of more powerful artillery and better-trained soldiers. If the line broke in one place, attacking soldiers could exploit the enemy's flanks and rear areas.

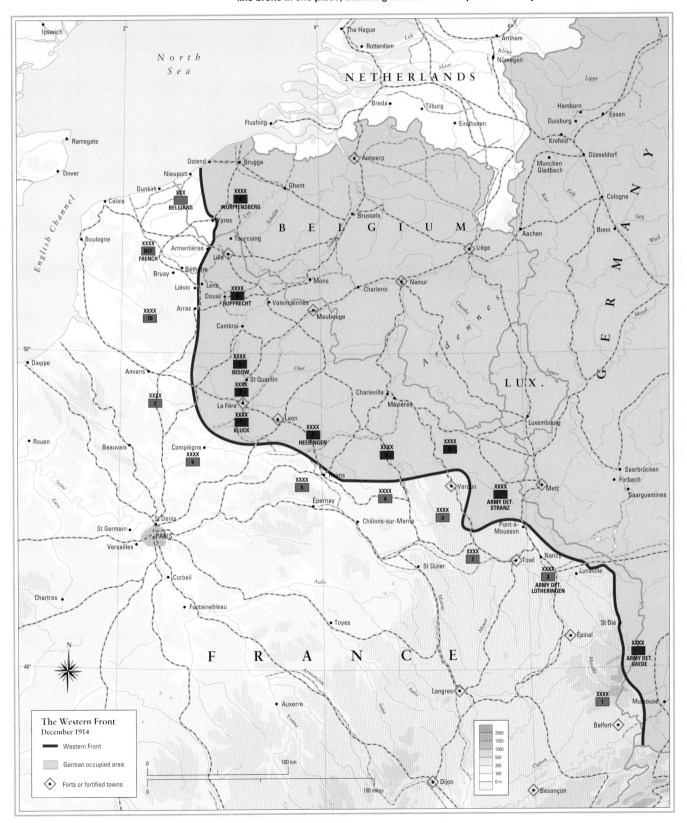

The Western Front
December 1914

— Western Front

▢ German occupied area

◇ Forts or fortified towns

0   100 km
0   100 miles

2500
1500
1000
500
200
100
0 m

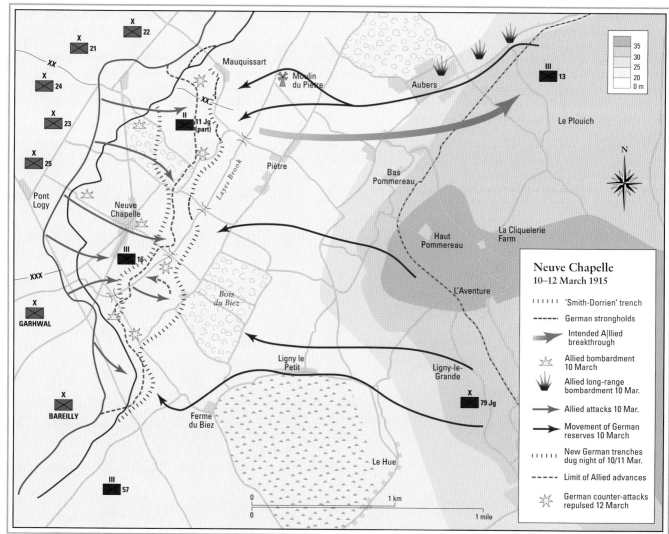

Neuve Chapelle
10–12 March 1915

Neuve Chapelle showed both promise and frustration. It began well but soon degenerated into chaos that the Germans exploited. By the end, the British gained little for heavy losses.

The operational goal of the Neuve Chapelle operation was to capture the rail line that lay just behind the German front lines. Without it, the Germans could not supply their men in the sector and would therefore have to retreat to the next parallel rail line. The British fired a short but intense artillery bombardment of just 35 minutes that nevertheless outweighed all the shells the British fired at Waterloo. The British took the town, but from there not much went well. They had too little artillery in reserve to solidify their gains. The Germans soon counter-attacked and, without enemy artillery to stop them, they quickly retook the town. They even took some territory that had been British before the battle. The British lost 13,000 soldiers and the Germans lost 15,000.

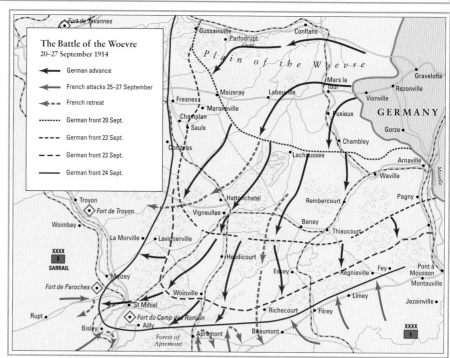

Second Battle of Ypres
22 April–25 May 1915

The Second Battle of Ypres is best known today for being the first battle in which poison gas was used on a large scale. The Germans introduced it in the hopes of compensating for their smaller numbers. It temporarily opened a hole in the line, but was not decisive.

The German forces had decided to make their main effort in the east in 1915 in a decision that became known as the Gorlice-Tarnow Offensive.

In order to make their plans work effectively, the Germans decided on a limited attack in the west to disguise their real intentions. They opened the offensive with 170 tonnes (168 tons) of chlorine gas that struck a French Territorial division – troops quickly fled in understandable terror. German soldiers were supposed to attack through the deadly chlorine gas cloud but, lacking any kind of protection, they refused the orders or at least moved with extreme caution. Canadian soldiers moved into the sector and helped to fill in the gap, thus negating any operational effect the gas might have given the Germans.

The Second Battle of Ypres did not produce any major gains for the Germans, but it did throw the Allies off balance and prevented them from detecting the transfer of German units to the east. Thus it did produce an important strategic effect for the Germans.

Increased Resources

It also led all of the great powers to increase the number of resources they put into both gas weapons and gas masks. Now that one side had used poison gas the others decided to follow suit. The Western Front was about to receive a new and deadly threat.

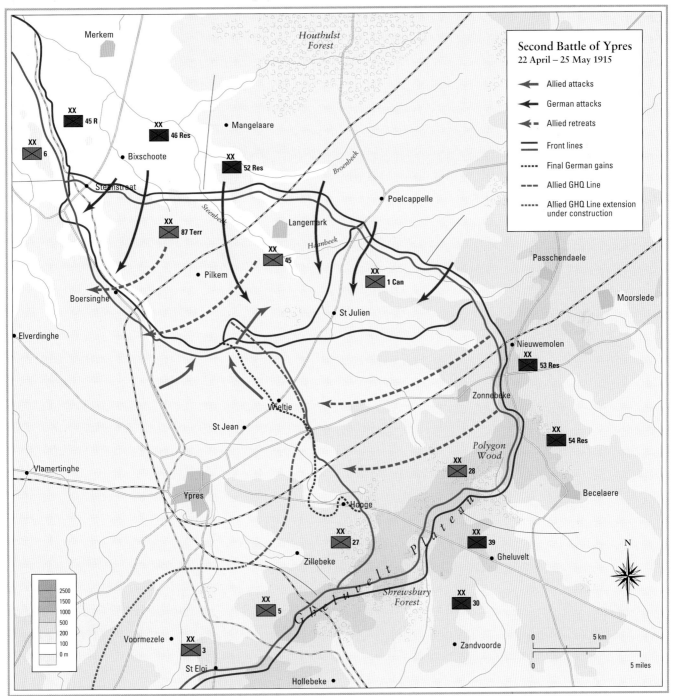

Aubers Ridge and Festubert March–December 1915

The Battle of Festubert was fought just north of the Neuve Chapelle sector. The methods the British used at Festubert differed from Neuve Chapelle, but did not produce the desired results.

The Battle of Festubert was part of the British contribution to a larger Allied offensive all along the Western Front. While the French attacked in the Arras sector near Vimy Ridge and Nôtre Dame de Lorette, the British First Army, which included large numbers of Canadians, would attack at Festubert and Aubers Ridge. In contrast to the short, sharp artillery barrage of Neuve Chapelle, at Festubert the British concentrated the fire of 400 guns for 60 hours. In all, they fired 100,000 shells into an area just 4.8km (3 miles) long. The British hoped that the sheer weight of shells fired would eliminate the German defences and allow their infantry to break the lines. But German defences held and were able to inflict massive casualties on the attackers for little gain.

Aubers Ridge

Aubers Ridge formed the main high ground of German defences, giving the Germans good observation over British and French lines. The ridge sat just 56km (35 miles) south of the Ypres salient; taking it would have the additional benefit of relieving much of the pressure at Ypres. Despite the weight of the artillery barrage, many of the shells failed to explode and the accuracy of the gunners was poor. The Germans retreated 2500m (8200ft) back to negate the power of the British artillery. Their infantry was thus intact when the Allies attacked, ruining the value of the artillery preparation. Although it began with high hopes, the Festubert/Aubers Ridge offensive failed.

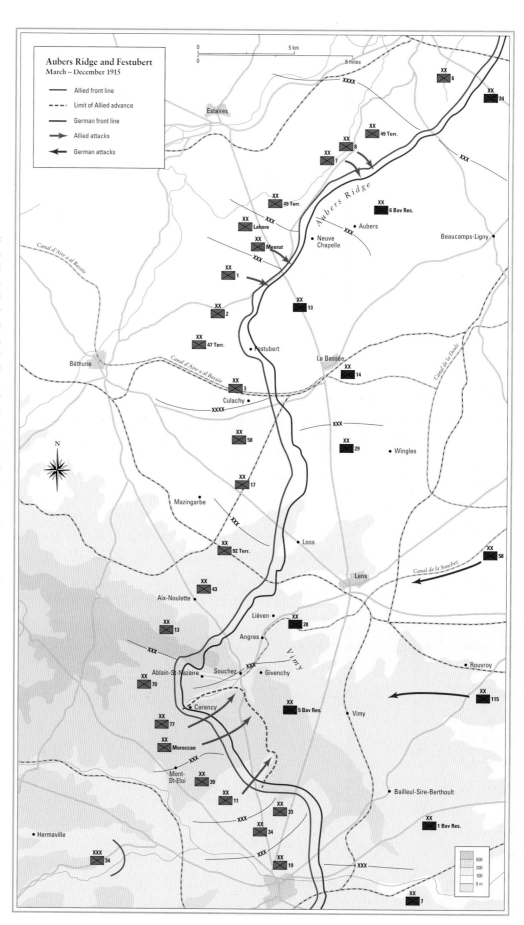

Aubers Ridge and Festubert
March – December 1915

— Allied front line
---- Limit of Allied advance
— German front line
→ Allied attacks
← German attacks

Second Battle of Champagne, 25–30 September 1915

The Allies planned a major series of offensives in the autumn of 1915 in the hopes of breaking German lines before poor winter weather began. The largest of the offensives was a massive 18-division assault in the Champagne region by the French Army. It is known today as the Second Battle of Champagne, but despite the size of the attack it failed to break the lines.

The French plan was sophisticated and relied on careful observation of the supposed weak points in the enemy line. Three days of heavy, well-placed artillery fire did tremendous damage to German front-line positions. The infantry advanced carefully and methodically, with specially trained teams carrying out specific missions. On the first day of the offensive the French managed to capture thousands of German soldiers and move the lines 4.8km (3 miles) in their favour. In some spots, French troops captured three separate lines of German defences, leading to hopes that the Allies might break into open ground as they had originally planned. After the first day, however, the Germans quickly recovered. They rushed reinforcements into the threatened sectors and established new defences. French soldiers discovered that they could not pursue as well as the Germans could defend. As the French moved forward, it became increasingly difficult to supply them. They could also not take advantage of trenches located in open ground, leaving them vulnerable to German artillery fire. They had learned the costly lesson of the war that sustaining offensive operations with tired troops and long supply lines was nearly impossible.

German Counter-attacks

From the German perspective, the French offensive came very close to succeeding. Dislodged from their defences and strategic high ground, the German Army felt exposed, vulnerable and at risk of losing the battle. In addition, more than 25,000 German soldiers had been taken as prisoners of war by the French, leading the German leadership to fear a creeping but profound breakdown in troop morale. They therefore decided to counter-attack with their recently arrived reinforcements in order to regain their positions. German forces recovered almost all of the territory they had lost before both sides became exhausted from combat. Even though the lines remained where they had been at the start of the battle, the cost had been high, with 145,000 French casualties and 95,000 German casualties.

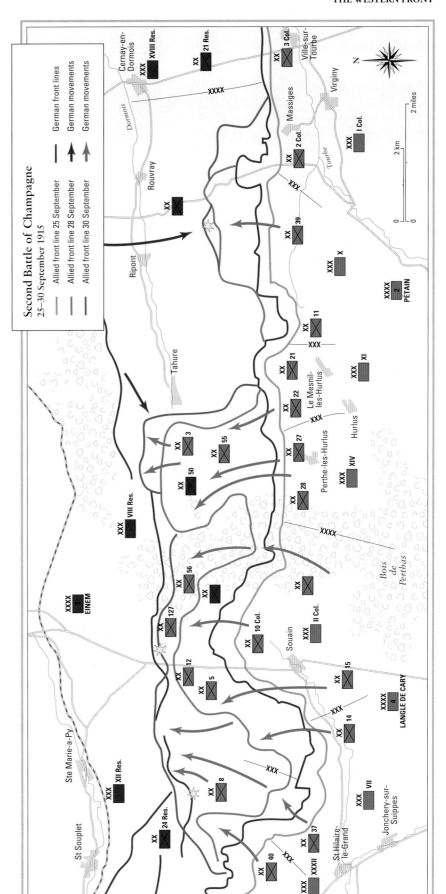

Battle of Loos
25 September 1915

Lacking artillery to clear passages in the German defences, the British used poison gas.

British use of gas opened up temporary holes in the German lines, but the British could not exploit them despite several days of attacks. Command problems complicated the use of reserves, which British commanders had kept far back from the front to protect them from gas. The Germans used their reserves skillfully, plugging holes in the lines and even counter-attacking. British casualties exceeded 50,000 men compared to Germany's 20,000. British gains were negligible.

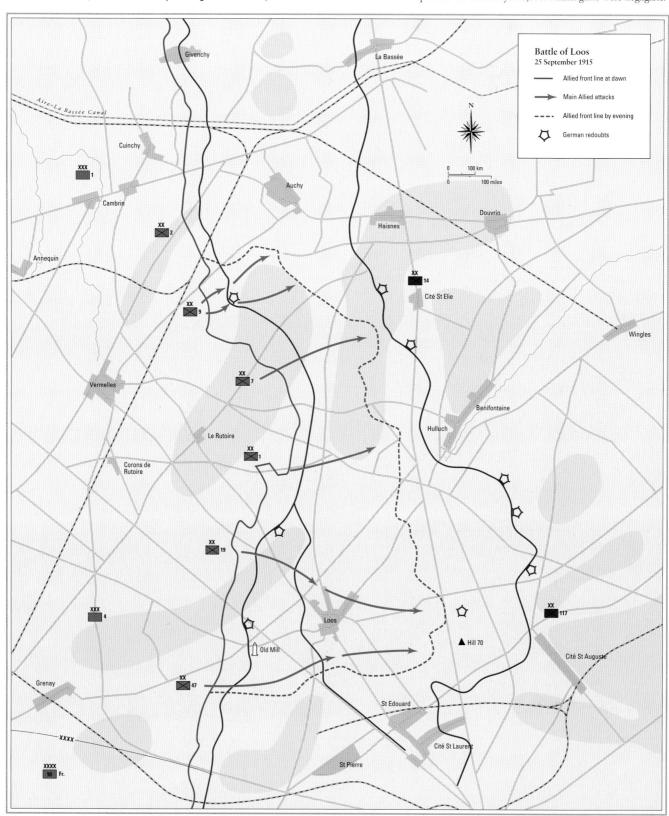

Battle of Loos
25 September 1915

— Allied front line at dawn

→ Main Allied attacks

--- Allied front line by evening

✧ German redoubts

0   100 km
0   100 miles

Battle of Artois 1915
25 September–8 October 1915

The Third Battle of Artois was designed to support the larger offensive in Champagne.

The offensive was part of a wider strategy that involved attacks along the Western Front and Italy. In theory, the Germans, who made their main effort in the east, should break somewhere, allowing for exploitation in open country. The French used a heavy four-day artillery bombardment at Artois. As had happened elsewhere in 1915 on the Western Front, however, the French learned that troops could survive a massive artillery onslaught and still have the strength to defeat an infantry attack.

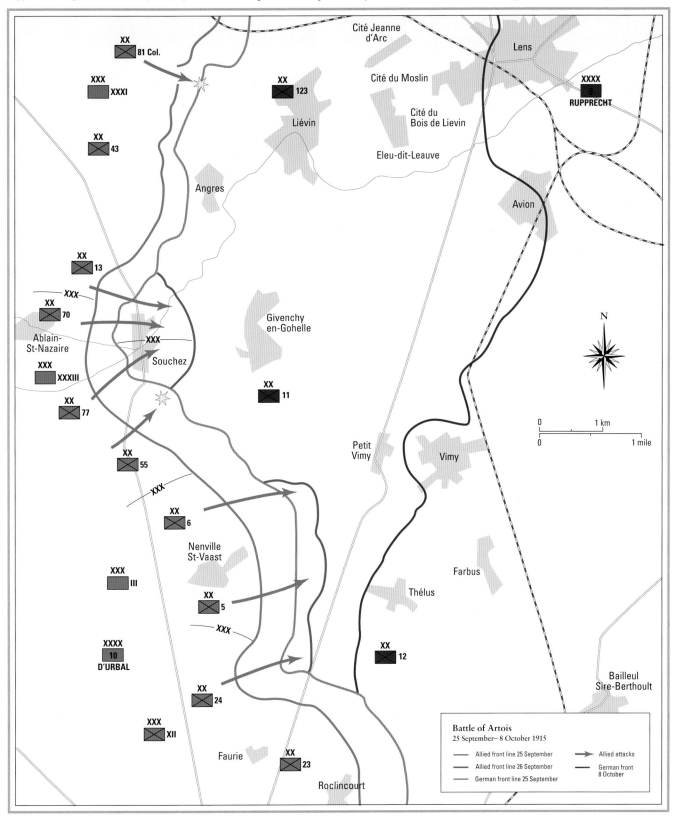

Battle of Artois
25 September– 8 October 1915

— Allied front line 25 September
— Allied front line 26 September
---- German front line 25 September

→ Allied attacks
— German front 8 October

Western Front 1915

The 1915 Western Front attacks featured heavier use of artillery to support infantry offensives. Almost all of them failed to break the lines.

The year 1915 seemed to prove two truths about the new way of war. First, armies could amass artillery and infantry to obtain temporary gains, but the power of enemy machineguns meant that even such limited successes were unacceptably costly. Second, the defenders could normally rush reserves into a threatened sector more easily than an attacker could because the attackers had to move over an active fighting sector. The defence had proven to be much stronger than the offense.

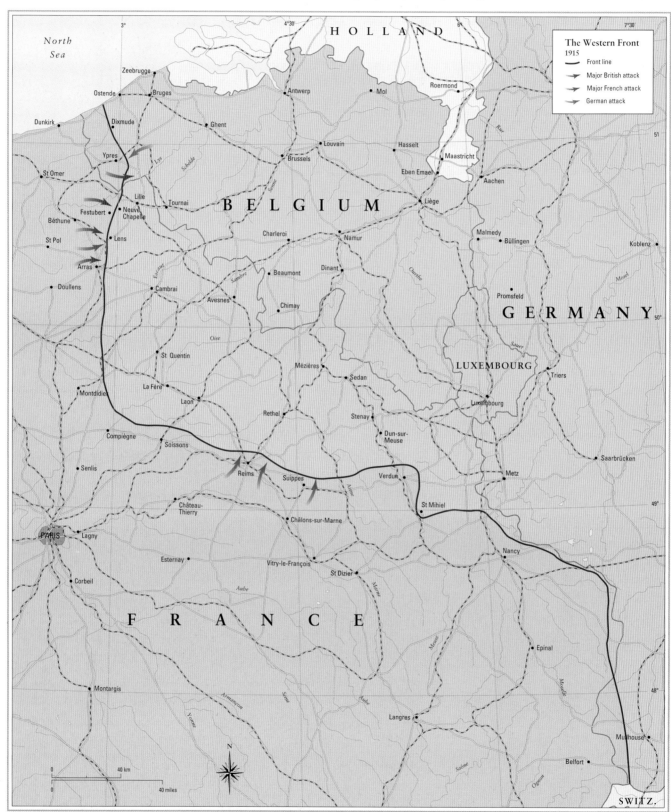

Plan of Fort Douaumont 1916

Fort Douaumont was the largest and most powerful fortification in the heavily fortified sector of Verdun. In 1914 it had the reputation of being the strongest fort in Europe. Reflecting the modern style, Douaumont was built deep underground to protect its defenders from artillery. Its top featured gun turrets and several feet of reinforced concrete and earth to minimize enemy shelling. Designed by France's best military engineers, it had 30,000m² (322,917ft²) of space. Douaumont was thus the lynchpin in Verdun's system of 19 major fortifications. A 1903 update had made it even stronger by reinforcing entrances and allowing for a larger garrison.

The easy capture of fortifications in Belgium by the Germans led many French strategists to argue that forts could not survive modern artillery. They advocated defending from trenches and abandoning the forts altogether. The loss of the forts, they argued, mattered little because soldiers could defend Verdun from trenches and other field defences. French Chief of Staff General Joseph Joffre agreed and withdrew most of Douaumont's heavy artillery pieces in order to support his offensives in 1915. Only two guns that were too difficult to remove remained. The French also removed the fort's garrison and replaced them with middle-aged reservists deemed unfit for duty in the trenches. Consequently, Douaumont and the other forts of Verdun were far weaker than they appeared.

Douaumont nevertheless featured as a key target in the German assault on Verdun in February 1916.

The Germans wanted to deny its use to the French as a depot and a place for French soldiers to get protection from both the enemy and the weather. Just days into the battle, German pioneers spotted an opening in the fort and daringly slipped in. They surprised the French defenders and took the most powerful fort in Europe without firing a shot. Even though the French leadership knew that the loss of the fort was not a major military disaster, they understood that it had become an important symbol and would need to be retaken.

French Attacks

The French pounded Douaumont with heavy and sustained artillery and, ironically, it held up very well, resisting the attackers and providing the Germans with protection. French soldiers finally retook its remains in October.

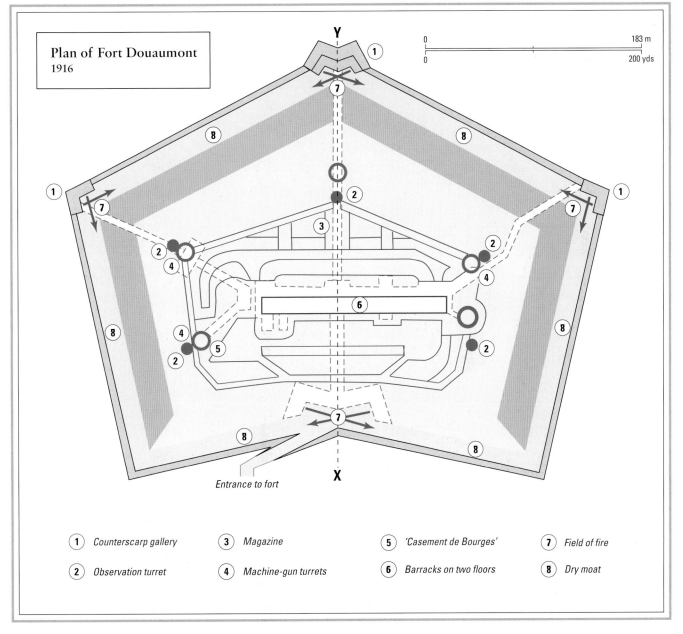

Plan of Fort Douaumont 1916

Entrance to fort

(1)	Counterscarp gallery	(3)	Magazine	(5)	'Casement de Bourges'	(7)	Field of fire
(2)	Observation turret	(4)	Machine-gun turrets	(6)	Barracks on two floors	(8)	Dry moat

Verdun

The ten-month Battle of Verdun became the war's longest and bloodiest. Scholars continue to debate the goals of the German attack – some think it was designed to attrite the French Army, others argue that the Germans hoped to shift momentum by forcing the Allies to attack in other sectors.

German Commander Erich von Falkenhayn designed the attack as part of a massive effort to win the war in 1916. He wanted to attack in February in order to forestall whatever plans the Allies had for the year ahead. He also argued unsuccessfully for the German Navy to resume unrestricted submarine warfare as part of a plan to pressure Britain into coming to the peace table with or without France. He chose Verdun because the Germans could more easily dominate the logistical lines going into the sector than could the French. He had hoped to bait the French into a battle on ground favourable to Germany.

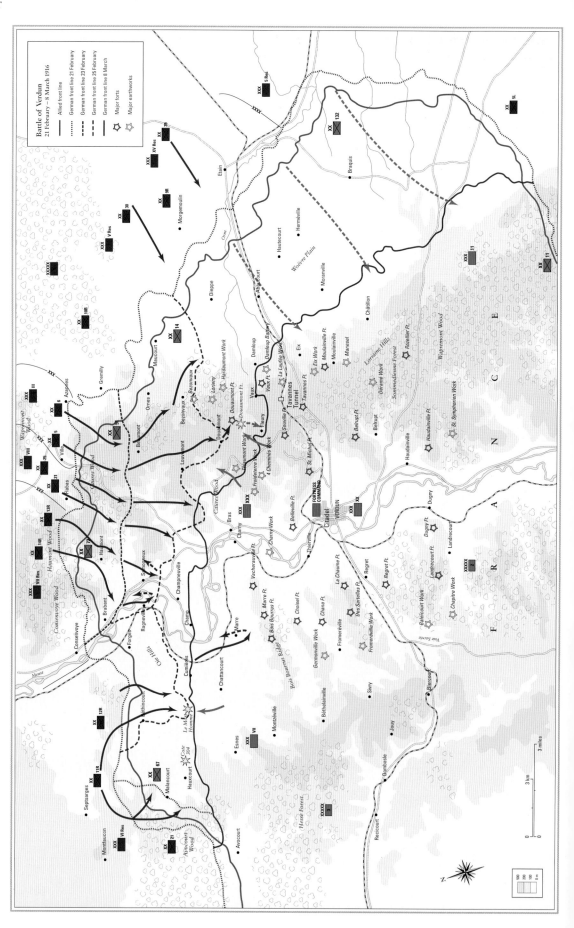

Verdun – French Counter-September–December 1916

Although some officers had predicted a German attack on Verdun, the offensive caught the French by surprise. Initial German successes at Fort Douaumont and elsewhere led the French to take the situation at Verdun more seriously than they had intended. Both sides soon fed all their resources into a battle whose symbolic value became greater than its military importance.

The German attack was unprecedented in its firepower. They unleashed the most powerful artillery assault in history. In six days, the Germans fired more than two million shells, some of them filled with poison gas. They fired another two million in the subsequent ten days. Dedicated air squadrons gave the Germans control of the skies and special infantry units infiltrated French units with new weapons, including flamethrowers. The seizure of Fort Douaumont and the exhaustion of the French defenders seemed to augur a collapse in the region. French commanders planned to abandon one bank of the Meuse River and demolish the fortifications rather than allow them to fall into German hands.

French leaders countermanded these decisions and ordered the defence of both banks of the river. They also changed commanders, sending General Henri-Philippe Pétain, a defensive specialist, to Verdun. Under his direction, the French redesigned their logistical networks and developed a rotational system for moving soldiers in and out of Verdun. His call, 'on ne passe pas,' ('they shall not pass') became the watchword of the battle for France. The Battle of Verdun quickly took on a life of its own. Both sides saw it as essential as much for morale reasons as for sound military reasons.

The French actions held Verdun and prevented it from falling into German hands. The battle quickly devolved into a bloody struggle of attrition with limited territorial gains. By mid-summer, the German leadership had grown frustrated with the combat and, having to fight the Battle of the Somme at the same time, tried to shut Verdun down. They dispatched Falkenhayn to Romania and replaced him with the duumvirate of Paul von Hindenburg and Erich Ludendorff, neither of whom believed that any success at Verdun could be worth the price.

French Counter-attacks

The French, however, had decided to keep the battle going in order to recover the ground they

had lost. French General Robert Nivelle developed new artillery methods designed to provide accurate and direct fire support to attacking infantry. General Charles Mangin led daring infantry assaults that were costly but ultimately successful. Throughout the late summer and early autumn, the French slowly but surely regained lost territory and turned the tide at Verdun. In October and November, the French launched a general offensive using the new methods. They retook Fort Douaumont and the number of German prisoners they captured led the French to believe that German morale might be close to breaking. Their own soldiers had suffered terribly as well, however, and the poor December weather made offensives difficult to sustain. The battle did not really end, however, as fighting there resumed in 1917 with the French retaking some strategic positions.

The Human Costs of Verdun

We still lack exact casualty figures from the battle. Estimates of French casualties range from 300,000 to 500,000 men, with approximately 150,000 of those killed in action. German casualties were probably slightly lower, but still between 280,000 to 430,000 men. In the end, the lines remained almost exactly where they had been at the start.

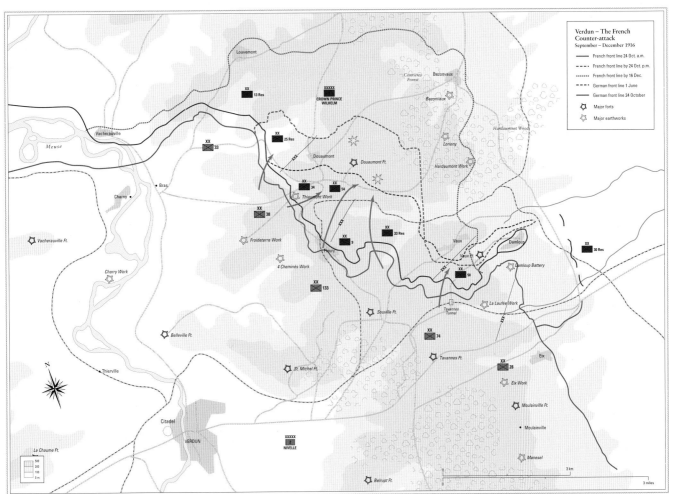

First Day of the Somme July 1916

Designed originally to be a primarily French battle with the British Army in support, Verdun turned the Somme into a mainly British battle with just eight French divisions attacking south of the Somme River.

The British Army was inexperienced and its commanders not fully in agreement with one another about the goals of the offensive. Some wanted to break through the German lines, while others hoped to seize high ground and entice the Germans into counter-attacking. Their French allies wanted an attack of any kind to relieve some pressure on Verdun. British artillery fired a preparatory barrage for an entire week at German positions on the Somme. Most officers expected that a barrage of that size would eliminate any German defenders and clear paths for the infantry. The plan for the first day involved another heavy artillery barrage, this one carefully coordinated with the advancing infantry, but many shells proved to be duds and many more failed to hit their intended targets. In many parts of the Somme battlefield, the Germans successfully protected themselves in deep underground bunkers. As a result, British infantry left their trenches without the proper protection and support from the artillery.

The Bloody First of July

Despite the sheer weight of the British barrages, enough Germans survived to sight their machineguns and decimate the advancing British infantry. In a few isolated places, the British achieved their objectives, but on the whole the day was a terrible and bloody failure. More than 60,000 British soldiers became casualties on that day, with 20,000 of them being killed. It was the worst day in the history of the British Army.

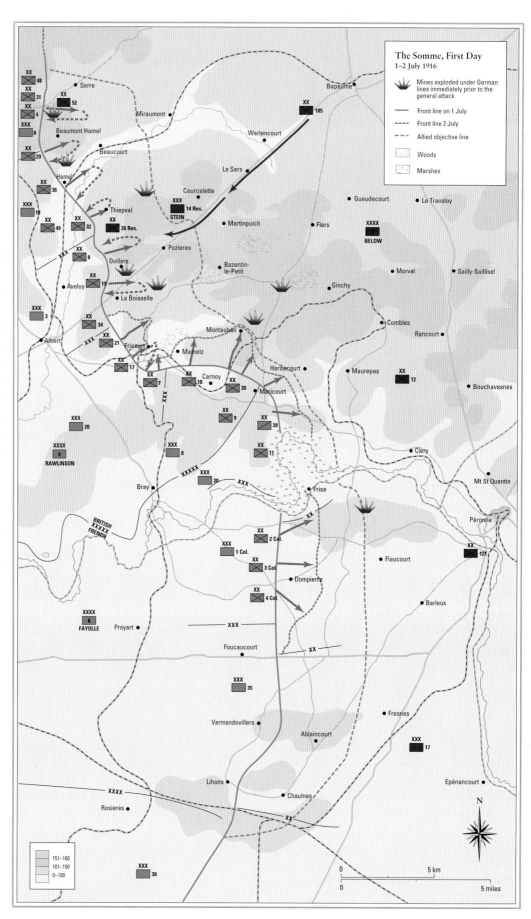

The Somme July–September 1916

The second phase of the battle featured actions for small parts of the battlefield. Some British generals hoped to break the enemy's line, while others hoped for a breakdown of German morale to gain victory.

French attacks south of the Somme river had generally fared better than the British attacks to the north because the French soldiers were more experienced and the terrain was slightly easier. The second phase of the campaign from July to September featured battles for Pozières, a village attacked by the Australians, and several large farms such as Guillemont Farm. The Germans made the unwise decision to try to recapture any ground lost to the British or French by counter-attacking. Their generals believed that restoring the line was critical to maintaining their positions across the front line. If the German line broke in any one place, they feared, then German units would have dangerously exposed flanks. The Germans also built second, third and even fourth lines of defences in case the British or French did break through. They suffered most of their losses during these counter-attacks, further proving the point that combat in 1916 favoured the defenders.

German Casualties

The German line held, but, in combination with the ongoing fighting at Verdun, the Somme was starting to wear down the German Army. One German officer later called the Somme the 'muddy field grave of the German Army'. To defend the insignificant village of Ginchy in early September the Germans took more than 100,000 casualties. Still, contrary to the reports from overly optimistic British intelligence officials, German morale did not break.

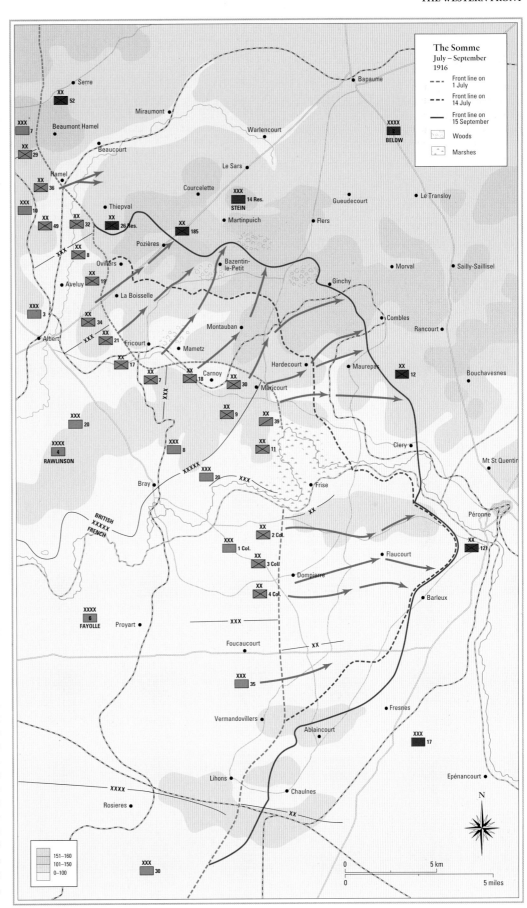

The Somme
July – September
1916

- – – – Front line on 1 July
- - - - Front line on 14 July
- ——— Front line on 15 September
- Woods
- Marshes

151–160
101–150
0–100

0 _____ 5 km

0 _____ 5 miles

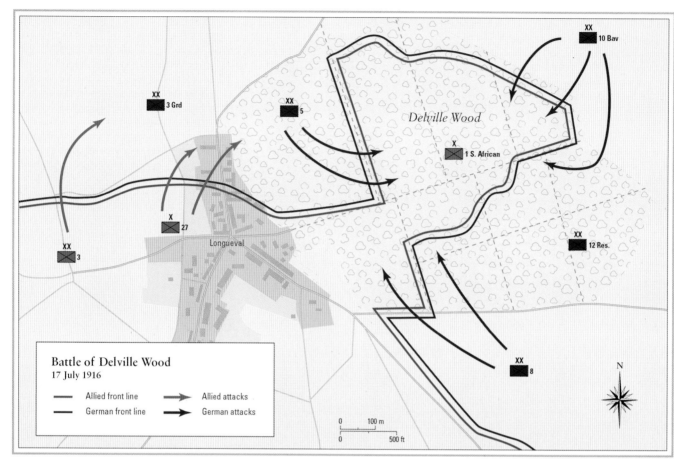

Battle of Delville Wood
17 July 1916

Allied front line — Allied attacks
German front line — German attacks

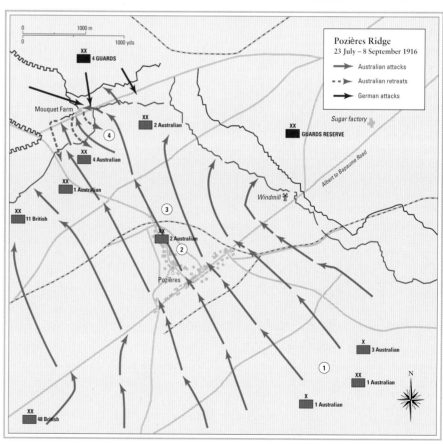

Pozières Ridge
23 July – 8 September 1916

→ Australian attacks
⇢ Australian retreats
→ German attacks

Battle of Delville Wood
17 July 1916

Delville Wood and High Wood were two forests that guarded the British right flank. The British needed to control them in order to advance further along the line. They did so in a battle that lasted from mid-July to early September.

South African troops and several British divisions led the battle for Delville Wood, a once picturesque small forest that the troops eventually called 'The Devil's Wood'. Heavy fighting occurred all through July, with large sections of the woods changing hands several times. The two sides fought hard for the area because it held the key to the strategic Thiepval Ridge, a feature that both sides considered the most critical high ground on the Somme front. The British took the wood, although its capture did not lead to an immediate advance on Thiepval. Casualties on both sides were enormous for such a limited geographical gain.

At the same time, Australian troops cleared the village of Pozières, hoping to force German troops off of the Thiepval ridge by advancing on an oblique angle. The Australians fought hard, but lost 23,000 men to secure one square mile of mostly muddy terrain. The Somme was killing men on both sides in enormous numbers, but the lines were hardly moving.

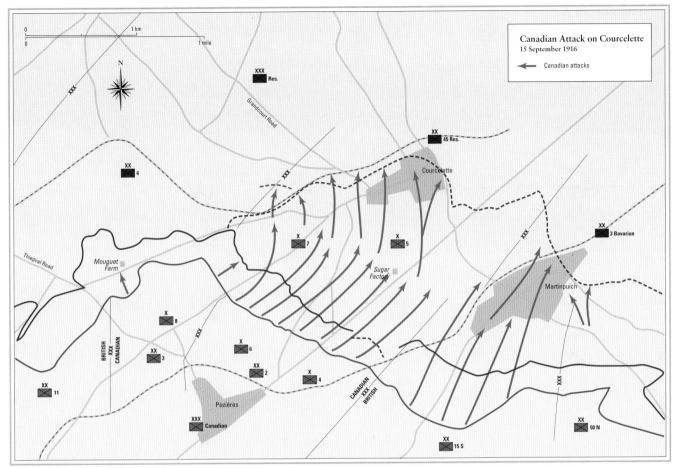

0 1 km
0 1 mile

XXX
Res.

XXX

N

XX 45 Res.

XX 4

Courcelette

XXX

X 7   X 5   XX 3 Bavarian

Thiepval Road

Mouquet Farm

Sugar Factory

Martinpuich

X 8

BRITISH XXX CANADIAN

XXX

X 6

XX 3

XX 2   X 4

CANADIAN XXX BRITISH

XX 11

Pozières

XXX Canadian

XXX

XX 50 N

XX 15 S

Flers-Courcelette
15 September 1916

This part of the Somme campaign has two claims to fame. It saw the first use of tanks as the British Army tried to surprise the Germans. It is also known for the success that the Canadian Corps had in capturing the village of Courcelette.

The British hoped that this battle would take advantage of the many casualties the Germans had experienced in 1916 at the Somme and Verdun. Tanks and artillery would pulverize German defences, allowing infantry to achieve the long-awaited breakthrough. Tanks proved to be too primitive, although they showed promise. Nine of the 45 tanks introduced at Flers never got to the front line; most of the others quickly broke down.

The Canadians, however, made excellent use of a creeping barrage, a technique whereby the artillery precedes attacking infantry, ideally pinning the enemy in his trenches long enough to give the infantry more time to advance through No Man's Land. The Canadians took Courcelette, a key strongpoint on the German line. They also held against a savage German counterattack. More than 7000 Canadians were casualties. Although very costly, Courcelette showed a way forward for the innovative Canadians.

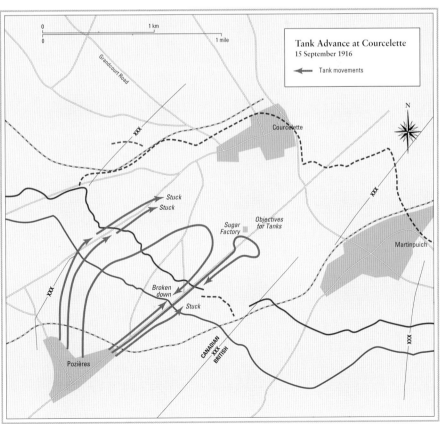

0 1 km
0 1 mile

Grandcourt Road

Courcelette

XXX

N

XXX

Stuck
Stuck

Sugar Factory

Objectives for Tanks

Martinpuich

XXX

Broken down

Stuck

Pozières

CANADIAN XXX BRITISH

XXX

The Somme September–November 1916

Despite new tactics and greater resources, the Allies failed to break the German lines as intended during July. Casualties on both sides mounted with little for either side to show to justify those losses.

The British forces adapted and innovated as the Somme campaign evolved. They undoubtedly learned to fight better, incorporating improved artillery procedures and learning how to fight from the air as well. They also introduced new technologies, most importantly the tank, which gave troops fire support without chewing up the ground over which they would need to advance. Tanks certainly did not solve the tactical problems of 1916, but they did show some promise for the future. Largely due to these improvements, September was the bloodiest month of the campaign for the German forces. The British captured key ground in the autumn, but the Germans had built new lines of defence, thus largely negating the value of that seized ground. Poor weather set in late in the campaign, making it harder for the Allies to attack. By the end of the Somme campaign in mid-November, the British Army was undoubtedly a much improved fighting force, although one that had been very badly bloodied.

Losses Justified?

British commander Sir Douglas Haig claimed at the end of the campaign that his goal by the middle of the Somme had been to attrite the Germans. In other words, by late summer he no longer aimed to pierce the German line, but to 'wear out' the German forces. Critics then and later accused Haig of inventing attrition as a justification to cover the enormous losses of his army on the Somme for minimal gains. This debate continues today.

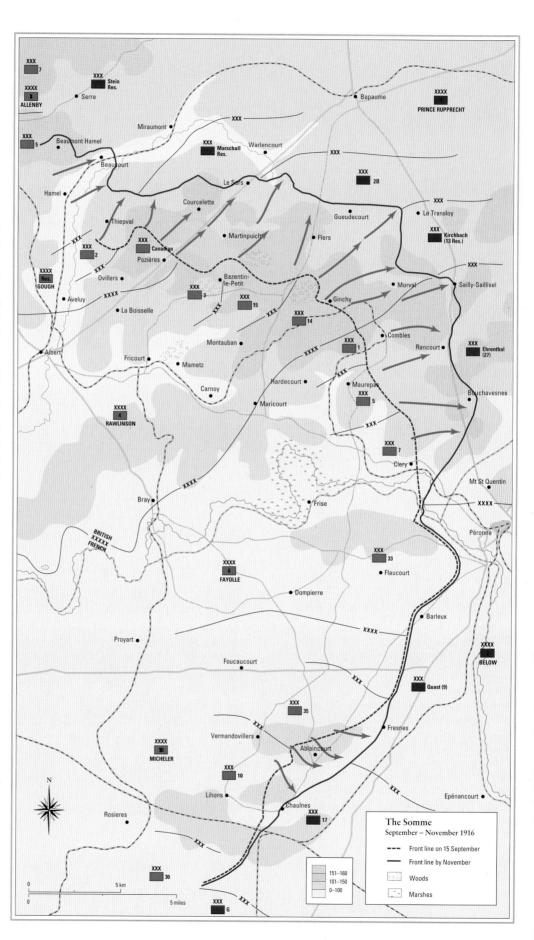

The Somme
September – November 1916

- - - Front line on 15 September
——— Front line by November

Woods

Marshes

151–160
101–150
0–100

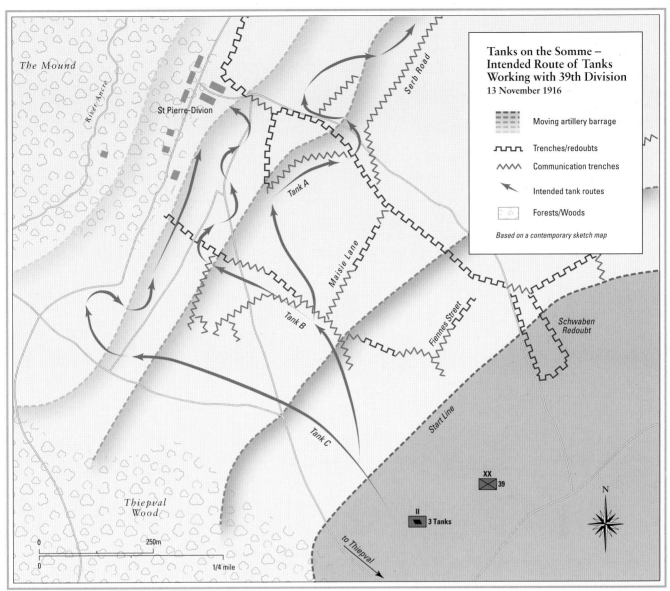

Tanks on the Somme –
Intended Route of Tanks
Working with 39th Division
13 November 1916

The Mound

St Pierre-Divion

Serb Road

Tank A

Maisie Lane

Tank B

Fiennes Street

Schwaben Redoubt

Tank C

Start Line

to Thiepval

Thiepval Wood

River Ancre

0   250m

0   1/4 mile

XX 39

II 3 Tanks

N

Moving artillery barrage

Trenches/redoubts

Communication trenches

Intended tank routes

Forests/Woods

Based on a contemporary sketch map

Ancre Heights
18 November 1916

**The Battle of Ancre
Heights was one of the last
engagements before winter.**

The Canadians took on the
assignment of attacking
the powerful Regina Trench, a
3000m- (9842ft-) long section
of German defences that had
resisted all attacks since the
start of the Somme campaign.
On 1 October the Canadians
attacked, piercing the German
lines but failing to break through
over several days. They took
20,000 casualties on the Somme
out of the 65,000 men engaged.

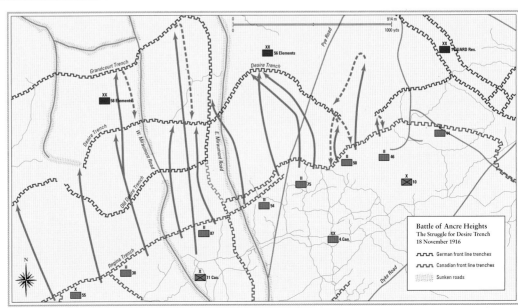

Battle of Ancre Heights
The Struggle for Desire Trench
18 November 1916

German front line trenches
Canadian front line trenches
Sunken roads

The Hindenburg Line
25 February–5 April 1917

The German Army decided after Verdun and the Somme that they could no longer afford to hold on to as much of the western front as it would like. They had lost too many soldiers and they still had to seek victory in the east. As a result the Germans made the decision to build a series of fortified lines behind which they hoped to defend against attacks by the British and French.

German war strategists decided to make their main offensive effort in 1917 on the Eastern Front. That decision made the idea of defending in the west seem even more logical. The Germans built the Hindenburg Line largely by using the forced labour of prisoners of war. It contained repeated lines of defence with barbed wire several metres deep and concrete trench lines. Underground communications systems connected the German positions, and observation posts gave German soldiers positions from which to observe the enemy and direct artillery and machinegun fire. The position of the Hindenburg Line allowed the Germans to straighten out the curved Western Front that jutted into France like a 'C.' It took advantage of natural terrain features such as hills, forests and rivers. The line thus greatly reduced the number of soldiers the Germans needed on the Western Front, a recognition of the high losses they had suffered in 1916.

The new German positions surrendered land back to the Allied forces, but the Germans believed that the land was not worth defending. However, they took great care to devastate everything they ceded, taking anything they could and destroying what they could not. French officials cited the intentional devastation of French land in the move back to the Hindenburg Line when they demanded reparations after the war.

Allied Strategy

The movement to the Hindenburg Line erased much of the strategic logic of the Allied plan for 1917, which was aimed at recovering ground that the Germans had recently ceded. The Allied forces did not change their plans, however. They still sought to attack in the sector.

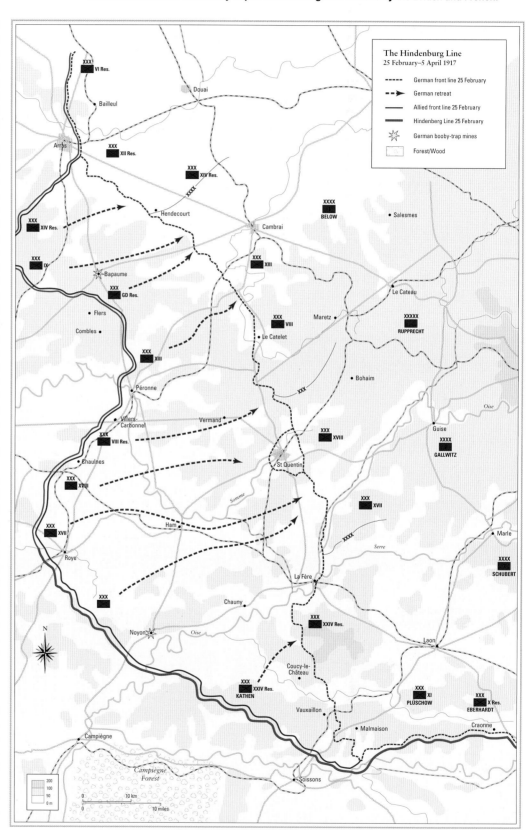

The Nivelle Offensive Early 1917

The new French commander, General Robert Nivelle, sought a major offensive in 1917 to pressure the Germans on two fronts. The British would attack in the north near Arras to draw resources away from the French attack along a ridge known as the Chemin des Dames. The Germans had, however, already moved back to the Hindenburg Line, rendering much of his plan less useful.

Despite the withdrawal to the Hindenburg Line, the Germans still had strong defences along the Chemin des Dames ridge. A formerly French fortress anchored one side of the ridge and a massive quarry in the centre served as a powerful subterranean position for the Germans. The ridge itself provided excellent observation of French preparations for an attack in the valley below. Nivelle attacked anyway, confident in the artillery methods he had developed at Verdun. Several generals in the French Army urged him to cancel the attack, but he went ahead. It proved to be a disaster, with only a few units getting anywhere near the ridge. Still Nivelle kept up the assault. French casualties mounted until President Raymond Poincaré intervened. Nivelle soon lost his command and was replaced by another hero of Verdun, Henri-Philippe Pétain, who inherited an army with a massive morale problem.

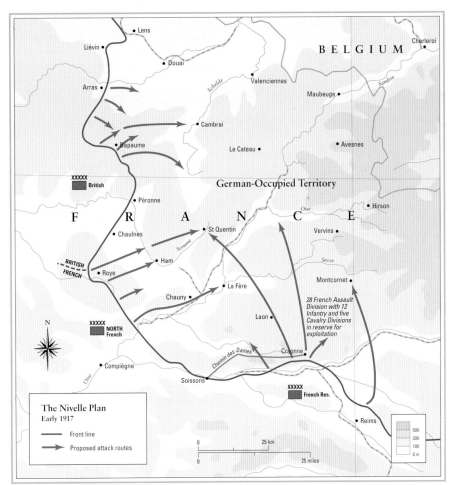

The Nivelle Plan
Early 1917
— Front line
→ Proposed attack routes

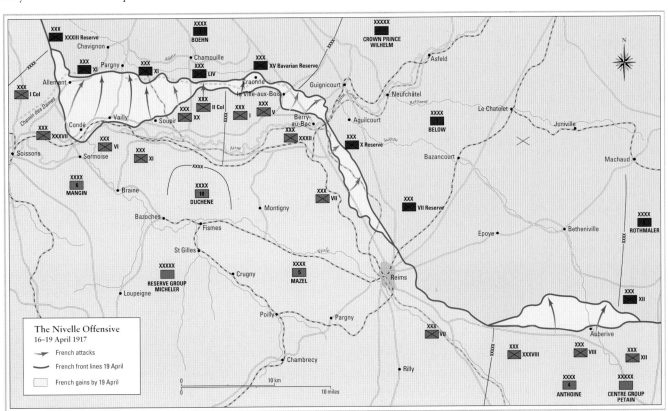

The Nivelle Offensive
16–19 April 1917
French attacks
French front lines 19 April
French gains by 19 April

Battle of Vimy Ridge
8–12 April 1917

The Canadian Corps, and the larger British Army to which it was attached, launched a carefully planned and well led assault on Vimy Ridge. The ridge had been in German hands since 1914 and had resisted several major assaults – it appeared impregnable. Yet the Canadians took it with one of the most skillful attacks of the war. Although a great local success, its larger value was diminished by the failure of the Nivelle Offensive.

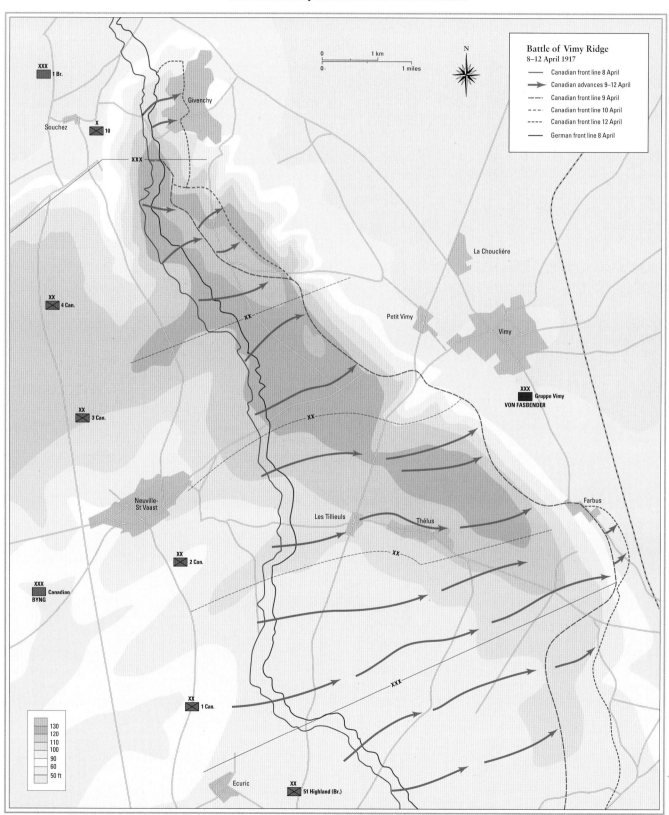

Battle of Vimy Ridge
8–12 April 1917

— Canadian front line 8 April
→ Canadian advances 9–12 April
- - - Canadian front line 9 April
- - - - Canadian front line 10 April
— — Canadian front line 12 April
— German front line 8 April

Arras and Vimy Ridge 9–13 April 1917

British forces also attacked on both banks of the Scarpe River in support of the Nivelle Offensive. These attacks gained ground, but they were only ever designed as large diversions to the main attack on the Chemin des Dames. When that attack failed, the British kept up the pressure near Arras in order to pin down the Germans. British generals resented having to lose more men to cover their ally, but they had little choice.

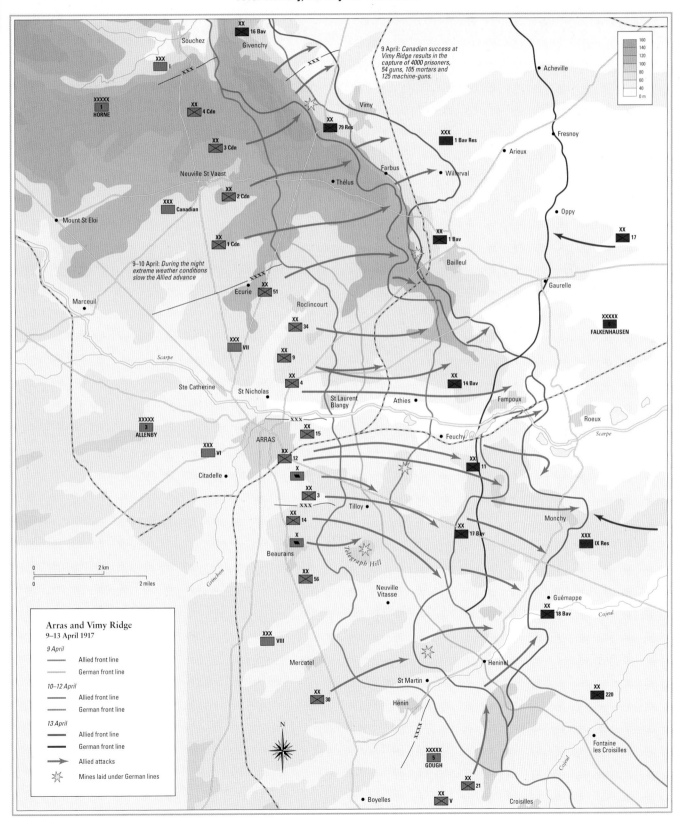

9 April: Canadian success at Vimy Ridge results in the capture of 4000 prisoners, 54 guns, 105 mortars and 125 machine-guns.

9–10 April: During the night extreme weather conditions slow the Allied advance

Arras and Vimy Ridge
9–13 April 1917

9 April
— Allied front line
— German front line

10–12 April
— Allied front line
— German front line

13 April
— Allied front line
— German front line

→ Allied attacks

✷ Mines laid under German lines

Battle of Messines June 1917

The Messines Ridge was not nearly as prominent a feature as Vimy Ridge, but in the relatively flat ground of Flanders it represented important terrain. If British forces were to advance out of the Ypres salient they needed to control it. Yet attacks in the area from 1914 to 1917 had failed to dislodge the German defenders. The British therefore designed a novel and innovative method for dealing with it. They sent teams of men who had been coal miners to tunnel under the ridge, carefully disguising their work from German observers. Then they packed the tunnels with explosives. If they could not take the ridge from above, they would try to eliminate it from below.

The plan to eliminate the Messines Ridge had the support of two of the British Army's most careful and creative generals, Sir Herbert Plumer and General Charles Harington. Harington, an engineer, quipped that the Messines operations might not change history, but it would certainly change geography. The massive explosion, featuring 508 tonnes (500 tons) of ammonal explosive, did all that Harington had hoped for and more, virtually removing the high ground from the Belgian plain. People as far away as London heard it and those in Lille thought there must have been an earthquake. Back near Messines, British artillery supported the advancing infantry with one of the most powerful barrages of the entire war. Aircraft flew overhead to keep German aircraft away and to correct the British artillery fire for improved accuracy.

British infantry thus went forward with everything on their side. Dazed German defenders reacted slowly to the attack. More than 10,000 Germans were killed or wounded by the explosion and another 7000 soon surrendered.

Plumer's methodical, careful infantry methods allowed British forces to move forward with maximum fire support. They quickly cleared what remained of the ridge and took the villages of Messines and Wytschaete. They had broken an important German defensive line, but as they advanced casualties began to mount alarmingly and the gains began to slow. The Germans moved their reserves into the region in response. Messines had nevertheless been a great success and the southern flank of the Ypres salient now sat in British hands.

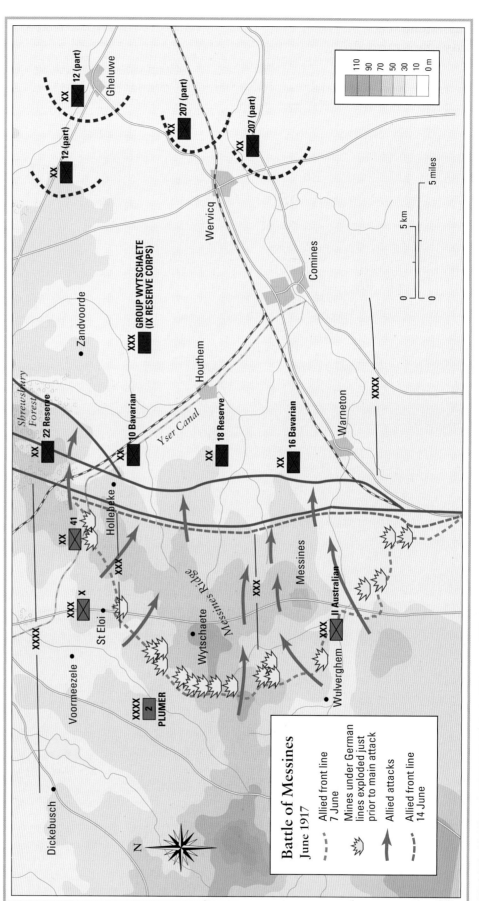

Passchendaele
July–November 1917

British forces moved slowly to exploit the success of Messines, and the British inexplicably replaced Plumer with the less talented Hubert Gough. The ensuing offensive at Passchendaele began with high hopes, but soon degenerated because of poor planning, leadership and weather. Instead of the breakthrough to the Belgian coast that Haig had promised, Passchendaele became another battle of attrition that cost enormous casualties for negligible gains of territory.

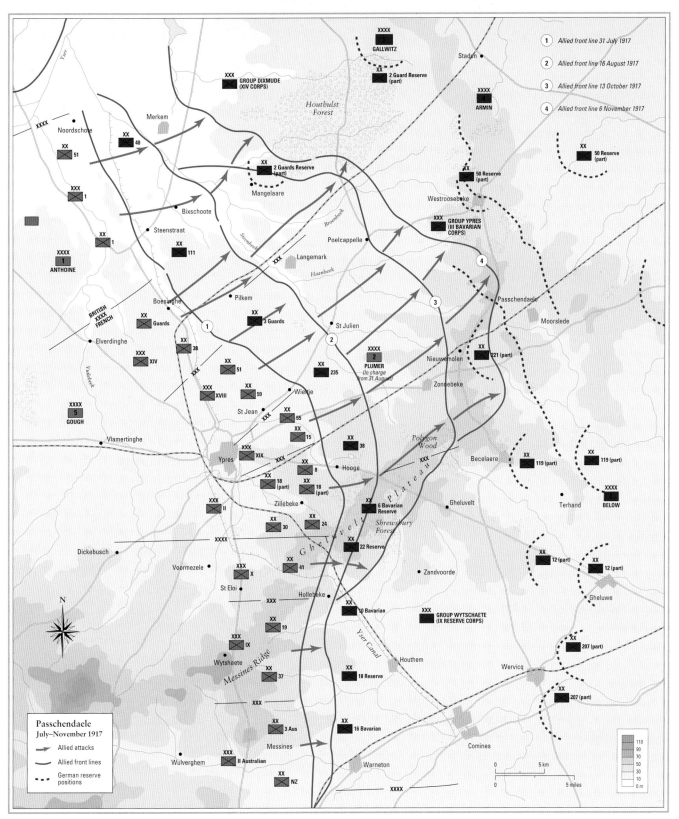

Battle of Cambrai
20–28 November 1917

Cambrai is best known today as the first battle that featured the mass use of tanks. Divided into units of three, the tanks helped to open up holes in the German lines, but the British lacked infantry reserves to exploit the holes and too many of the vehicles suffered from mechanical problems. Cambrai pointed the way to a new kind of war, but also showed that tanks alone were not the solution to the western front.

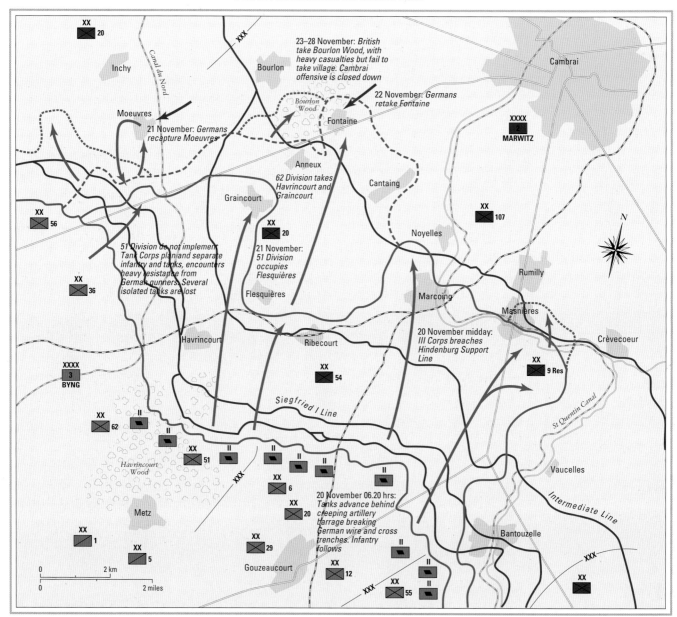

23–28 November: *British take Bourlon Wood, with heavy casualties but fail to take village. Cambrai offensive is closed down*

22 November: *Germans retake Fontaine*

21 November: *Germans recapture Moeuvres*

62 Division takes Havrincourt and Graincourt

51 Division do not implement Tank Corps plan and separate infantry and tanks, encounters heavy resistance from German gunners. Several isolated tanks are lost

21 November: *51 Division occupies Flesquières*

20 November midday: *III Corps breaches Hindenburg Support Line*

20 November 06.20 hrs: *Tanks advance behind creeping artillery barrage breaking German wire and cross trenches. Infantry follows*

The British plan for Cambrai combined 476 tanks with more than 1000 artillery pieces in support of infantry. The heavy losses at the Somme and at Passchendaele forced the British to rely on a more industrial method of warfare because those previous battles had greatly reduced infantry reserves. The initial plan counted on overwhelming firepower to win the battle in 48 hours. If they had not achieved success by then, the British generals pledged to stop the battle.

Tank crews underwent an ordeal in their machines, but they provided direct fire support and helped troops move over enemy trenches. They were

devastating against infantry untrained in methods to deal with them. Troops who had learned to widen their trenches and use artillery against tanks generally fared better. At Cambrai, 179 British tanks broke down or were taken out by German action.

The British advanced as far as 6.4km (4 miles) in places, creating a deep salient into German lines. After the first day, however, the surprise of the tanks was gone and German troops no longer panicked. Generals ordered counter-attacks against exposed British positions in the Cambrai salient. Without trenches to protect them, the British had no choice but to retreat to their original lines. For

a time it appeared as though the Germans might even break the British Third Army's line. In the end, each side suffered approximately 40,000 casualties for minimal changes in the front line.

Debates in the British Army

Cambrai pitted the advocates of mechanization, including Winston Churchill, against those leaders who thought that tanks alone were no solution to the problems of the western front. Tanks, they argued, had to be tied closely into existing infantry and artillery systems in order to be effective. And that would take time.

The German Offensive 21 March–17 June 1918

Germany had successfully forced Russia out of the war, giving the German Army the ability to focus mainly on one front for the first time in the conflict. Nevertheless, the German home front was under strain from the blockade and the entry of the Americans gave the Allies an important source of manpower. The Germans thus gambled everything on one more offensive in the west.

The German offensives began in March 1918, as soon as the weather permitted. They are known either as the Spring Offensives or the Ludendorff Offensives after the general largely responsible for their design and execution. Erich Ludendorff had experienced a meteoric rise since gaining fame by taking the Belgian fortress at Liège then winning the battle of Tannenberg in 1914. He knew that the Spring Offensives were likely Germany's last chance to win the war. He therefore was willing to throw everything into making them successful before the Americans arrived en masse. Still, his offensives had no larger strategic goal. He hoped to break a hole

somewhere in the Allied line then win by exploiting the open flanks thus created. Rather than capture a key position or threaten Paris, he hoped that he might inflict enough casualties on the Allies to bring them to the bargaining table on terms favourable to Germany, even if he had not thought out what those terms might include.

Hutier Tactics

The key to the German attacks lay in tactics successfully used at Riga on the Eastern Front and at Caporetto in Italy in 1917. The Germans could not rely on massed artillery or tanks because German industry could no longer produce them in the numbers required. Instead, new German artillery methods would target the command and control centres of Allied units with short, sharp barrages. They would feature heavy use of poison gas. The goal was to immobilize the enemy's 'brain'. Then, specially-trained elite soldiers called stromtroops would advance past the enemy front line and attack the now weakened enemy command centres. Only then would regular infantry advance. If the system worked and the enemy's officers had been eliminated, then the Germans would be fighting enemy troops unsupported by heavy artillery or

reserves. In this way, German regular troops would stand a fighting chance.

The new Hutier tactics, named for General Oskar von Hutier, relied heavily on a small number of men trained in the new way of war. As they were killed or wounded in the early offensives, the Germans would be less likely to succeed. Thus time and speed were of the essence. Eventually, the Germans would run out of both men and resources to fight such a high-intensity and high-casualty method of war.

Deciding Where to Attack

Ludendorff assumed that if he broke the British lines, British troops would retreat toward the Channel coast to protect their supply bases. If he broke French lines, then the French would head toward Paris. The most logical place for him to attain such an outcome was the rail juncture of Amiens, which was also the meeting point of the French and British armies. Still, Ludendorff chose not to attack Amiens, aiming his first blow instead at the British Fifth Army south of Amiens. It was commanded by Hubert Gough, who had led poorly at Passchendaele, and it also lacked proper defences to meet the kind of attack the Germans were preparing to unleash.

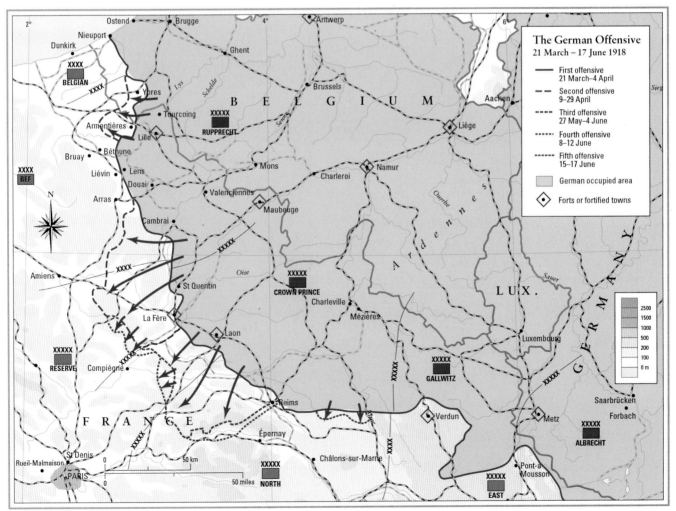

Operation Michael
21 March–4 April 1918

More than 6600 artillery pieces and 3500 trench mortars supported the first of the German attacks, codenamed Michael. A heavy morning fog further added to the confusion. British lines broke in several places and the Fifth Army took heavy casualties. Gough ordered a retreat back to an emergency defensive line on the Somme River. The Allies defended Amiens rather than reinforce the Fifth Army, which took 38,500 casualties. Germany had clearly won the first round.

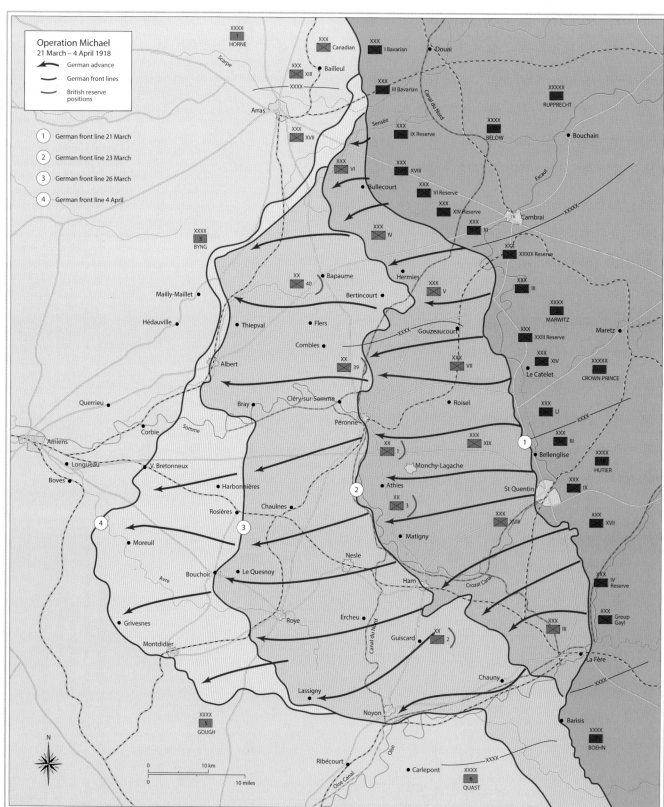

Other German Spring Offensives April–July 1918

The second German offensive struck in Flanders, targeting the British once again. The British Second Army yielded 8km (5 miles) and took heavy casualties, but the line did not break. German casualties were also rising, however, and attacking in Flanders gave tired British troops near the Amiens front a badly-needed chance to rest. French troops rushed to provide reserves and help to stem the tide.

The German offensives had gained ground and led French politicians to contemplate the abandonment of Paris, but German gains looked better on maps than they did on the ground. Although they had restored movement to a war so long dominated by stasis, the Allies managed to hold the most strategic parts of the Western Front. Much of the ground the Germans regained was worthless, having been devastated by German hands in the retreat to the Hindenburg Line the previous year. As the Germans advanced, their supply problems grew. They could not live off the territory they captured.

The Allies also adjusted to German tactics. They put in place defences that were better able to absorb attacks. They also better protected their command and control centres. French units stretched their lines north to allow the British to concentrate their own forces into threatened sectors. The Americans also began to arrive in larger numbers. They may not have been fully trained, but they provided a critical margin of manpower. In many cases, they took over sectors that were relatively quiet so that experienced French troops could go to more active areas. Where they did fight they fought well, earning the respect of their Allies and their enemies alike.

Foch and Supreme Command

The most important change the Allies made was naming a supreme commander, French General Ferdinand Foch. Foch had been arguing for putting one person in charge of the strategic direction of the Western Front so that the British, French and Americans did not fight three separate wars. A supreme commander could direct reserves, coordinate withdrawals and align attacks. But Foch's job was difficult as he had no power to command any of the armies. He led by force of personality and an innate understanding of the movements of the German Army. He projected confidence and understood that the Germans would reach breaking point. He was an ideal choice for the assignment.

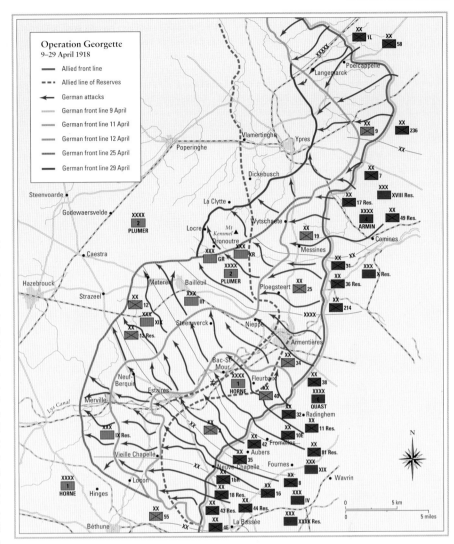

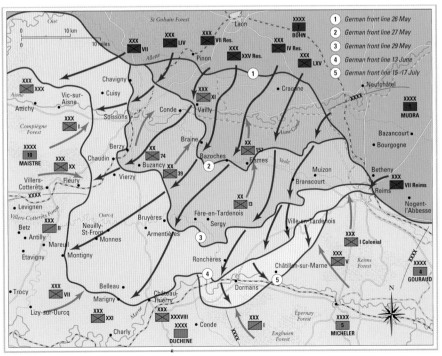

Franco-American Counter-attacks

German momentum finally stopped on the Marne River in July. French intelligence had divined the outlines of the German attack in the region and Foch designed both a defence and a counteroffensive to defeat it. His plan worked brilliantly and thereafter the Germans did not win a major engagement for the rest of the war.

French officers divined the exact time of the German attack from intelligence reports and the capture of critical German deserters. The French opened up a massive artillery barrage on German lines ten minutes before the German attack was to begin. The barrage destroyed the German assault before it even had a chance to begin. A few isolated German units managed to cross the Marne, but they had no support from their own artillery and were doomed. Earlier German attacks had left them stuck in the Marne sector with a dangerously exposed salient. As soon as he knew that the German attack had definitely failed, Foch ordered the French Tenth Army to attack the defenceless western end of that salient. Shortly thereafter, troops from the French, British and American armies attacked the salient on all sides. They soon reduced it, although the Germans fought well in the broken terrain of the Marne sector once they recovered their balance.

The attack caught the Germans completely by surprise and changed the momentum of the war in a day. A dejected Ludendorff cancelled his next planned offensive and began to order his units to defend instead. Foch then implemented a general counteroffensive aimed to put pressure on the Germans all along the Western Front. If one offensive slowed down, he would stop it and start another. With the arrival of the Americans, the Allied armies were soon in a position to take advantage of their superiority of manpower as well as their increasing advantages in armour, artillery and aviation.

Pershing and the AEF

The Second Battle of the Marne also proved the fighting ability of the American Expeditionary Forces (AEF). Its commander, General John Pershing, had allowed American divisions about 20,000 men each to fight as part of French corps and armies. Under this arrangement, the French could handle much of the sophisticated staff work needed to make armies move and fight. But the stubborn Pershing insisted on the Americans receiving their own dedicated part of the front with a fully American chain of command. After the Second Battle of the Marne, Foch agreed as long as the Americans conformed to his general strategic vision. The Americans were ready to take the offensive.

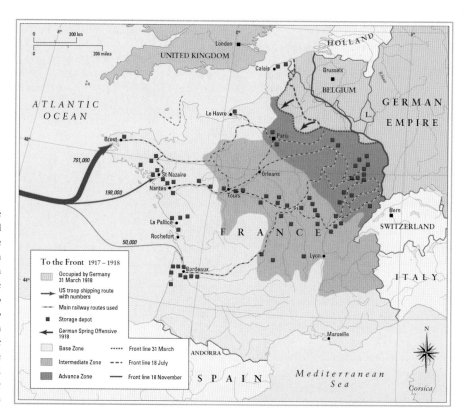

To the Front 1917–1918

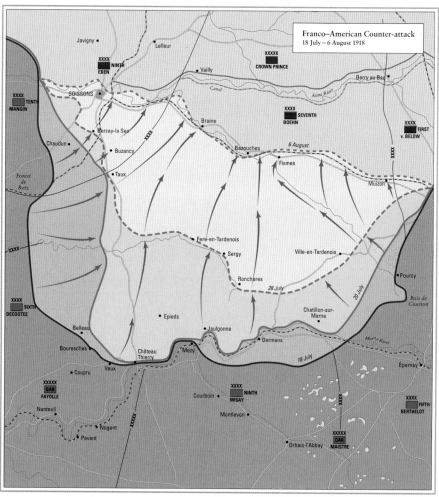

Franco–American Counter-attack
18 July – 6 August 1918

Black Day of the German Army 8 August 1918

The next major Allied offensive cleared German troops away from the critical rail juncture of Amiens. Ludendorff later called the loss at Amiens the 'black day' of the German Army because of the high number of men who surrendered.

The British attack relied on all of the new methods of warfare. It used intelligent and meticulous planning to maximize the chances of success. British artillery methods had become much more sophisticated, allowing for a much higher degree of accuracy. Using a technique called sound ranging, the British forces had identified the location of 504 of the 530 German heavy artillery pieces at Amiens. British gunners could therefore target and destroy them in a process known as counterbattery fire. More than 400 German artillery pieces were thus eliminated early in the battle. Some of the problems with tanks had also been worked out, giving the British troops the firepower they needed. A talented Australian general named John Monash worked out the details for the battle. For the loss of 9000 British casualties, the Germans lost in excess of 27,000 men.

The New Allied Strategy

The twin victories of the Second Battle of the Marne and Amiens convinced Foch that the Allies could win the war in 1918 if they pushed hard enough. They would need to smash through the Hindenburg Line before the arrival of winter if they hoped to achieve this, however. The two great summer victories seemed to show the superiority of the Allied methods of mass over the German stormtroop method. The high numbers of prisoners of war in both battles also suggested that the German Army's morale was cracking.

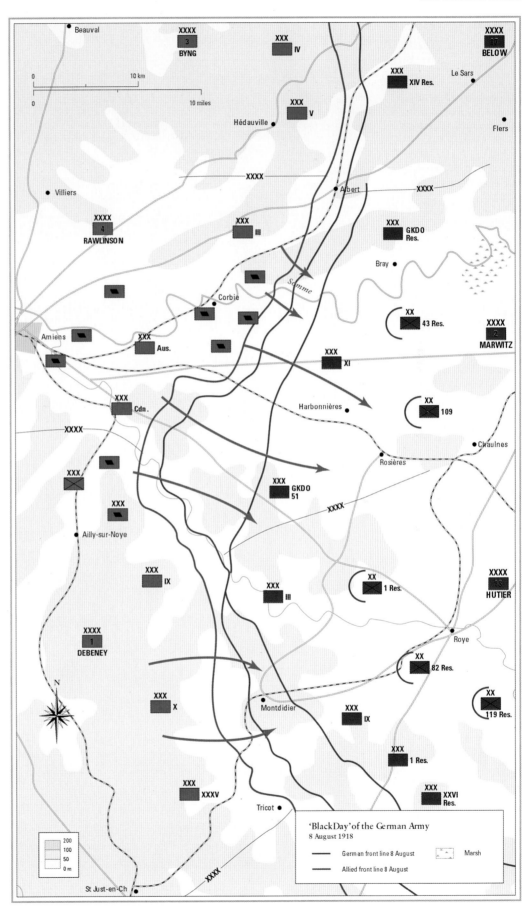

'Black Day' of the German Army
8 August 1918

— German front line 8 August

— Allied front line 8 August

Marsh

St. Mihiel 12–18 September 1918

The attack into St. Mihiel represented the first major offensive directed and led by the U.S. Army. If they succeeded they could provide another force to hammer away at German positions across the western front.

The St. Mihiel salient had bulged into Allied lines since 1914. The U.S. attack aimed to reduce it and then pressure the key rail centre of Metz. The Germans found they could not devote as many divisions to its defence as they wanted. Still, the difficult terrain of the region made an attack awkward, and the Germans had added strong trenches several layers thick.

The Americans, with the French in support, aimed to solve the problem from the air. They amassed more than 1400 aircraft, then the largest air armada ever assembled. It cleared the skies of enemy planes and helped artillery to target positions.

The Germans quickly realized that they could not hold the salient and began a withdrawal. The Americans retook 518km² (200 miles²) of French territory while capturing 15,000 soldiers.

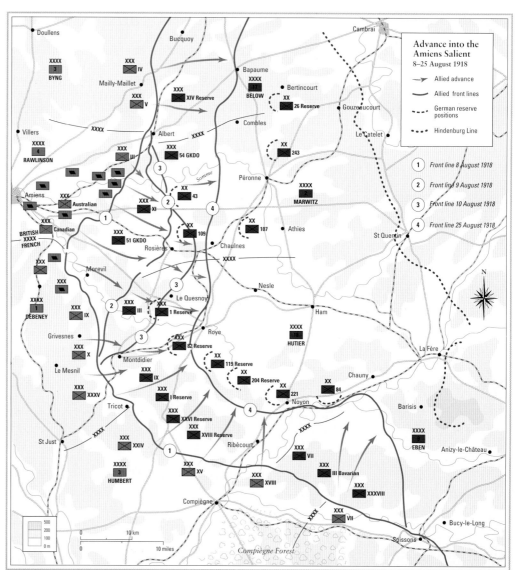

Advance into the Amiens Salient
8–25 August 1918

→ Allied advance
— Allied front lines
--- German reserve positions
···· Hindenburg Line

① Front line 8 August 1918
② Front line 9 August 1918
③ Front line 10 August 1918
④ Front line 25 August 1918

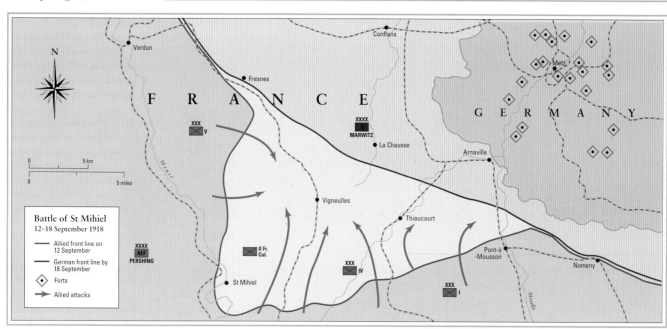

Battle of St Mihiel
12–18 September 1918

— Allied front line on 12 September
— German front line by 18 September
◇ Forts
→ Allied attacks

Meuse-Argonne Offensive 26 September–11 November 1918

After the victory at St. Mihiel, Pershing wanted to advance the AEF toward Metz, but Foch overruled him and ordered the Americans into the extremely difficult terrain adjoining the Argonne Forest and the Meuse River. The Americans hoped to smash quickly past the heights of Montfaucon and through the German lines, but the Germans held their ground well, turning the Meuse-Argonne into a bloody slogging match that lasted until the end of the war.

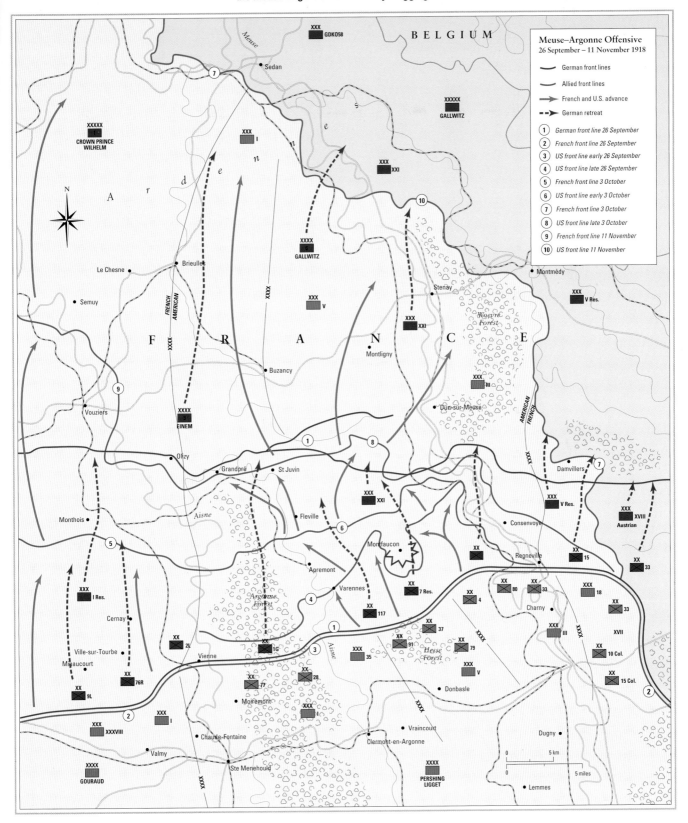

Meuse–Argonne Offensive
26 September – 11 November 1918

- German front lines
- Allied front lines
- French and U.S. advance
- German retreat

1 German front line 26 September
2 French front line 26 September
3 US front line early 26 September
4 US front line late 26 September
5 French front line 3 October
6 US front line early 3 October
7 French front line 3 October
8 US front line late 3 October
9 French front line 11 November
10 US front line 11 November

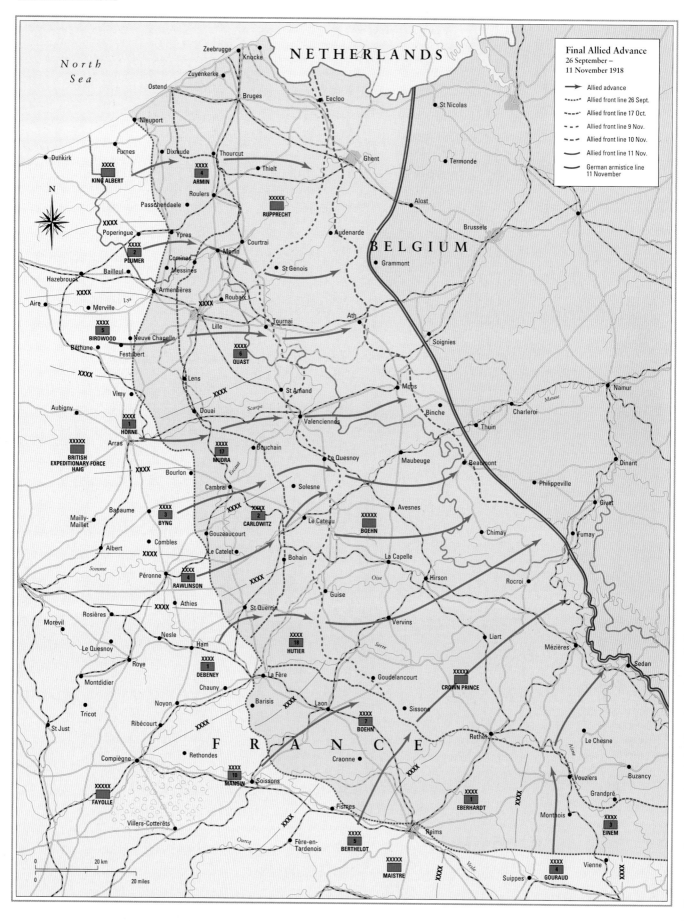

North Sea

NETHERLANDS

Final Allied Advance
26 September –
11 November 1918

→ Allied advance
···· Allied front line 26 Sept.
-·-· Allied front line 17 Oct.
-- Allied front line 9 Nov.
-- Allied front line 10 Nov.
— Allied front line 11 Nov.
— German armistice line
11 November

Zeebrugge
Knocke
Ostend
Zuyenkerke
Bruges
Eecloo
St Nicolas
Dunkirk
Furnes
Dixmude
Thourout
Ghent
Termonde
Nieuport
XXXX 4 KING ALBERT
XXXX 4 ARMIN
Thielt
Roulers
Passchendaele
XXXXX RUPPRECHT
Alost
Brussels
Poperinghe
XXXX
Ypres
Courtrai
Audenarde
BELGIUM
XXXX 2 PLUMER
Comines
Menin
St Genois
Grammont
Bailleul
Messines
Hazebrouck
Armentières
Roubaix
Ath
Soignies
Aire
Merville
Lys
XXXX
Lille
Tournai
XXXX 5 BIRDWOOD
Neuve Chapelle
Mons
Namur
Béthune
Festubert
XXXX 6 QUAST
St Amand
Binche
Charleroi
Meuse
XXXX
Lens
Valenciennes
Thuin
Vimy
XXXX
Douai
Scarpe
Dinant
Aubigny
XXXX 1 HORNE
XXXX 17 MUDRA
Bouchain
Le Quesnoy
Maubeuge
Beaumont
Philippeville
Arras
XXXXX BRITISH EXPEDITIONARY FORCE HAIG
Escaut
Givet
XXXX
Bourlon
Cambrai
Solesne
Avesnes
Fumay
Bapaume
XXXX 3 BYNG
XXXX
XXXX 2 CARLOWITZ
Le Cateau
XXXXX BOEHN
Chimay
Mailly-Maillet
Gouzeaucourt
Le Catelet
La Capelle
Rocroi
Albert
Combles
Bohain
Oise
Hirson
XXXX
Somme
Péronne
XXXX 4 RAWLINSON
XXXX
Guise
Vervins
Liart
Mézières
Rosières
XXXX
Athies
St Quentin
Sedan
Morevil
Nesle
Ham
Serre
Le Quesnoy
XXXX 18 HUTIER
Goudelancourt
Le Chesne
Roye
XXXX 1 DEBENEY
XXXXX CROWN PRINCE
Rethel
Montdidier
Chauny
La Fère
Laon
Sissone
Buzancy
Noyon
Barisis
Vouziers
Tricot
XXXX
Grandpré
St Just
Ribécourt
Aisne
Montmois
XXXX 3 EINEM
Compiègne
Rethondes
F R A N C E
Craonne
XXXX 10 MANGIN
Soissons
XXXX
XXXX 1 EBERHARDT
XXXXX FAYOLLE
Fismes
Reims
XXXX 4 GOURAUD
Villers-Cotterêts
Ourcq
XXXX 5 BERTHELOT
Fère-en-Tardenois
Vesle
Vienne
XXXXX MAISTRE
Suippes
XXXX

The Western Front 1918

The growing strength of the U.S. Army gave the Allies strategic options that the Germans no longer had. Allied armies were getting bigger and better, with more and more modern weaponry. The German decision to seek an armistice came in large part from their awareness that they stood little chance of keeping the Allies out of Germany itself in 1919.

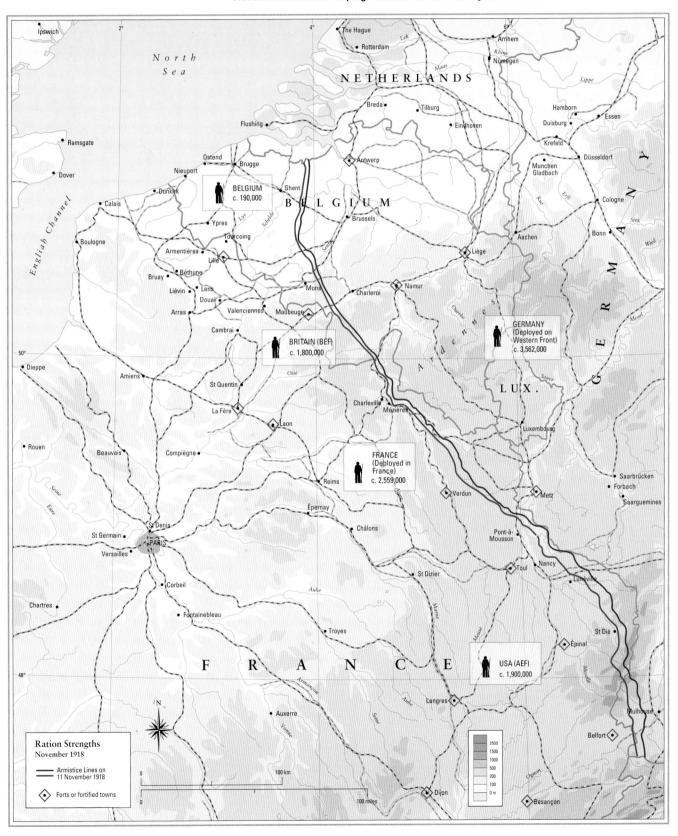

Ration Strengths
November 1918

— Armistice Lines on 11 November 1918

◇ Forts or fortified towns

0   100 km

0   100 miles

BELGIUM c. 190,000

BRITAIN (BEF) c. 1,800,000

GERMANY (Deployed on Western Front) c. 3,562,000

FRANCE (Deployed in France) c. 2,559,000

USA (AEF) c. 1,900,000

Austrian soldiers pose for the camera outside their dug-in positions near Tolmino, Italy, during the battle of Caporetto.

THE
WIDER
WAR

This world war impacted every part of the world. Scholars are only now starting to understand the ways that military service and the horrors of war changed global social, economic and political patterns. Men from the French, British, and German overseas empires volunteered or were drafted into military service thousands of miles from their homes.

Borders changed, civilians suffered and empires crumbled. In one of the most famous examples, British forces entered Jerusalem at the end of 1917, ending many centuries of Muslim control there and shifting the religious dynamic of the region. Neutral countries also found it difficult to remain above the fray. In the most important case, the United States finally entered the war after nearly three years of neutrality, changing the war in an instant.

Russian artillery, Azerbaijan
Soldiers defending Baku, Azerbaijan. In summer 1918, the oil-rich region was the scene of a multi-state competition that included revolutionary Russia, the British and other Russian forces still loyal to the Tsar.

East African *Askaris*
World War I devastated African communities. Shown here are *Askaris*, locally recruited troops under German command in Dar Es Salaam, Tanzania, which was then part of German East Africa.

Teasing a sniper
A Royal Irish Fusilier teases a Turkish sniper at Gallipoli, ca. 1915. The Gallipoli campaign brought together soldiers from all over the world in an ultimately futile Allied attempt to open a sea lane to Russia and knock the Ottomans out of the war.

Fight for Jerusalem
Austro-Hungarian forces near Jerusalem in 1916 support their Ottoman allies. The British took the city and the whole of Palestine the following year, radically changing the history of the region.

Easter Rising, 1916
British troops man a barricade during the Irish Easter Rising in 1916. At first unpopular with the Irish people, the brutal British military response to the insurgency led many Irish to seek independence.

Mexico intervention
American infantry take position outside of the American-occupied port city of Vera Cruz, Mexico, in 1917. Rumours of German support for anti-American leaders in Mexico increased American anxieties.

The Ottoman Empire November 1914

Largely due to the Ottoman Empire's fear of Russian desires for control of the Dardanelles Straits and Constantinople, they cast their lot with the Germans. Years of heavy diplomatic, economic, cultural and military engagement from Berlin paid off when the two powers became allies.

Ottoman defeats in three major wars since 1911 made the Empire look like 'the sick man of Europe' to many contemporaries, but the Ottomans retained a great deal of strength. The Empire, however, had to guard a number of critical frontiers, including Palestine, Mesopotamia, Thrace and the Caucasus. These regions were too far apart to allow forces in one to support the others. The Ottoman Empire also had long, exposed coastlines that enemy fleets could exploit. The Ottoman Army contained a dizzying number of ethnicities, not all of which were loyal to the Sultan or the new 'Young Turk' movement that sought political reform in the pre-war years.

Ottoman Strategy

The Ottoman Empire did not attempt to use the war to recover their lost Balkan territories. Ottoman military strategists instead sought to increase their power over the regions they still controlled. They aimed to pressure the British in the Suez Canal region as a way to cut Britain's lifeline to India and to reassert their power in Egypt. The Empire's biggest security concern, however, was always Russia. The Germans gave the Ottoman Navy two modern warships to patrol the Black Sea and to encourage the majority of the Ottoman Army to move east into the Caucasus where Turkish nationalists sought to reach out to ethnic Turks inside Russia.

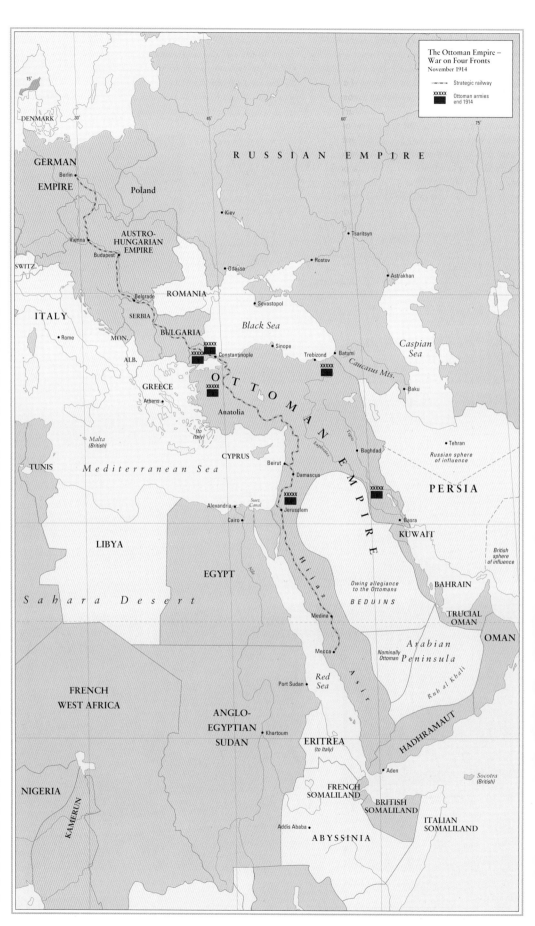

Caucasus Campaign November 1914

The Caucasus contained a number of ethnic groups whose loyalties stretched across the Turkish–Russian border. On the Turkish side sat the Christian Armenians and on the Russian side sat many Turkish Central Asian peoples. Nationalists on both sides demanded annexations of territory to protect people they saw as kinsmen from a foreign government. Even if much of the official rhetoric – especially on the Russian side – proved to be empty, it nevertheless added fuel to a smoldering fire in wartime.

The terrain of the Caucasus made any major military operation extremely difficult to conduct. High altitudes and frigid weather caused massive casualties to frostbite. Logisticians struggled to get supplies through the heavy snows to their lightly-clad troops in a region with few paved roads and even fewer rail lines. Both sides suffered terribly from cold and even from wild animal attacks. The front line in the Caucasus focused on fortifications such as Erzerum, and key towns such as Sarakamish. The Ottomans placed so much importance on their eastern front that Minister of Defence Enver Pasha came east personally to lead.

The Russians moved first, crossing the border and hoping to capture key forts quickly to give their troops protection from the coming winter. The first battle in the east occurred in temperatures as low as -25 degrees Celsius. An outbreak of typhus hit both sides, adding to the misery of the troops. Enver hoped to use three corps, one of which would fix the Russians in place while two more surrounded them and cut off their avenues of retreat.

Difficult Plan to Execute

The plan looked elegant on paper, but in the mountains and snow it proved impossible to execute. The Russians won the first major battle in the Caucasus, the Battle of Sarakamish, which turned into a brutal and costly clash that left the Russians in control of parts of the region.

Lower Mesopotamia November–December 1914

While the Ottomans clashed with the Russians in the Caucasus, they also faced the British in their Mesopotamian province. Britain sought to secure the region mainly with Indian troops led by British officers. Ambitious British officials saw Lower Mesopotamia as a bridge between the Egyptian and Indian axes of Britain's Empire. Ottoman officials hoped to hold a region that they had at least nominally controlled since the sixteenth century. For both sides, however, Mesopotamia was at best a secondary theatre.

Relying on its advantage in sea power, the British moved men, supplies and ships into the Shatt-al-Arab waterway that connects the historic Tigris River to the Persian Gulf. Then, with an Indian division in the lead, British forces began their advance toward Basra, the most important city in Lower Mesopotamia. The proximity of India allowed the British to concentrate thousands of their soldiers in the region without weakening their forces in France. In November 1914 British and Indian forces brushed aside a nominal Ottoman force guarding the outdated fortress at Fao at the mouth of the Tigris River. With a secure foothold in the region, the British began a build up of troops and supplies.

The Road to Basra

Suphi Bey, the Ottoman governor of the Basra region and de facto commander in the area, knew his forces could not match the numbers, the training or the firepower of the British. His small force of barely 350 men had been accustomed to routine garrison duties, not high-intensity combat. In late November, Suphi Bey ruefully abandoned Basra after a brief but intense fight and retreated up the Tigris River to the town of Qurna. From there, he hoped to be resupplied and reinforced by river. The British moved into Basra and began to establish authority in the town. At the same time they decided to move upriver and attack Suphi Bey's remaining forces at Qurna.

Ottoman Raid on the Suez Canal 3–5 February 1915

The Suez Canal represented one of the most important arteries for the British Empire. Without it, British ships sailing to India increased their time at sea from days to weeks. If the Ottoman Empire's forces could seize it or at least interdict British shipping through it, they could perform an invaluable service to themselves and their German allies. The Ottomans also hoped to spark an uprising in Egypt against the British forces based there.

At the start of the war, Egypt remained a nominal province of the Ottoman Empire, but since the 1880s the British had effective control over it. Ottoman leaders sought to change that situation and to control navigation rights on the Suez Canal. Political confusion in Egypt led the British to depose the pro-Ottoman ruler of Egypt and replace him with a pro-British figurehead. The Egyptian people did not actively oppose these moves, but popular disaffection with the British was evidently growing in late 1914, putting the British on their guard. The Ottomans opted for light patrols and raids on the canal that year, hoping to test British defences and provide at least some encouragement to the anti-British forces in Egypt.

The British surrendered the wide-open spaces of the Sinai Peninsula to the Ottomans, opting to defend the canal on the water line itself. British gunships provided mobile fire support, although only on the coast could they use their largest warships. Unable to rely on native Egyptian troops for its defence, the British brought in two divisions of Indian troops.

Battle for the Canal

In February 1915 the Ottomans attacked, aiming at the centre of the canal in order to avoid the deepest water where the heaviest British gunboats might lurk. Djemal Pasha, a tough Ottoman commander, pushed his men forward with his usual aggressiveness, but only two companies of Ottoman troops managed to get across the water. They could not hold the bridgehead they had created against British counter-attacks. Perhaps more importantly, the attack did not create the much-anticipated revolt of the Egyptian people against the British.

Although they held the canal, the British grew anxious about its security as well as the safety of their positions in Egypt in general. They soon increased the size of their forces in Egypt to 150,000 and sent the newly formed Australia and New Zealand Army Corps (ANZAC) to Egypt to train and provide a reserve. The British began to plan for a new forward defence of the Suez Canal that involved advancing into Sinai and pushing the Ottomans away from the lifeline of their Empire.

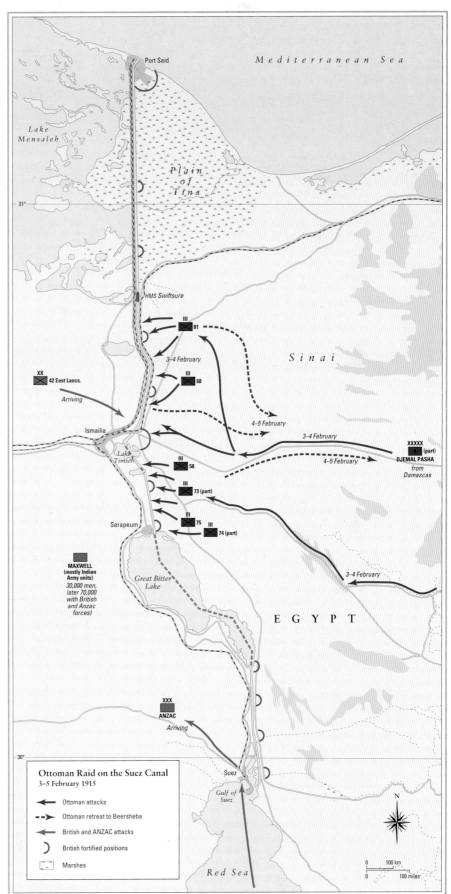

113

Naval Attack in the Dardanelles 18 March 1915

Winston Churchill hoped that the Royal Navy could rush the Dardanelles Straits, leading to the defeat of the Ottomans, the security of the Suez Canal and a direct supply line between the western Allies and a Russia in need of help.

British battleships could not move through the Dardanelles because of minefields, while minesweepers could not do their work because of gunfire from Ottoman forts. Many of those forts had German-trained gunners. Churchill thus hoped to use the army to land on the Gallipoli peninsula and take out the Ottoman guns.

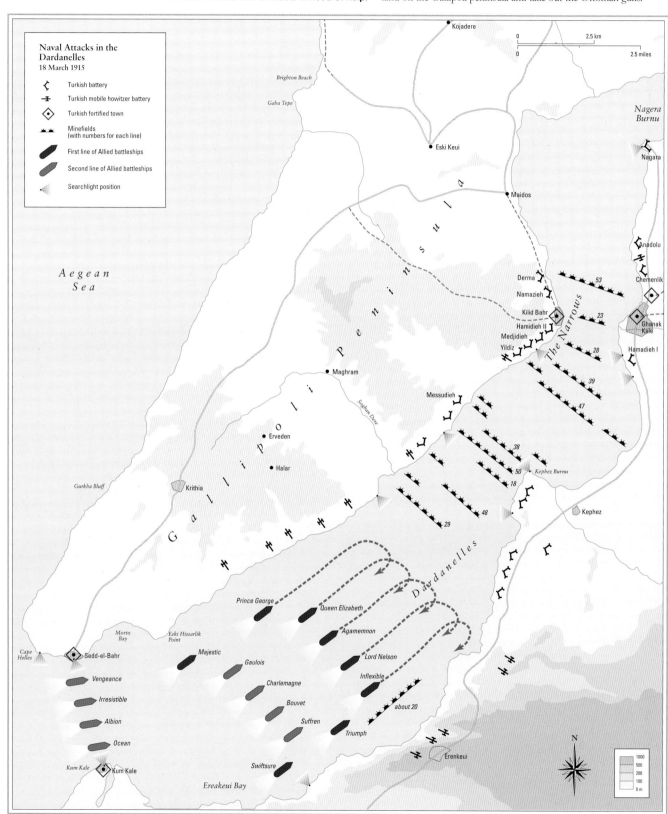

Naval Attacks in the
Dardanelles
18 March 1915

- Turkish battery
- Turkish mobile howitzer battery
- Turkish fortified town
- Minefields (with numbers for each line)
- First line of Allied battleships
- Second line of Allied battleships
- Searchlight position

Kojadere

Brighton Beach

Gaba Tepe

Eski Keui

Maidos

Nagera Burnu

Nagara

Anadolu

Chemenlik

Derma

Namazieh

Kilid Bahr

Hamidieh II

Medjidieh

Yildiz

Ghanak Kale

Hamadieh I

Aegean
Sea

Maghram

Messudieh

Soghan Dere

Erveden

Halar

Gurkha Bluff

Krithia

Kephez Burnu

Kephez

P e n i n s u l a

G a l l i p o l i

D a r d a n e l l e s

The Narrows

53

23

28

39

47

38

50

18

48

29

Prince George

Queen Elizabeth

Agamemnon

Lord Nelson

Inflexible

about 20

Morto
Bay

Eski Hissarlik
Point

Cape
Helles

Sedd-el-Bahr

Majestic

Gaulois

Charlemagne

Bouvet

Suffren

Triumph

Vengeance

Irresistible

Albion

Ocean

Kum Kale

Kum Kale

Swiftsure

Ereakeui Bay

Erenkeui

1000
500
200
100
0 m

Gallipoli Campaign
18 March–13 July 1915

The British, using many ANZAC troops, landed in six different places hoping to confuse the Ottoman defenders. But those same defenders had had time to prepare and they had the benefit of excellent defensive ground. They were also fighting to defend their own territory, not some distant province of the Empire. The British landings were confused and disorganized. They also ran into the determined leadership of future president of Turkey, Lt. Col. Mustafa Kemal.

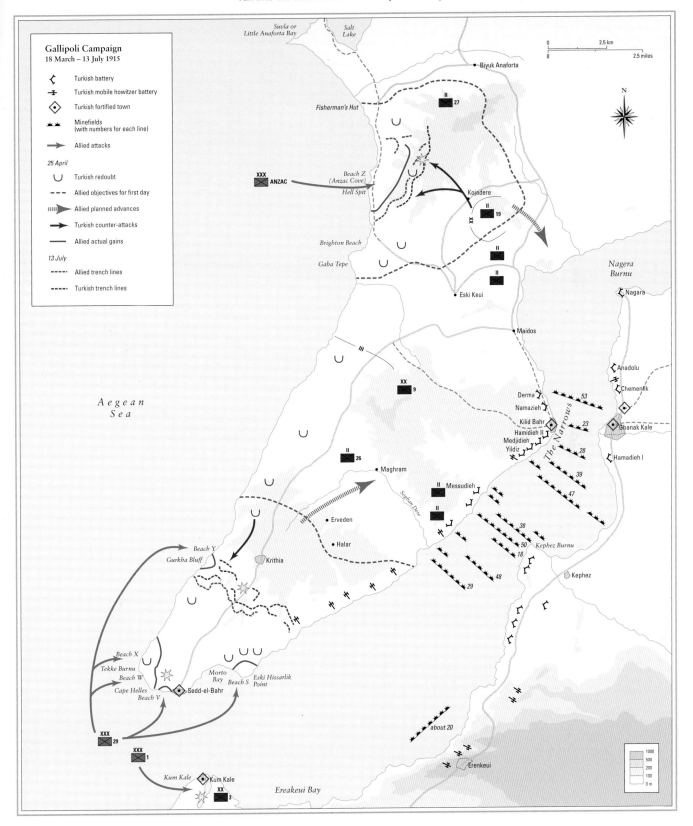

Gallipoli Campaign
18 March – 13 July 1915

- Turkish battery
- Turkish mobile howitzer battery
- Turkish fortified town
- Minefields (with numbers for each line)
- Allied attacks

25 April
- Turkish redoubt
- Allied objectives for first day
- Allied planned advances
- Turkish counter-attacks
- Allied actual gains

13 July
- Allied trench lines
- Turkish trench lines

0   2.5 km
0   2.5 miles

N

Suvla or Little Anaforta Bay
Salt Lake
Biyuk Anaforta
Fisherman's Hut
27
Beach Z (Anzac Cove)
Hell Spit
Kojadere
19
XX
ANZAC
XXX
Brighton Beach
Gaba Tepe
Eski Keui
Maidos
Nagera Burnu
Nagara
Anadolu
Chemenlik
Derma
Namazieh
53
Kilid Bahr
23
Hamidieh II
Medjidieh
Yildiz
Ghanak Kale
28
Hamadieh I
39
9
XX
Aegean Sea
26
Maghram
Messudieh
47
Erveden
Halar
Soghan Dere
38
50
Kephez Burnu
18
Beach Y
Gurkha Bluff
Krithia
48
29
Kephez
Beach X
Tekke Burnu
Beach W
Cape Helles
Beach V
Sedd-el-Bahr
Morto Bay
Beach S
Eski Hissarlik Point
about 20
29
XXX
1
XXX
Kum Kale
3
XX
Ereakeui Bay
Erenkeui

1000
500
200
100
0 m

The Cape Helles Front
April 1915–January 1916

Landing at Cape Helles at the tip of the Gallipoli peninsula gave British forces few options but to charge forward up narrow ridges against defenders on high ground. Ottoman forces pressed the British back, but lacked the strength to expel them from Gallipoli. Poor supply systems, a confused command arrangement and brutal weather added to the misery of the British. They needed another attack somewhere else at Gallipoli to break what had become a frustrating stalemate.

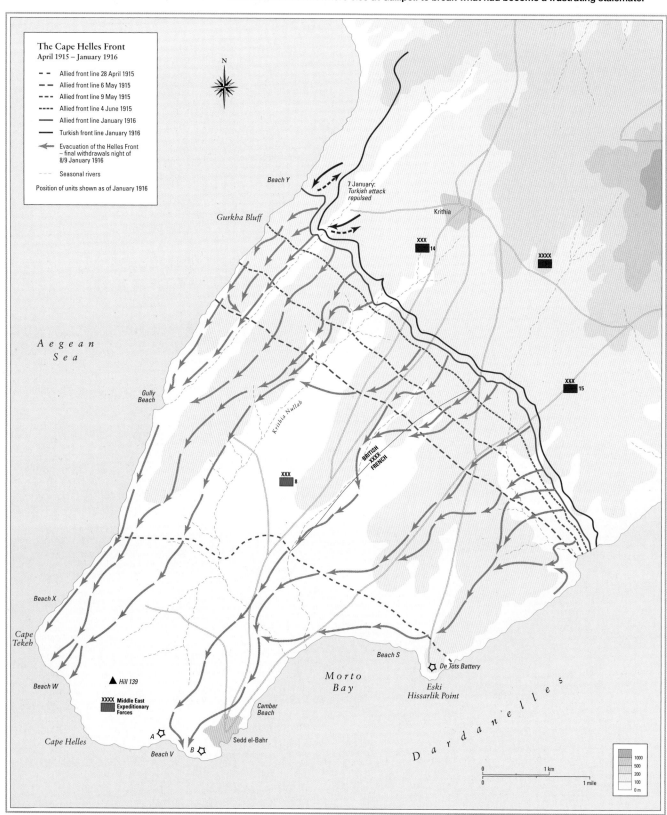

The Cape Helles Front
April 1915 – January 1916

– – Allied front line 28 April 1915
– – Allied front line 6 May 1915
– – – Allied front line 9 May 1915
· · · · Allied front line 4 June 1915
——— Allied front line January 1916
——— Turkish front line January 1916
→ Evacuation of the Helles Front – final withdrawals night of 8/9 January 1916
- - - Seasonal rivers

Position of units shown as of January 1916

N

Beach Y

7 January: Turkish attack repulsed

Gurkha Bluff

Krithia

XXX 14

XXXX

Aegean Sea

Gully Beach

XXX 15

Krithia Nullah

BRITISH
XXXX
FRENCH

XXX 8

Beach X

Cape Tekeh

Beach W

▲ Hill 139

XXXX Middle East Expeditionary Forces

Beach S

De Tots Battery

Morto Bay

Eski Hissarlik Point

Camber Beach

A ✩

B ✩

Sedd el-Bahr

Cape Helles

Beach V

Dardanelles

0   1 km
0   1 mile

1000
500
200
100
0 m

Suvla Bay and Anzac Cove
6 August–30 December 1915

The British tried to change the momentum of the faltering Gallipoli campaign with a landing in the wide Suvla Bay in August. Ships landed in the wrong places and dispersed British troops across the bay. Despite a huge edge in manpower, the British could not advance far from Suvla, although their command of the sea protected their men from Ottoman counter-attacks. By winter, the British had decided to evacuate Gallipoli and give up on the expedition.

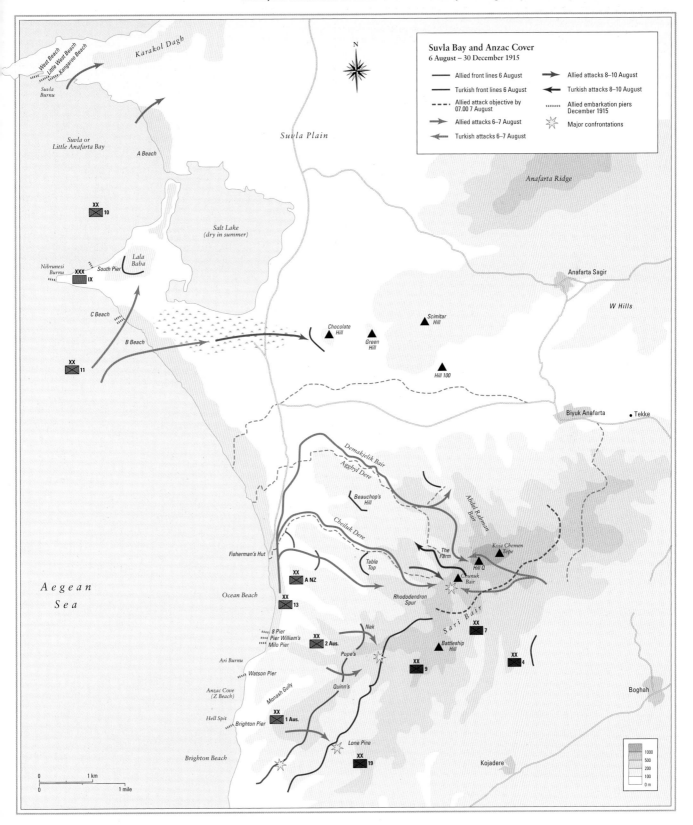

Suvla Bay and Anzac Cover
6 August – 30 December 1915

—— Allied front lines 6 August

—— Turkish front lines 6 August

- - - Allied attack objective by 07.00 7 August

→ Allied attacks 6–7 August

← Turkish attacks 6–7 August

→ Allied attacks 8–10 August

← Turkish attacks 8–10 August

······ Allied embarkation piers December 1915

✶ Major confrontations

Russian Capture of Trebizond 5 February–18 April 1916

Trebizond was one of the key economic centres of the Black Sea region. Once a terminus of the Silk Road from China, by 1914 it had become a key centre of transportation for the Caucasus oil industry. The British and Russians both had economic investments there. The city had been part of the Ottoman Empire for almost 450 years and had a multi-ethnic population that included thousands of Armenian Christians. The Russians wanted it for economic and ethnic reasons, and set it as one of the goals of the Caucasus campaign. In early 1916 Russian Grand Duke Nicholas took command in the sector and began a campaign to take Trebizond.

Ottoman persecution and deportation of the local Christian Armenian community in Trebizond added to the tensions in the region, although it is not clear that they directly motivated the Russians to act. By the time of the campaign's start in 1916, virtually all of the city's once thriving Armenian population had been removed by force. In February, an advance on Trebizond became possible when the Russians captured the fortified city of Erzurum. With 40,000 men and 235 artillery pieces defending 20 separate fortifications, the Ottoman leadership thought Erzurum invincible. But the Russians took it, along with 15,000 Ottoman prisoners, in a surprising lightning advance. The fall of Erzurum allowed the Russians to move north toward the Black Sea coast and Trebizond. The loss of Erzurum stunned Ottoman leaders, who ordered Mustafa Kemal, the hero of Gallipoli, to come to the Caucasus in an effort to change Ottoman fortunes there.

Kemal did not arrive in time to stop the Russians from advancing north out of Erzurum and directing a two-pronged attack toward Trebizond. Grand Duke Nicholas, sent to the Caucasus after the humiliation of Gorlice-Tarnow, carefully prepared his supply lines and assembled a large, confident force. Building on their success at Erzurum, they marched north while at the same time the Russian Navy sailed south across the Black Sea in support. The Ottomans rushed what units they could toward Trebizond overland while sending ships east from Istanbul to challenge the Russians.

Fall of Trebizond

On both land and sea the Russians won the race, outflanking the Ottomans and capturing the city. The Russians caused destruction on a huge scale in the city, blowing up mosques and forcing Muslims to leave. The destruction suggests that perhaps the Russians were in fact avenging the Armenians.

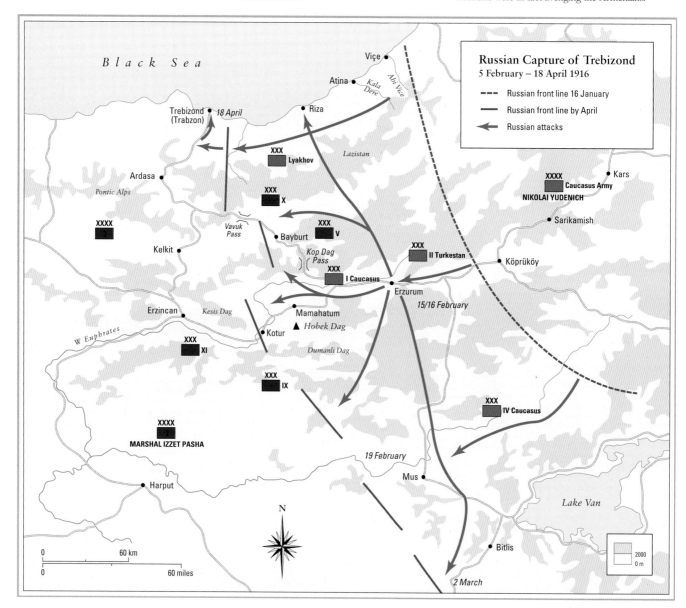

Mesopotamia Overview 1915–18

The Ottomans formed a new army to hold the British in lower Mesopotamia. Germany sent an experienced general, Colmar von der Goltz, to command the force. He envisioned pushing the British forces out of Mesopotamia then invading Persia and possibly India.

Although the British, Germans and Ottomans all understood that Mesopotamia could never become their primary theatre, they all saw the advantages of a campaign there. Sitting close to the Persian Gulf, Arabia, Persia and India, Mesopotamia had a vital geographic location. The British Anglo-Persian Oil Company had also begun to extract oil in the region at a time when militaries and civilian economies alike were becoming more dependent on oil. The British also saw a value in increasing their prestige among the Sunni and Shia Muslims of the region, most of whom had only nominally accepted Ottoman suzerainty in the area.

Military Options

The difficult terrain of Mesopotamia limited military forces. Advancing along the Tigris and Euphrates Rivers was the easiest way to transport men and supplies. That gave the British an edge, although the further they moved from their supply centres, the more dangerous movements upriver became. The British took the town of Kut in September 1915. As the British moved north, they moved further from safety. The focus of operations quickly became the capital of Baghdad. The Ottomans based their defences on the river town of Ctesiphon just 32km (20 miles) south of Baghdad, using the Tigris to secure one flank. British forces moved toward the town in November 1915 expecting a rapid success.

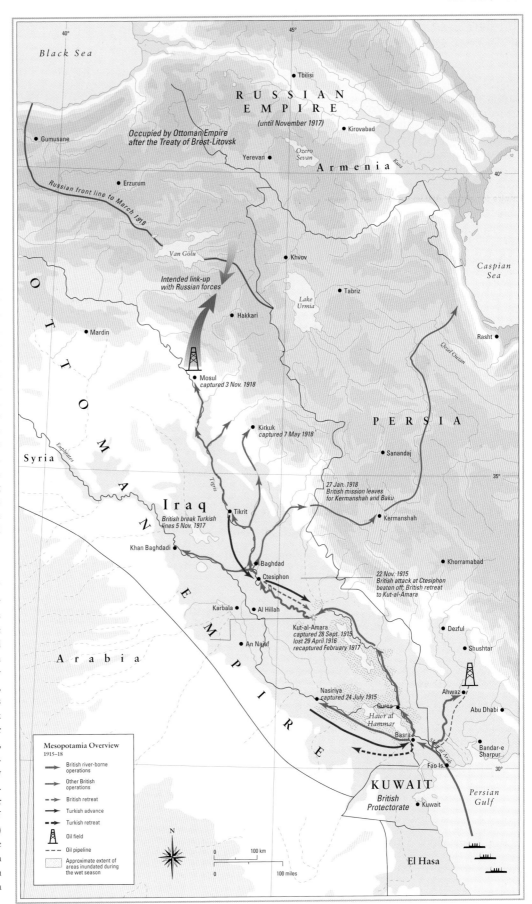

Black Sea

RUSSIAN EMPIRE
(until November 1917)

Occupied by Ottoman Empire
after the Treaty of Brest-Litovsk

• Tbilisi

• Kirovabad

• Gumusane

• Yerevan

Armenia

Ozero
Sevan

Caspian
Sea

Russian front line to March 1918

• Erzurum

• Khvov

• Tabriz

Van Gölu

Lake
Urmia

• Rasht

Intended link-up
with Russian forces

• Hakkari

• Mardin

O T T O M A N

Mosul
captured 3 Nov. 1918

P E R S I A

Euphrates

• Kirkuk
captured 7 May 1918

• Sanandaj

Syria

Tigris

27 Jan. 1918
British mission leaves
for Kermanshah and Baku

Iraq

• Tikrit

British break Turkish
lines 5 Nov. 1917

• Kermanshah

E M P I R E

Khan Baghdadi •

• Khorramabad

• Baghdad
Ctesiphon

22 Nov. 1915
British attack at Ctesiphon
beaten off; British retreat
to Kut-al-Amara

Karbala

• Al Hillah

• Dezful

Kut-al-Amara
captured 28 Sept. 1915
lost 29 April 1916
recaptured February 1917

• Shushtar

• An Najaf

Arabia

Nasiriya
captured 24 July 1915

Ahwaz •

Qurna

Hawr al
Hammar

• Abu Dhabi

Basra

• Bandar-e
Sharpur

Fao Is.

KUWAIT
British
Protectorate • Kuwait

Persian
Gulf

Mesopotamia Overview
1915–18

→ British river-borne operations
→ Other British operations
⇢ British retreat
→ Turkish advance
⇢ Turkish retreat
⛏ Oil field
– – Oil pipeline
▨ Approximate extent of areas inundated during the wet season

N

0   100 km

0   100 miles

El Hasa

Capture of Qurna
3–9 December 1914

After the defeat at Basra, a large part of the Ottoman forces retreated to Qurna, a town that sat at the juncture of the Tigris and Euphrates Rivers. From there they could threaten British positions in southern Mesopotamia and impede any British movements to the north.

Ottoman forces set up their main position astride both rivers, forcing the British to make two crossings if they wanted to fight a battle. The Ottomans thus had excellent terrain to defend, but they had only 1000 men ready for battle under an inexperienced commander. The British could assemble twice that number immediately and reinforce with thousands more in a few weeks' time. They had an experienced commander and better supply lines, as British gunboats could bring supplies up the Tigris from Basra. Those gunboats could also shell Ottoman positions from almost any direction. If the British could seize Qurna, they could secure southern Mesopotamia and the Abadan oil fields.

The British plan called for relying on the gunboats to shell the Euphrates side of the Qurna position while the infantry crossed the Tigris to its north. The first British attempts to take the town failed as the Ottoman defensive positions proved to be too strong. On 8 December, however, two regiments found a place to cross the Tigris that the Ottomans had not properly defended. As British ships shelled the Ottomans from the Euphrates, British land forces closed in. Recognizing that they could not hold the town for long, the Ottomans sent a ship down the Euphrates to negotiate surrender terms.

The Ottoman envoys offered to surrender the town in exchange for the British allowing the garrison to leave. The British officer who received them refused their demands and insisted that the entire garrison surrender. They pressed their case, but eventually yielded with 42 Ottoman officer and 989 enlisted men becoming prisoners of war. British casualties were light.

First Battle of Kut

Their successes in Basra, Qurna and elsewhere convinced British officers to move even further north to the town of Kut on the Tigris River. British politicians encouraged the advance, in part to compensate for the bad news coming from other fronts in 1915. In September, British forces outflanked Ottoman defences and entered Kut. The fall of the town worried the Ottomans as much as it encouraged the British. The Ottomans sent reinforcements to protect Baghdad and, when possible, to launch a counter-attack. British forces immediately planned an advance on Baghdad through the town of Ctesiphon. British commander General Sir Charles Townshend worried about the size of his force and its slender lines of supply but moved forward anyway.

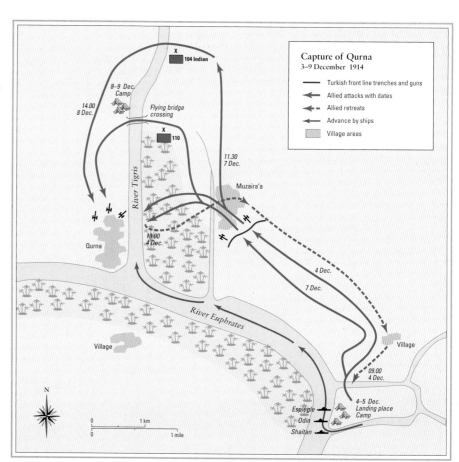

Battle of Ctesiphon 22–25 November 1915

Although they were more than 563km (350 miles) from their main supply base at Basra, the British pushed on toward Ctesiphon. It sat on the Tigris River, 24km (15 miles) south of Baghdad. Capturing it would virtually guarantee the British control of the approaches to Baghdad and its eventual seizure. Ctesiphon thus enticed the British forces, but it sat on good defensive ground and the Ottoman Empire had more men in the city than they had had in past battles such as Qurna and Basra.

Ottoman forces had nearly two months to prepare the ground in front of them. They built two solid lines of defences manned by more than 18,000 troops and equipped with modern artillery pieces. Some of these troops were among the most experienced and elite soldiers in the Ottoman Army. The British pushed forward in three columns from the east and northeast. They were confident because they had little respect for the Ottoman commander and they thought that Ottoman morale was low. The British had hoped to outflank the Ottoman lines but instead found themselves attacking solid formations.

The three British columns attacked the Ottoman army left flank while a fourth British formation awaited instructions to circle around the Ottoman right to attack with support from British gunboats. The plan quickly unraveled, however, after the gunboats turned back due to mines in the river, and two of the British columns failed to break the enemy lines. The third column, made up mostly of Indian soldiers, broke through the first line but got no further.

British Regroup

The British attacked again on the second day of the battle, inflicting heavy casualties on the Ottomans but still failing to break through the line. Unable to remain where they were, the British retreated to Kut to regroup.

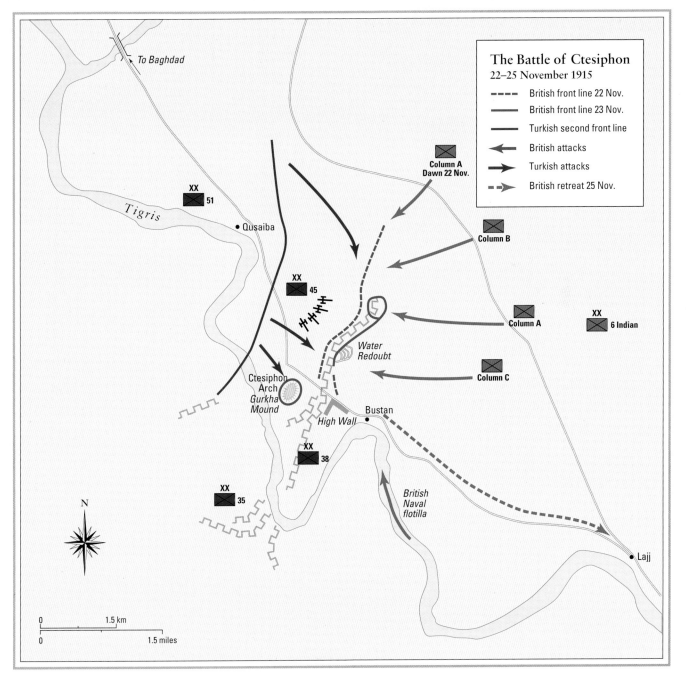

The Battle of Ctesiphon
22–25 November 1915

- - - - British front line 22 Nov.
——— British front line 23 Nov.
——— Turkish second front line
◄——— British attacks
———► Turkish attacks
- - -► British retreat 25 Nov.

To Baghdad

Tigris

XX 51

• Qusaiba

Column A
Dawn 22 Nov.

XX 45

Column B

Column A

XX 6 Indian

Water
Redoubt

Column C

Ctesiphon
Arch
Gurkha
Mound

Bustan

High Wall

XX 38

XX 35

British
Naval
flotilla

• Lajj

N

0   1.5 km

0   1.5 miles

Retreat to Kut November–December 1915

The retreat to Kut, which British troops reached on 3 December, offered the British little protection. Despite their heavy casualties, the Ottomans pursued the retreating British down the Tigris where they found themselves pinned alongside a bend in the river. The British force comprised 11,600 soldiers and 10,000 civilians. Ottoman forces cut the roads in and out of Kut, leading to a siege. The British had 60 days of rations by which time they expected a relief expedition to rescue them.

The British had time to send most of their cavalry out of the city before the Ottomans completed their encirclement on 9 December. The Ottomans had 11,000 men, enough to seal the British into the town of Kut and put men on the opposite bank of the river. More Ottoman troops soon followed. On Christmas Eve the Ottomans attacked, hoping to take the town before British reinforcements could arrive, but they failed to make much progress. A major British relief expedition of 19,000 men set out soon thereafter, advancing on both sides of the river. In January, it pushed Ottoman forces back but they did not break. Heavy rains helped the Ottomans by slowing down the British pursuit. Two more overland rescue expeditions by the British also failed.

The British then tried to aid the garrison by water. They sent ships with 274,332 tonnes (270,000 tons) of food and supplies upriver. The Ottomans shelled the ships and blocked the Tigris with an enormous metal chain. Meanwhile, the better-supplied Ottomans wore down the British with small but persistent attacks around the perimeter of the British positions. Cholera and dwindling food stocks weakened the British forces, and as the siege went into March the British government began to panic. More relief efforts failed and even the first airdrop of supplies in history failed to help. The British made an offer through T. E. Lawrence (Lawrence of Arabia) to ransom the trapped soldiers for £2 million in gold. The Ottomans refused.

Capitulation

The British took the unusual step of asking the Russians to send a rescue effort from northern Persia. The Russians agreed but it was too late. On 29 April, the emaciated and exhausted British garrison of Kut surrendered. More than 2500 British and 7000 Indian soldiers became prisoners of war. It was then the largest surrender in the history of the British Army and a deep humiliation for their leadership. The majority of the men died in captivity, adding to the tragedy and embarrassment. Many Indian soldiers joined the Ottoman Army in exchange for freedom; they later fought against the British. The surrender at Kut set back British plans in Mesopotamia and proved a huge disappointment for a campaign that had begun with high hopes.

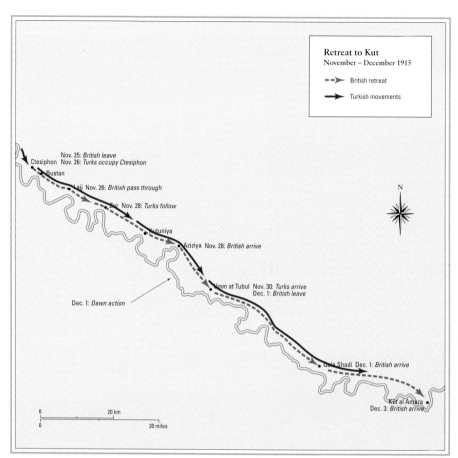

Retreat to Kut
November – December 1915

- - - ➤ British retreat
——➤ Turkish movements

Nov. 25: *British leave*
Ctesiphon Nov. 26: *Turks occupy Ctesiphon*
Bustan
Lajj Nov. 26: *British pass through*
Zor Nov. 28: *Turks follow*
Kutuniya
Aziziya Nov. 28: *British arrive*
Umm at Tubul Nov. 30: *Turks arrive*
Dec. 1: *British leave*
Dec. 1: *Dawn action*
Qala Shadi Dec. 1: *British arrive*
Kut al Amara Dec. 3: *British arrive*

0   20 km
0   20 miles

N

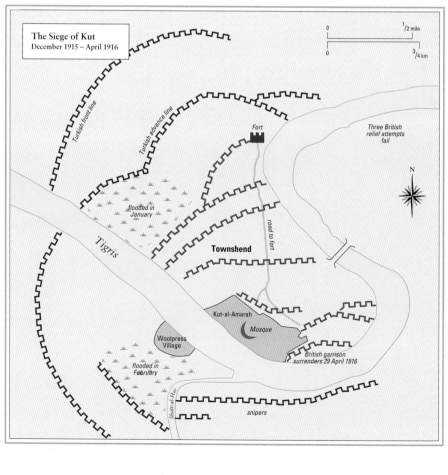

The Siege of Kut
December 1915 – April 1916

0   1/2 mile
0   3/4 km

Turkish front line
Turkish advance line
Fort
Three British relief attempts fail
flooded in January
Tigris
Townshend
road to fort
Kut-al-Amarah
Mosque
Woolpress Village
flooded in February
British garrison surrenders 29 April 1916
Shatt-al-Hai
snipers

N

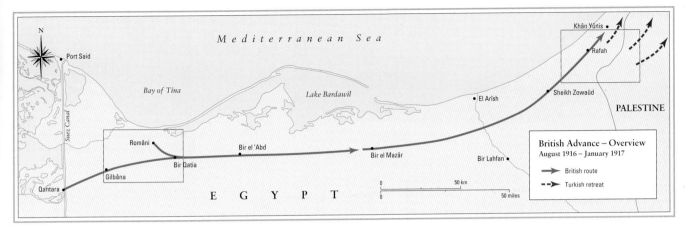

British Advance – Overview
August 1916 – January 1917

→ British route
⇢ Turkish retreat

Sinai and Palestine
August 1916–January 1917

After turning away another determined Ottoman attack on the Suez Canal, the British decided to advance into Sinai in order to take the pressure off of the canal itself. After a small victory at Români, the British decided to target Gaza and Palestine hoping for help from Arabs in the region who opposed Ottoman rule.

In April 1916 the Ottomans, with help from the Germans, tried once again to cross the canal. The British forces turned the attack aside and went on the offensive. They moved along the north coast of Sinai, close enough to get fire support from British warboats offshore. They moved deliberately and methodically, digging water wells and building roads as they went. In early August, the British reached the town of Români, about 32km (20 miles) east of the canal. The Germans and Ottomans decided to fight to stop the British advance. In brutal summer heat the British forces defeated the attacks, but could not pursue in any numbers. The Ottomans began a retreat toward Palestine.

Again moving carefully and deliberately, the British forces pressured the Ottomans. At Rafah in January 1917 the British made a risky cavalry attack, counting on superior speed to overcome their relative lack of ammunition and heavy artillery. Moving quickly and carefully, Australian, New Zealand and British infantry and cavalry forces surrounded Rafah and cut off the avenues of retreat. British aggressiveness and daring paid off – all but 200 of the 1700-man Ottoman force surrendered. The British seemed to have found a way to win in the Sinai desert. The Germans responded by launching a major air raid that inflicted heavy casualties on the badly exposed cavalry.

Aftermath

To advance much further required more secure logistics. The British continued the process of building roads, digging wells and laying rail lines. They next targeted Gaza, the coastal route into the historic and strategic region of Palestine.

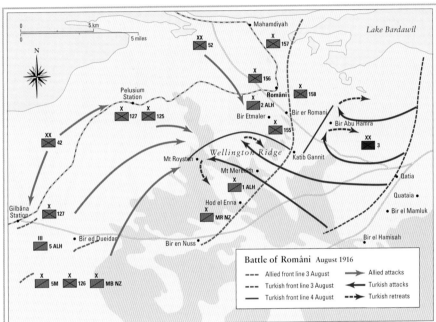

Battle of Români August 1916

--- Allied front line 3 August   → Allied attacks
--- Turkish front line 3 August   ← Turkish attacks
— Turkish front line 4 August   ⇢ Turkish retreats

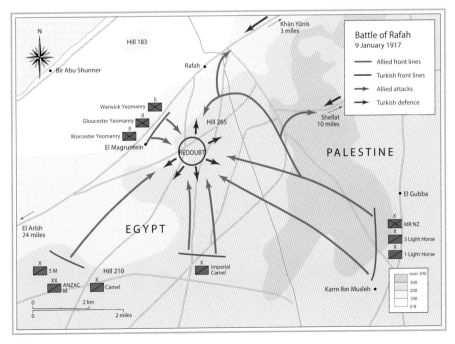

Battle of Rafah
9 January 1917

— Allied front lines
— Turkish front lines
→ Allied attacks
→ Turkish defence

The Arab Revolt
June 1916–June 1917

The revolt was the result of intense negotiation between the Hussein family of the Hejaz and an eccentric British officer named T. E. Lawrence. The Husseins wanted British support for their rule over a large Arab kingdom after the war. Lawrence wanted the Arabs to act as a guerrilla force, weakening Ottoman troops with speed and lightning attacks on isolated garrisons. Not all Arabs supported the revolt, but it provided the British with important military help.

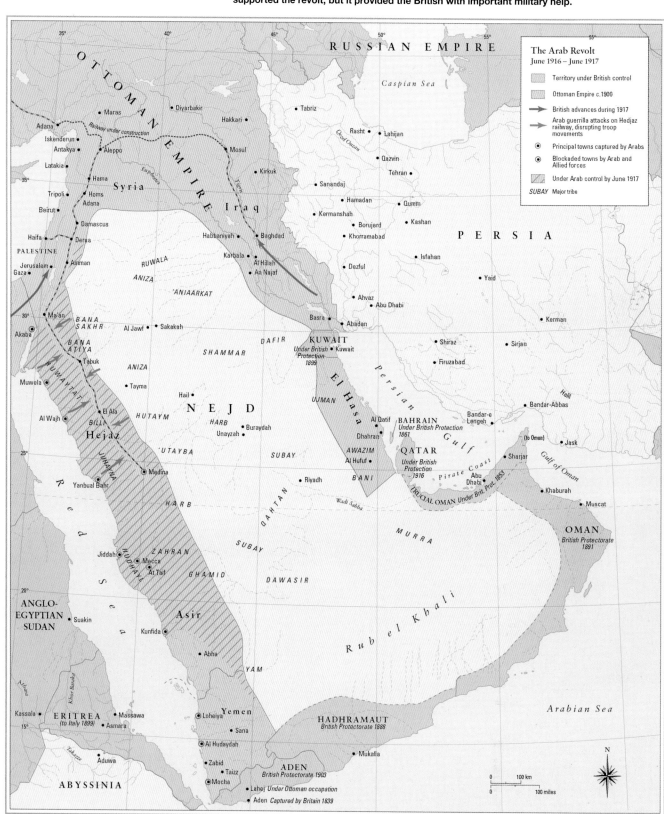

The Arab Revolt
June 1916 – June 1917

- Territory under British control
- Ottoman Empire c.1900
- → British advances during 1917
- → Arab guerrilla attacks on Hedjaz railway, disrupting troop movements
- ⊙ Principal towns captured by Arabs
- ⊙ Blockaded towns by Arab and Allied forces
- Under Arab control by June 1917
- *SUBAY* Major tribe

Palestine
October 1917–October 1918

A new British commander in Palestine, Edmund 'The Bull' Allenby, pushed into Gaza in 1917. Unlike his predecessor, he led from the front instead of a headquarters in Cairo and he inspired his men to greater efforts. Officials in London, hungry for victories, sent Allenby more resources, even though commanders on the Western Front were opposed. Allenby rewarded the politicians by advancing through Gaza and winning victories with his combined force of infantry and cavalry.

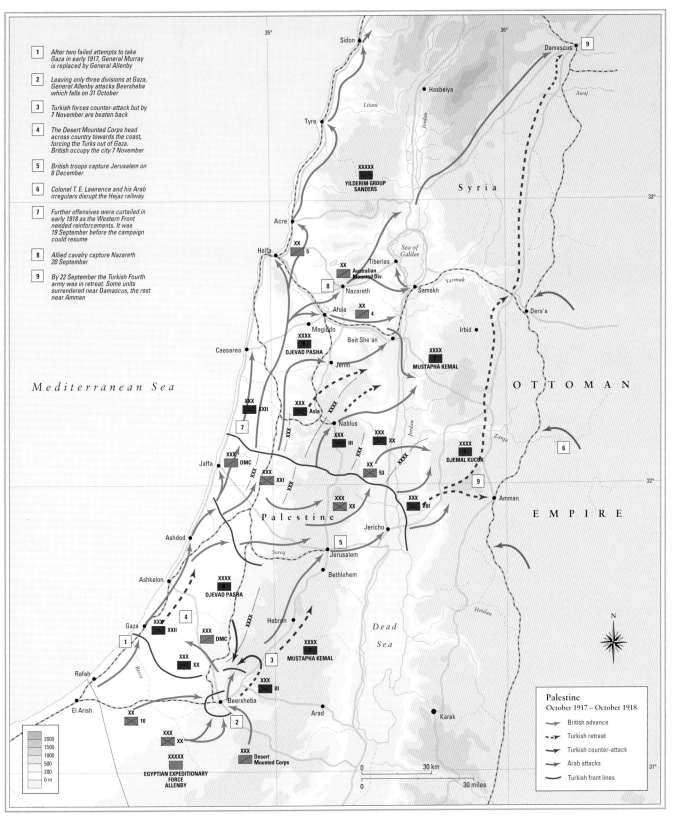

1 After two failed attempts to take Gaza in early 1917, General Murray is replaced by General Allenby

2 Leaving only three divisions at Gaza, General Allenby attacks Beersheba which falls on 31 October

3 Turkish forces counter-attack but by 7 November are beaten back

4 The Desert Mounted Corps head across country towards the coast, forcing the Turks out of Gaza. British occupy the city 7 November

5 British troops capture Jerusalem on 8 December

6 Colonel T. E. Lawrence and his Arab irregulars disrupt the Hejaz railway

7 Further offensives were curtailed in early 1918 as the Western Front needed reinforcements. It was 19 September before the campaign could resume

8 Allied cavalry capture Nazareth 20 September

9 By 22 September the Turkish Fourth army was in retreat. Some units surrendered near Damascus, the rest near Amman

Palestine
October 1917 – October 1918
British advance
Turkish retreat
Turkish counter-attack
Arab attacks
Turkish front lines

Gaza and Beersheba October–November 1917

Allenby drove his troops forward in two large columns. One moved through Gaza with the support of gunboats off shore, the other towards the critical rail juncture of Beersheba, without which the Ottomans could not hold on to southern Palestine. The Ottomans and even the Germans sent reinforcements. Although it did not have the strategic importance of France, Palestine became symbolically important to both sides.

German General Erich von Falkenhayn established defensive positions on high ground where he could find it, but the British had superior numbers, better cavalry and momentum on their side. Outnumbered Ottoman forces also had to expend energies locating and fighting the Arab irregulars loyal to the Husseins and T. E. Lawrence. Allenby moved quickly and kept up the pressure on the tired Ottoman defenders. With a full moon to aid them, Allenby's cavalrymen launched a daring night raid on Beersheba on 31 October with the Australian Light Horse leading the charge. British artillery and gunboats also opened an assault in Gaza. Falkenhayn did not have enough resources to handle both.

The British attack on Beersheba worked almost exactly to plan. British units moved into the town so quickly that they captured the critical water wells intact. Thus the British could use Beersheba as a reliable base from which to move on the port city of Jaffa. They took Jaffa on 16 November. The way was now clear for Allenby to think about a movement on Jerusalem. Ottoman morale had begun to collapse and Allenby's force had learned the right combat methods for dealing with the desert

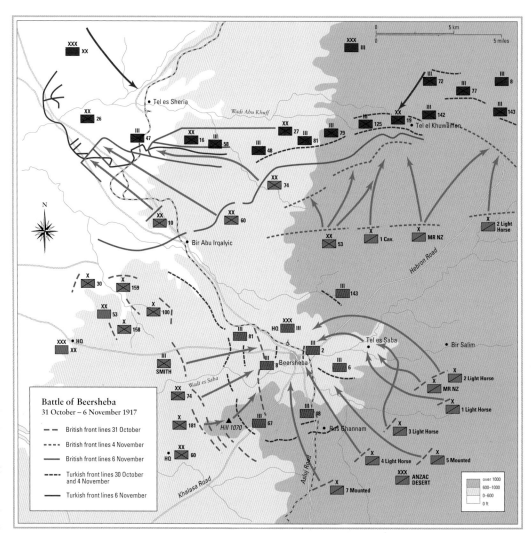

Battle of Beersheba
31 October – 6 November 1917

- – – – British front lines 31 October
- · · · · British front lines 4 November
- ——— British front lines 6 November
- – – – Turkish front lines 30 October and 4 November
- ——— Turkish front lines 6 November

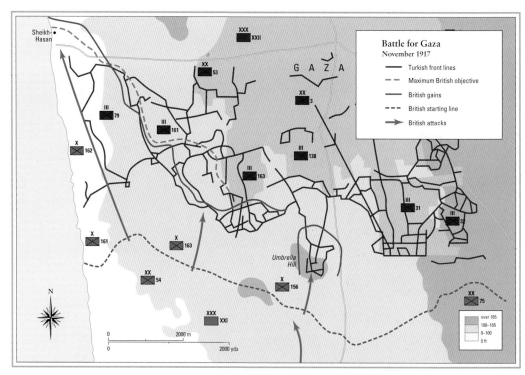

Battle for Gaza
November 1917

- ——— Turkish front lines
- – – – Maximum British objective
- ——— British gains
- · · · · British starting line
- ➤ British attacks

Conquest of Jerusalem 7 November– 9 December 1917

Allenby began his advance on Jerusalem almost immediately after the capture of Beersheba. He knew that its capture would be a major coup for Britain. He moved carefully but quickly, capturing key high ground on the approach to the Holy City. He hoped to do most of the fighting outside the city to spare it any damage. His men had also broken through in Gaza, sending Ottoman forces in retreat.

The Ottoman and German commanders in Palestine knew they could not hold the city indefinitely. Bad weather and heavy rains slowed Allenby for a while, but he clearly had the power to take Jerusalem. As a result, on 8 December the Ottomans left and declared Jerusalem an open city. Two British corps were then in the hills outside Jerusalem. Local religious officials came out to surrender the city to the first two British soldiers they came across. Three days later Allenby famously entered Jerusalem on foot through the Jaffa gate to show his humility in conquering this majestic and multi-ethnic city. The British politicians finally had their prize, and just in time for Christmas.

Diplomatic Documents

The headaches had only just begun, however. Three separate secret diplomatic documents led three different groups to believe that they had rights to the city of Jerusalem. The Jews had the Balfour Declaration to support their claim, the French had the secret Sykes-Picot Agreement promising them a share of Palestine and Sherif Hussein had agreements he made in return for originally starting the revolt. Allenby, however, had no intention of ceding control to any of them.

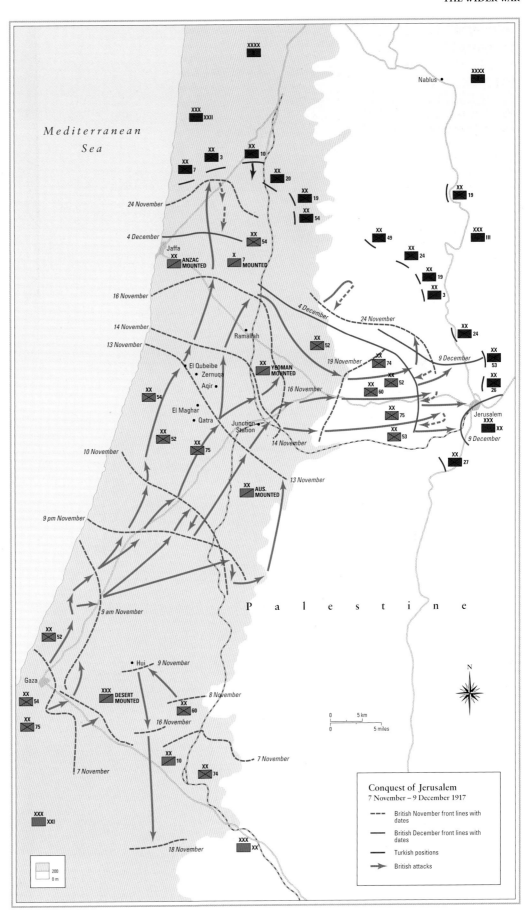

Central Mesopotamia September 1917– April 1918

After the humiliation at Kut, the British changed commanders in Mesopotamia and sent additional resources to the region. British forces moved deliberately and aggressively on both sides of the Tigris River, forcing the Ottomans out of their defences. They got a degree of revenge for Kut in March 1917 when they took Baghdad and captured 15,000 Ottoman soldiers in the process. The British forces then moved north in three columns to secure the major towns and cities of central Mesopotamia. The death of their commander to cholera slowed operations in the winter of 1917–18, but in the spring they began moving north again, pressuring the Ottoman defenders.

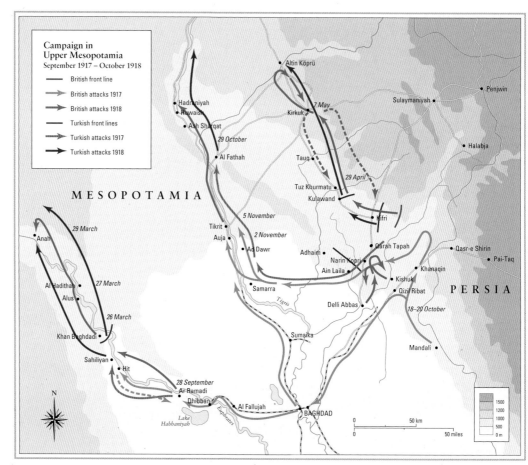

Campaign in
Upper Mesopotamia
September 1917 – October 1918

—— British front line
—→ British attacks 1917
—→ British attacks 1918
—— Turkish front lines
⇢ Turkish attacks 1917
⇒ Turkish attacks 1918

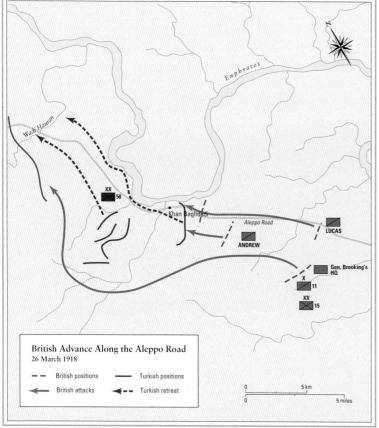

British Advance Along the Aleppo Road
26 March 1918

– – – British positions   —— Turkish positions
←— British attacks   ◀┅ Turkish retreat

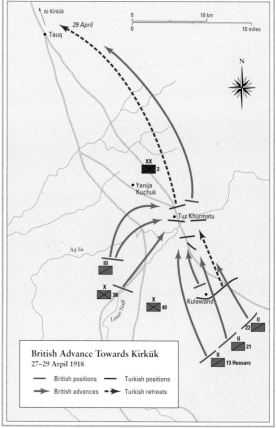

British Advance Towards Kirkük
27–29 Arpil 1918

—— British positions   —— Turkish positions
—→ British advances   ⇢ Turkish retreats

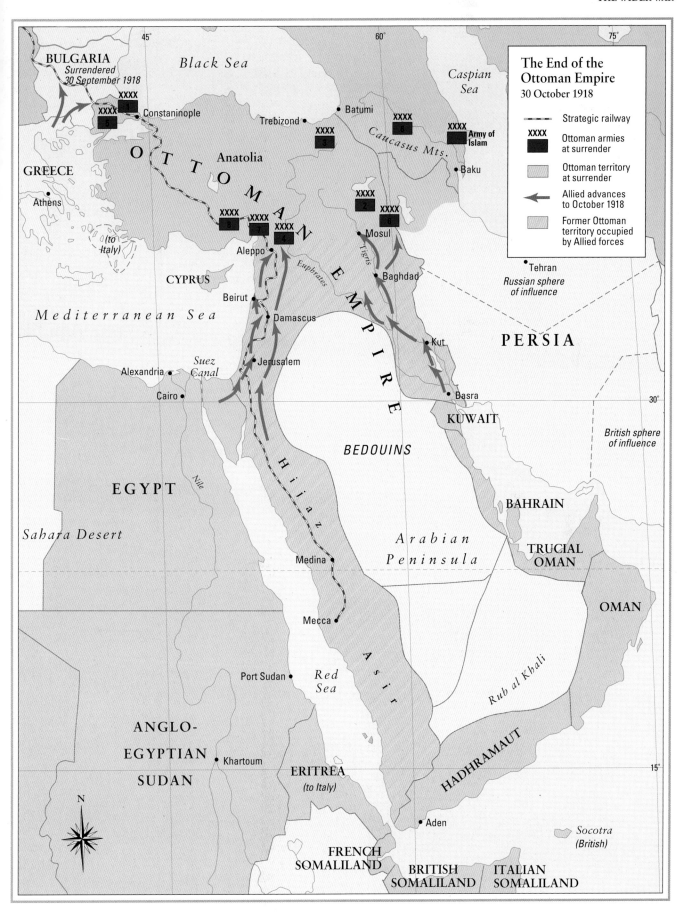

**The End of the
Ottoman Empire**
30 October 1918

- - - · Strategic railway
XXXX Ottoman armies
at surrender
Ottoman territory
at surrender
→ Allied advances
to October 1918
Former Ottoman
territory occupied
by Allied forces

BULGARIA
*Surrendered
30 September 1918*

Black Sea

*Caspian
Sea*

XXXX 1
Constaninople

Trebizond • • Batumi

XXXX 6

Caucasus Mts.

XXXX
**Army of
Islam**

XXXX 5

O T T O

Anatolia

XXXX 3

M

• Baku

GREECE

• Athens

A N

XXXX 8

XXXX 7

XXXX 4

XXXX 2

XXXX 8

CYPRUS

Aleppo

E

Euphrates

Tigris

Mosul •

(to
Italy)

M

Beirut •

P

Baghdad •

• Tehran
*Russian sphere
of influence*

PERSIA

M e d i t e r r a n e a n   S e a

Damascus •

I R E

Kut •

Suez
Canal

• Jerusalem

Alexandria •

Cairo •

• Kut

• Basra

30°

KUWAIT

*British sphere
of influence*

BEDOUINS

EGYPT

Nile

Hijaz

BAHRAIN

Sahara Desert

*A r a b i a n
P e n i n s u l a*

**TRUCIAL
OMAN**

Medina •

OMAN

Mecca •

A s i r

Rub al Khali

Port Sudan •

*Red
Sea*

HADHRAMAUT

**ANGLO-
EGYPTIAN
SUDAN**

• Khartoum

ERITREA
(to Italy)

15°

N

*Socotra
(British)*

• Aden

**FRENCH
SOMALILAND**

**BRITISH
SOMALILAND**

**ITALIAN
SOMALILAND**

Italy and
its Empire
1914

Although it was one of the weakest of Europe's seven great powers, Italy had a modern navy, an alliance with Germany and Austria-Hungary, a strategic location astride main shipping routes and borders with two other powers.

Italy dramatically added to the tensions in Europe by invading Ottoman-held Libya in 1911. No other European state supported the invasion. The war was also unpopular in Italy and threatened to destabilize the continent by making the Ottomans look weak. Soon thereafter, the Balkan states united in war against the Ottomans.

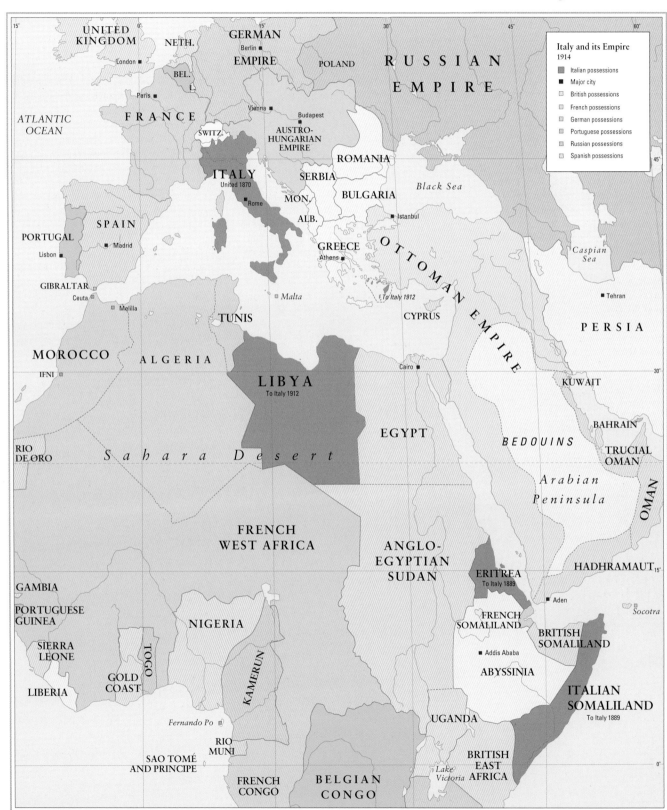

Italy and its Empire 1914
- Italian possessions
- Major city
- British possessions
- French possessions
- German possessions
- Portuguese possessions
- Russian possessions
- Spanish possessions

UNITED KINGDOM
London

NETH.
BEL.
L.
FRANCE
Paris

ATLANTIC OCEAN

GERMAN EMPIRE
Berlin

POLAND

RUSSIAN EMPIRE

SWITZ.
Vienna
AUSTRO-HUNGARIAN EMPIRE
Budapest

ITALY
United 1870
Rome

MON.
SERBIA
ALB.
ROMANIA
BULGARIA
Black Sea
Istanbul

GREECE
Athens

OTTOMAN EMPIRE

Caspian Sea

Tehran

PORTUGAL
Lisbon

SPAIN
Madrid

GIBRALTAR
Ceuta
Melilla

Malta

To Italy 1912

CYPRUS

PERSIA

TUNIS

MOROCCO
IFNI

ALGERIA

LIBYA
To Italy 1912

Cairo

EGYPT

KUWAIT

BAHRAIN
BEDOUINS
TRUCIAL OMAN

RIO DE ORO

Sahara Desert

Arabian Peninsula

OMAN

FRENCH WEST AFRICA

ANGLO-EGYPTIAN SUDAN

HADHRAMAUT

ERITREA
To Italy 1889

Aden

Socotra

GAMBIA
PORTUGUESE GUINEA

NIGERIA

FRENCH SOMALILAND

BRITISH SOMALILAND

SIERRA LEONE

TOGO
KAMERUN

Addis Ababa

ABYSSINIA

LIBERIA
GOLD COAST

Fernando Po

ITALIAN SOMALILAND
To Italy 1889

RIO MUNI
SAO TOMÉ AND PRINCIPE

UGANDA

FRENCH CONGO

BELGIAN CONGO

Lake Victoria

BRITISH EAST AFRICA

Italian Front May–August 1915

Italy had been a signatory to the Triple Alliance with Germany and Austria-Hungary, but that alliance had been largely designed to protect Italy from French designs. As 1914 approached, Franco-Italian relations had improved and Italy no longer needed the alliance as it was designed. At the same time, Italian nationalists sought to add territory in Dalmatia and Istria that was home to large numbers of ethnic Italians. That land sat inside the Austro-Hungarian Empire. German diplomats tried to square the circle between their two allies, but they knew that Italy was becoming ever more unreliable. When the crisis of 1914 began in earnest, Italy decided that Austria-Hungary had been the aggressor and that Italy therefore had no obligation to fulfil its part in the alliance. The Germans were not surprised, and they pressured Austria-Hungary to make territorial concessions that might keep Italy on their side. The Austro-Hungarians reacted with fury at what they saw as Italian perfidy in the empire's moment of great need. Italy then followed a policy of pure self-interest, listening to offers from both sides.

The British and French governments saw the value of Italy as an ally, mostly for geographic reasons. An unfriendly Italy could complicate British supply lines through the Suez Canal to and from India. France also saw the value of having its southeastern front secure. Russia hoped that Italy could force the Austro-Hungarian Army to pull forces away from the Carpathians. British, Russian and French strategic interests lined up well with those of Italy.

For its part, Italy had several reasons to sign an alliance with the British and French. The Allies could promise Italy the parts of Austria-Hungary that Italian nationalists coveted. An alliance with the two great naval powers in the Mediterranean also secured the long and exposed Italian coastlines, allowing the Italians to focus their naval strength in the Adriatic. Britain and France also pledged aid in the form of weapons, money and natural resources such as iron and coal. Russia, too, offered the Italians the enticing promise of renewed offensives in the Carpathians to draw off Austro-Hungarian troops from the Italian front.

Unprepared for War

Still, the Italian Army was unprepared for war, and belligerence was unpopular with many Italians, especially in the rural south. The death of the Italian commander-in-chief just before the start of operations further impaired Italian preparations. Command fell to Luigi Cadorna, a stubborn and

unimaginative general who rashly pledged that his men would 'walk to Vienna' once they breached the enemy line. But the enemy line ran through the difficult terrain of the Julian Alps and the Isonzo river valley.

Austria-Hungary, already engaged in the Carpathian Mountains and in the Balkans, now prepared for another front. Most subjects of the Empire despised the Italians for entering the war in order to acquire Austro-Hungarian territory. Soldiers of all ethnicities supported the war against Italy and morale sat squarely on the side of the Austro-Hungarians.

The Austro-Hungarian leadership knew that the Italians could focus all of their manpower on the Isonzo front while they themselves could only make the Isonzo a third priority at most. They therefore decided on a purely defensive strategy that utilized the high ground of the Alps as compensation for their inferiority of numbers. They sent a defensive specialist, Svetozar Boroevic, to command. He had led well in the Carpathian campaigns and had shown an aptitude for war in the mountainous terrain there. He hoped to repeat his success in the Alps.

Seeing that the Austro-Hungarians were setting up defences in the mountains, the Italians put their hopes on a quick offensive. If successful, they could push through the Alps and the Isonzo valley before the Austro-Hungarians could organize their defences. If they failed, they faced a long, difficult battle against solid defences.

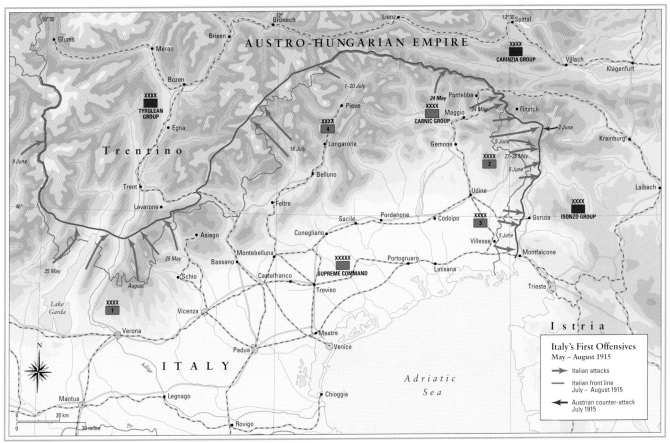

The Isonzo Battles 1915–17

The difficult terrain of the Isonzo valley and the Julian Alps were ideally suited for a defensive-minded general like Boroevic. Italy, on the other hand, had to attack in order to capture the ground that they sought to annex.

General Luigi Cadorna's war plan for the Italian Army was unimaginative, but the terrain gave him few options. He employed rudimentary tactics and reacted with anger when units failed to achieve the goals he set for them. He lived by the motto hung in his headquarters, 'The supreme commander is always right, especially when he is wrong.' He ordered the execution of random members of disappointing units and fired thousands of officers.

Still, for Cadorna and other Italian leaders, the Isonzo valley held out tremendous allure. If they could break through the line they could then move into Trieste, a city that Italian nationalists demanded. Trieste was also a major port for the Austro-Hungarians and its loss would have huge strategic importance. An Italian breakthrough would also force the Austro-Hungarian Army to move men from the Carpathian and Balkan fronts. It might also force the German Army to move men from the western front. Thus could Italy play a major role in the larger alliance victory, then use that victory to gain territory at the peace table.

Difficult Terrain

Thus Cadorna persisted in ordering repeated offensives on the Isonzo front despite the immense difficulty of the terrain. Cadorna also believed that Austro-Hungarian morale was declining and that repeated assaults might win by attrition what previous assaults had failed to gain by breakthrough. The result was a difficult, bloody series of battles in mountainous terrain.

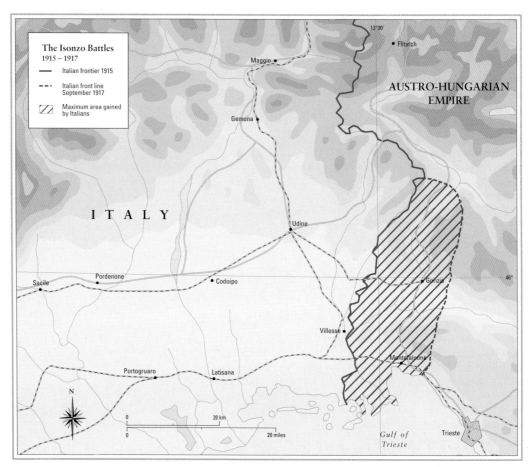

The Isonzo Battles 1915 – 17

Battles	Dates	Italian Casualties	Austrian Casualties
First	23 June – 7 July 1915	15,000	10,000
Second	18 July – 3 August 1915	42,000	46,600
Third	18 October – 4 November 1915	67,000	71,700
Fourth	10 November – 2 December 1915	49,000	
Fifth	11–15 March 1916	2700	2000
Sixth	6 – 17 August 1916	51,250	41,850
Seventh	14–17 September 1916	75,500	63,000
Eighth	10–12 October 1916		
Ninth	1–4 November 1916		
Tenth	12 May – 5 June 1917	132,000	52,300
Eleventh	17 August – 12 September 1917	148,000	56,000

The Isonzo Battles June 1915–March 1916

This time period coincides with the First to Fifth battles of the Isonzo. They share in common the feature of Italian numerical superiority against stronger Austro-Hungarian positions. At the end of this period, the lines had barely moved despite heavy losses.

The general trend in the first five battles of the Isonzo showed Italy relying more on artillery. That artillery, however, was not usually enough to make much of a difference in the mountains, leaving infantry to advance with little firepower protection. The Italians hoped to capture the road junctures around the region's most important town, Gorizia. The Austro-Hungarians managed to repulse most attacks despite their inferior numbers. Italy chose to widen its front in an effort to keep Austria-Hungary guessing about the exact location of the next attack while Austria-Hungary could focus on defending the valleys and mountain passes.

Savage Fighting

In places, the fighting on the Isonzo front became savage, particularly in the Karst plateau where bitter hand-to-hand combat became the norm. The Fourth Battle of the Isonzo was fought in winter conditions that limited supply and troop movements, and led to high levels of casualties due to frostbite and diseases. Despite these frustrations, the French and British urged Cadorna to attack for a fifth time, both to keep up the pressure on Austria-Hungary for Russia's sake and in the hopes of relieving German pressure on Verdun. Although Germany was not technically at war with Italy, the German forces did begin to consider moving men to the Isonzo front to assist their faltering ally. Although the Italians had not yet broken through, every offensive seemed to hold out that possibility anew.

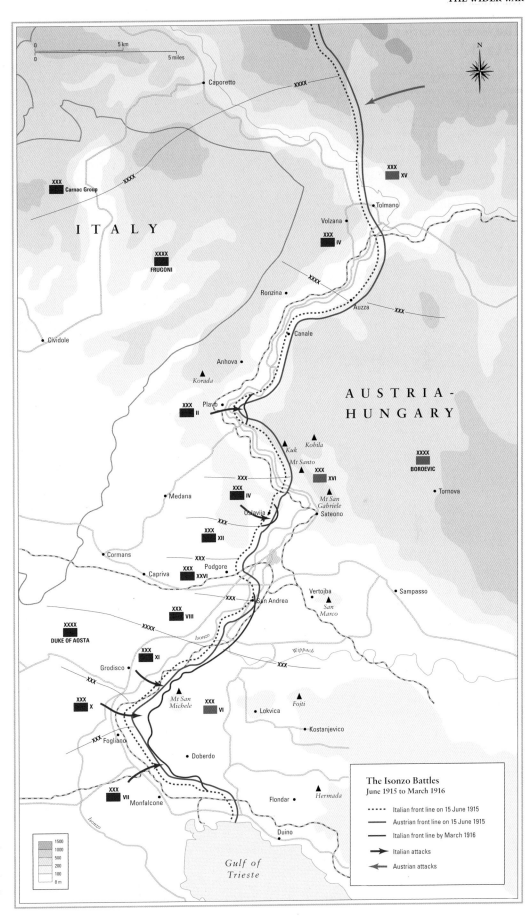

The Isonzo Battles
June 1915 to March 1916

- - - - Italian front line on 15 June 1915
———— Austrian front line on 15 June 1915
———— Italian front line by March 1916
→ Italian attacks
← Austrian attacks

Trentino Offensive May–June 1916

Hoping to reduce pressure on the Isonzo, Austro-Hungarian forces went on the offensive in the Trentino, an area with many ethnic Germans whom the Austro-Hungarians hoped might help them to win a major victory.

The offensive began well for the Austro-Hungarians. The centre of the Italian line retreated, temporarily opening up the possibility of an advance on the line Verona–Vicenza–Padua–Venice and threatening Italian positions on the Isonzo from the rear. But Russian success in the Brusilov Offensive forced Austria-Hungary to call off the attack.

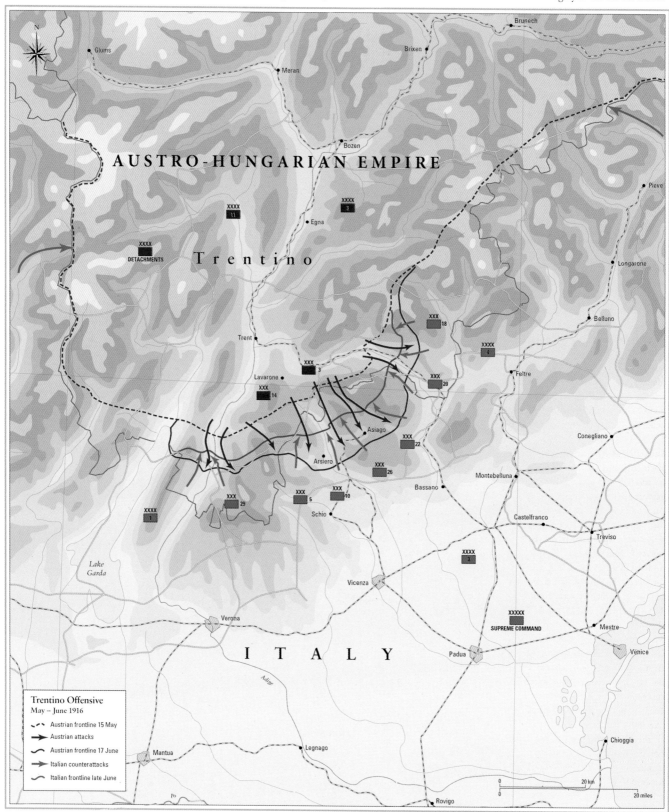

Trentino Offensive
May – June 1916

- Austrian frontline 15 May
- Austrian attacks
- Austrian frontline 17 June
- Italian counterattacks
- Italian frontline late June

The Isonzo Battles March 1916– September 1917

Despite no success in the first five offensives, Cadorna kept up the pressure. He hoped that the Austro-Hungarian lines in the Isonzo would break. Each Italian offensive gave just enough results to convince him to keep trying.

The sixth battle of the Isonzo showed some success as the Italians at last took the key town of Gorizia. It had cost Italy 21,000 lives, and while its capture did not yield the spectacular results Cadorna had hoped for, it did encourage Italy to try again. The seventh, eighth and ninth battles turned into bloody slugging matches that did not produce decisive victory for either side. The total casualties in the three battles amounted to 81,000 for Italy and 73,000 for Austria-Hungary. Because Austria-Hungary lacked the manpower to reinforce the Isonzo sector, the numbers encouraged Cadorna to believe that victory was close.

Lack of Manpower

Each side's major allies believed it, too. The Germans showed grave concern over the weakening Austro-Hungarian position in the Isonzo. At the same time, the British and French proved willing to send men and material to Italy in the hope of getting the breakthrough they could not get on the western front. The casualties in the tenth and eleventh battles on the Isonzo were enormous. In the tenth Italy took 150,000 casualties to Austria-Hungary's 75,000. In the eleventh, Italy took 148,000 casualties to Austria-Hungary's 105,000. Both sides were worn out and demoralized. Despite all the bloodshed, Italy had still not produced the breakthrough it wanted. The Italians looked forward to the winter to rest and refit. The Germans, however, had other ideas.

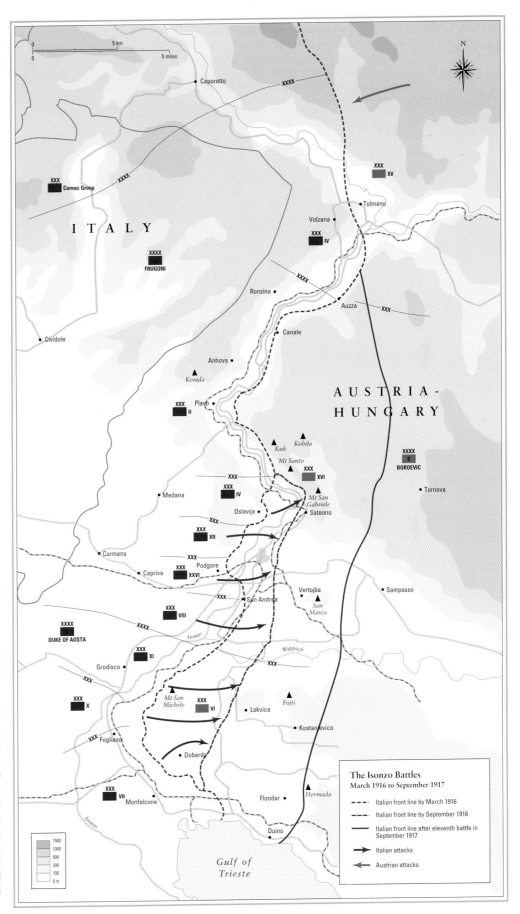

The Isonzo Battles
March 1916 to September 1917

- - - Italian front line by March 1916
- - - Italian front line by September 1916
——— Italian front line after eleventh battle in September 1917
→ Italian attacks
← Austrian attacks

Trentino Offensive June 1917

Italy attacked in the Trentino sector to ensure that the Austro-Hungarians could not threaten the Isonzo front from the rear again. Italy had numerical superiority and expected to at least improve their positions in the region.

Italy targeted the relatively flat region to the west of Asiago. They had a three-to-one edge in men and artillery, but defences were stronger than estimated. The Austro-Hungarians had also divined the broad features of the Italian plan. As a result, the Italians advanced into a region where the Austro-Hungarians had concentrated their artillery.

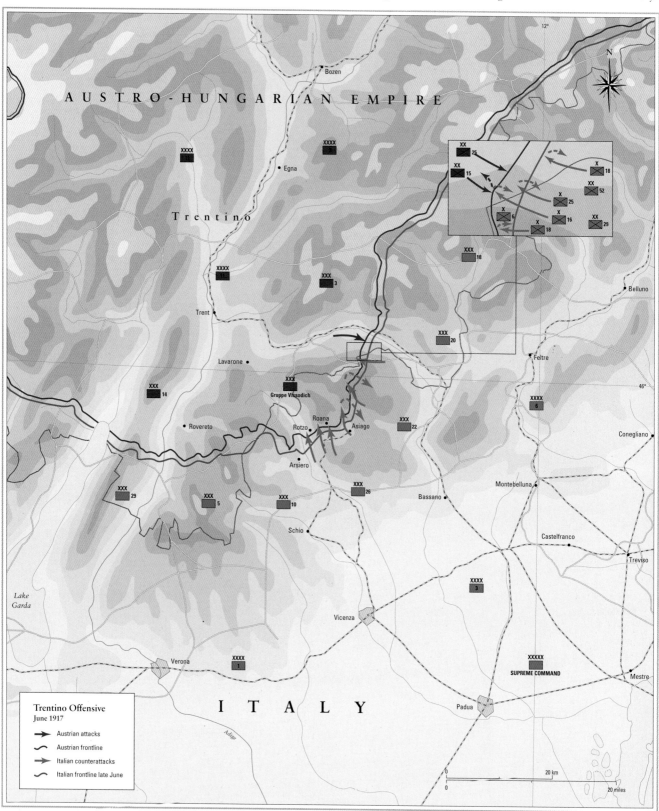

Trentino Offensive
June 1917

→ Austrian attacks
⌢ Austrian frontline
→ Italian counterattacks
⌢ Italian frontline late June

Caporetto 24 October– 1 November 1917

The Germans grew concerned enough about the Austro-Hungarian position in the Isonzo to plan an attack, even though they had little intention of staying there. They sought only to help alleviate the immediate crisis in the sector.

German forces used the same infiltration tactics they had employed at Riga to smash holes in the Italian line. They also used overwhelming artillery support, introduced air squadrons and fired 1000 gas shells in a theatre that had not seen much use of gas weapons. Italy was caught by surprise and a mass retreat began.

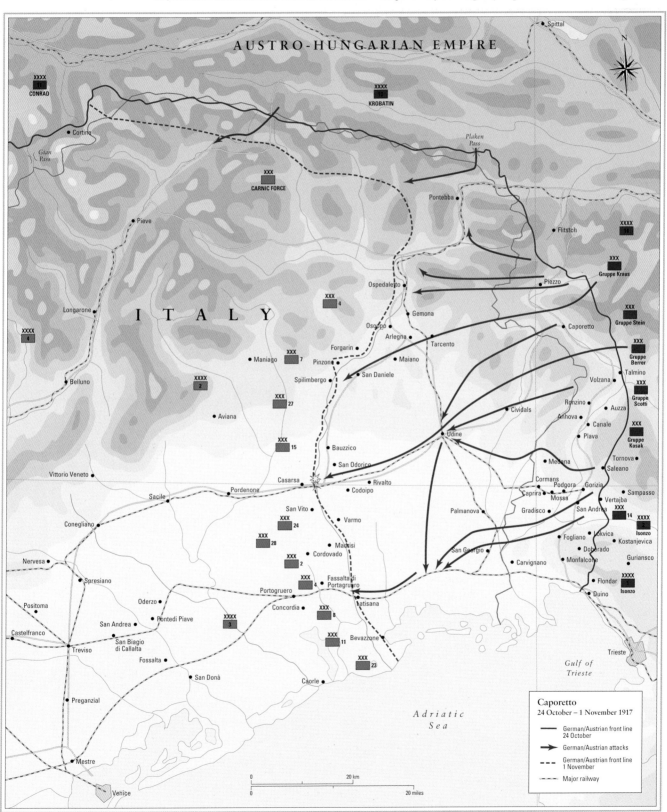

AUSTRO-HUNGARIAN EMPIRE

ITALY

Caporetto
24 October – 1 November 1917

— German/Austrian front line 24 October
→ German/Austrian attacks
--- German/Austrian front line 1 November
-·-· Major railway

0   20 km
0   20 miles

Caporetto
1–12 November
1917

The chaotic retreat resulted in 275,000 Italians surrendering and almost 350,000 deserting. The army lost half of their artillery pieces and thousands of machineguns. Caporetto became one of the most lopsided victories of the war.

The Italian retreat did not stop until it reached the Piave River. Some German officers wanted to pursue across this, but they had made no plans to operate that deep into enemy territory. Moreover, they had dealt what seemed like a mortal blow to the Italians, and they saw no strategic goals worth pursuing south of the Piave.

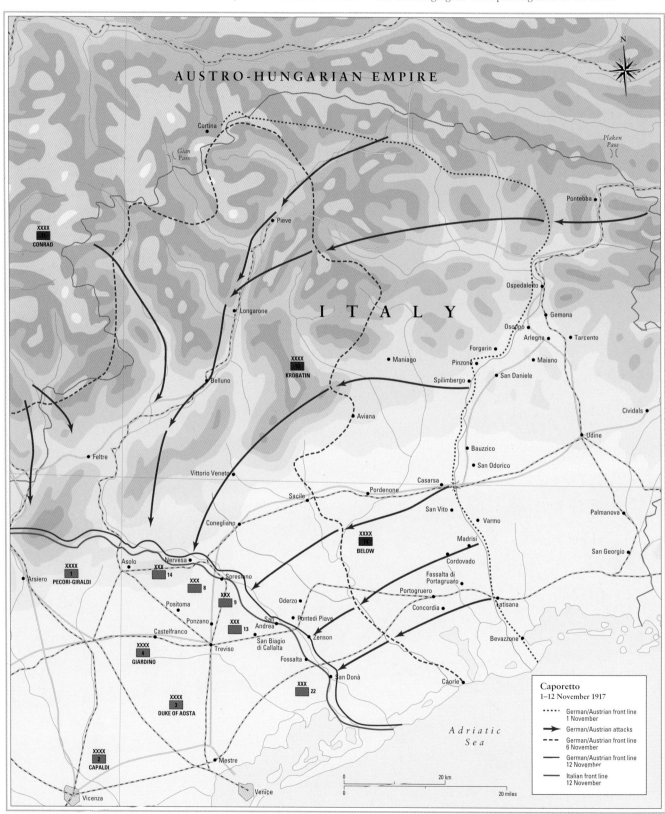

Caporetto
1–12 November 1917

······· German/Austrian front line
1 November

➤ German/Austrian attacks

- - - German/Austrian front line
6 November

——— German/Austrian front line
12 November

——— Italian front line
12 November

Piave Offensive June–July 1918

Italy eventually recovered. Cadorna was replaced by Armando Diaz, who boosted morale and managed to get many deserters to return. Britain and France helped by sending men and supplies to stabilize the line.

A demoralized Austro-Hungarian Army decided to cross the Piave and finish off the Italians. The exhausted Italians, however, had prepared for the attack. They disrupted it with artillery and limited Austro-Hungarian gains. They counter-attacked and retook the lost territory. The Italians gained confidence and went on the offensive.

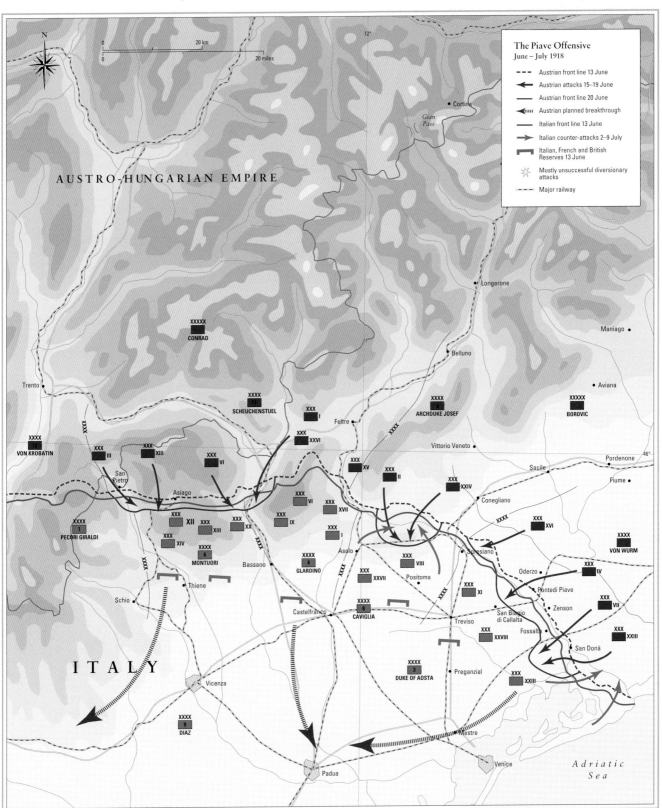

The Piave Offensive June–July 1918

- – – – Austrian front line 13 June
- ◀── Austrian attacks 15–19 June
- ─── Austrian front line 20 June
- ◀··· Austrian planned breakthrough
- ─── Italian front line 13 June
- ──▶ Italian counter-attacks 2–9 July
- ▬ Italian, French and British Reserves 13 June
- ✳ Mostly unsuccessful diversionary attacks
- ─·─ Major railway

Africa
c. 1914

Imperial issues did not cause the war, as most disputes had been settled long before 1914. Africa, however, provided Britain, France and Germany with manpower. The Allies had the advantages of more populous colonies, more wealth in Africa itself and a favourable geographic position. War in Africa led to high casualty levels not only from direct combat, but also from disease and exhaustion in the unforgiving climate. Casualty rates among human porters were especially high.

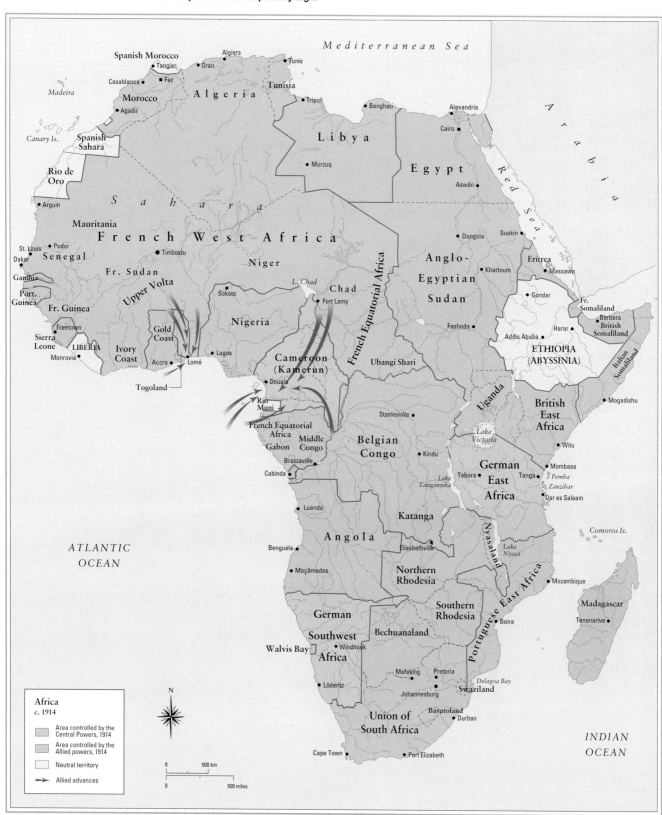

Mediterranean Sea

Spanish Morocco
Algiers
Tangier
Oran
Tunis
Casablanca
Fez
Tunisia
Morocco
Algeria
Tripoli
Agadir
Benghazi
Alexandria
Madeira
Libya
Cairo
Canary Is.
Spanish Sahara
Egypt
Rio de Oro
Murzuq
Aswân
Sahara
Arabia
Arguin
Red Sea
Mauritania
Dongola
Suakin
French West Africa
St. Louis
Podor
Timbuktu
Anglo-Egyptian Sudan
Eritrea
Massawa
Senegal
Niger
Khartoum
Dakar
Fr. Sudan
Gondar
Fr. Somaliland
Gambia
Upper Volta
L. Chad
Berbera
British Somaliland
Port. Guinea
Sokoto
Chad
Fort Lamy
Fashoda
Harar
Fr. Guinea
Nigeria
Addis Ababa
Freetown
Gold Coast
Lagos
ETHIOPIA (ABYSSINIA)
Sierra Leone
LIBERIA
Accra
Lomé
Cameroon (Kamerun)
Monrovia
Ivory Coast
Togoland
Douala
Ubangi Shari
French Equatorial Africa
Mogadishu
Uganda
British East Africa
Rio Muni
Stanleyville
Lake Victoria
Witu
French Equatorial Africa
Middle Congo
Belgian Congo
German East Africa
Gabon
Kindu
Mombasa
Brazzaville
Tabora
Tanga
Pemba
Zanzibar
Cabinda
Lake Tanganyika
Dar es Salaam
Luanda
Katanga
ATLANTIC OCEAN
Angola
Elisabethville
Lake Nyasa
Comoros Is.
Benguela
Nyasaland
Moçâmedes
Northern Rhodesia
Mozambique
Madagascar
German Southwest Africa
Southern Rhodesia
Portuguese East Africa
Tananarive
Walvis Bay
Windhoek
Bechuanaland
Beira
Mafeking
Pretoria
Delagoa Bay
Lüderitz
Swaziland
Johannesburg
Basutoland
Durban
Union of South Africa
INDIAN OCEAN
Cape Town
Port Elizabeth

Africa
c. 1914

Area controlled by the Central Powers, 1914

Area controlled by the Allied powers, 1914

Neutral territory

Allied advances

N

0   500 km

0   500 miles

East Africa
August 1914–November 1918

In East Africa, German General Paul von Lettow-Vorbeck led a force of 3000 Germans and 11,000 African troops called askari. He utilized the terrain of Africa to evade a British force several times his size, leading them on a chase that lasted for four years and earning the grudging admiration of his opponents with his skill. He held out until the end of the war, but the campaign devastated the parts of Africa he traversed.

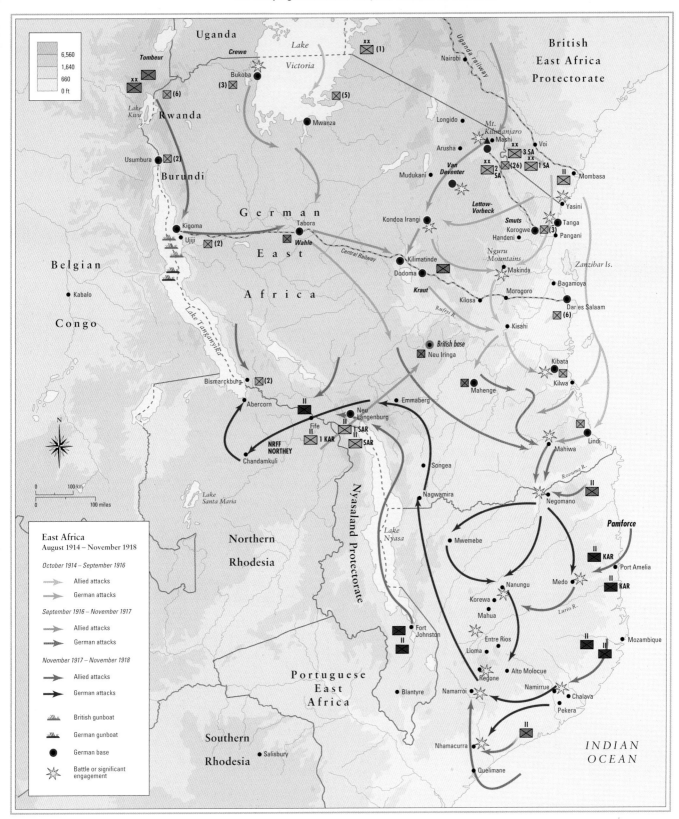

Easter Rising
25 April 1916

As the British became increasingly distracted on the Continent, some militant Catholic Republicans argued for using that distraction to make a statement in favour of Irish independence. They led a Rising in Dublin during Easter 1916.

The Easter Rising was not initially popular among most people in Ireland. Some saw it as unnecessarily provocative, while others argued that the timing was wrong given the number of Irishmen serving on the Western Front. But the British government reacted brutally to the Rising, shocking people in Ireland and beyond. The British response may have temporarily crushed the Republican movement, but it provoked the surviving leaders into

further action. It also angered many of the same Irishmen and women who had initially not supported the Rising. As a result, it soon became a symbol of Irish opposition to an unjust British government that was willing to fight for 'poor little Belgium', while simultaneously suppressing poor little Ireland. All sides in the Irish conflict prepared for the civil war that seemed likely to begin when the world war ended.

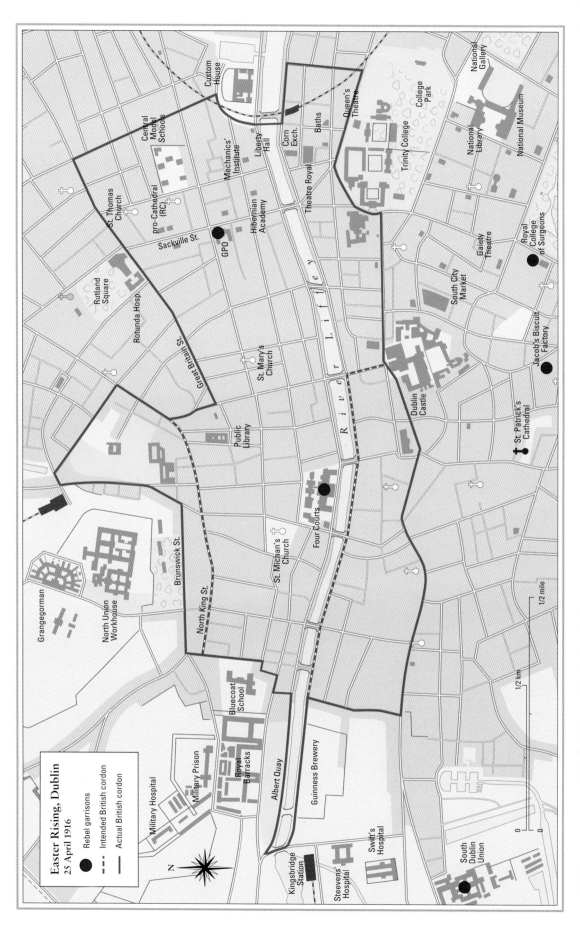

Easter Rising, Dublin
25 April 1916

● Rebel garrisons
- - - Intended British cordon
—— Actual British cordon

U.S. Soldiers by State, 1917–18

The American military system relied heavily on local units. In 1916 the United States passed a law that allowed the President to nationalize local units in the event of an emergency.

Most American soldiers went to war as part of state-based National Guard divisions that were integrated into the larger U.S. Army. These units had identities that symbolized these local roots. The New York division, for example, was known as the Liberty Division (and had the Statue of Liberty as its emblem), and the Pennsylvania division was known as the Keystone Division.

Both names recalled traditional associations for those states. The U.S. also created the famous 42nd 'Rainbow' Division that included National Guard soldiers from around the nation. A few American divisions were from the Regular Army and composed mainly of draftees. These had no local connections. This hybrid system caused tensions but worked well enough for the duration of the war.

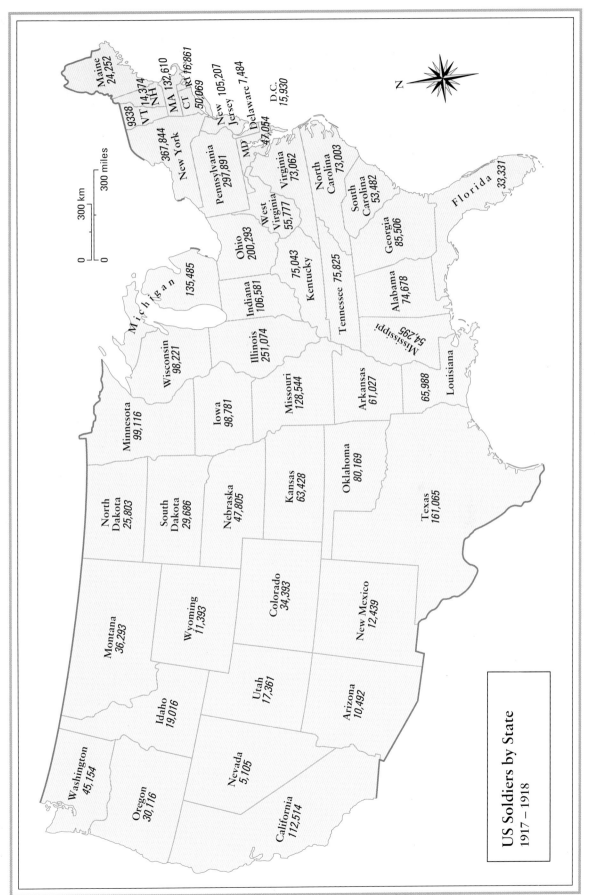

US Soldiers by State
1917 – 1918

Central and South America in World War I

Brazil was the only Latin American country to engage in military operations.

Despite their neutrality, the states of Latin America felt the impact of the war. Their commerce to Europe was cut off or greatly reduced, creating economic dislocations. Mexico unwittingly became a focal point of the war for a time in 1917 as a result of the Zimmerman Telegram, in which Germany promised Mexico American territory in the event of war. Brazil, which saw much of its shipping sunk by U-boats, declared war on Germany in 1917, although few Brazilians wanted it.

Central and South America in World War I

World War I

- Broke diplomatic relations with Central Powers, with date
- Declared war on Central Powers, with date
- Remained neutral

The League of Nations

- ★ Founding country
- ★ Country admitted after January 1920
- ☆ Country admitted after January 1921

UNITED STATES OF AMERICA
1917
Los Angeles
Washington
Dallas

NORTH ATLANTIC OCEAN
Tropic of Cancer

MEXICO
Mexico City

Havana
CUBA
DOMINICAN REP.
HAITI

HONDURAS
July 1918
left 1936

GUATEMALA
April 1918 *left 1936*
NICARAGUA
March 1918
left 1936
EL SALVADOR
COSTA RICA
May 1918 *left 1924*

PANAMA
April 1918

Caracas
VENEZUELA
left 1938
British Guiana
Surinam
French Guiana

COLOMBIA
Bogotá

Quito
ECUADOR
December 1917

Manaus
Belém

PERU
October 1917
Lima

BRAZIL
October 1917

PACIFIC OCEAN

BOLIVIA
April 1917
La Paz

Rio de Janeiro
São Paulo
Tropic of Capricorn

left 1937
PARAGUAY
Asunción

left 1938
ARGENTINA
URUGUAY *October 1917*
Montevideo

Santiago
Buenos Aires

CHILE

SOUTH ATLANTIC OCEAN

Falkland Islands
to UK

South Georgia
to UK

Mexican Revolution 1910–17

For most of the period 1914–17, Americans were more concerned with events in Mexico than Europe. The U.S. intervened militarily to prevent the discord in Mexico from impacting on America and, in President Wilson's words, to teach the Mexicans to elect good men.

Mexico had been run since 1876 by strongman Porfiro Diaz. He had prevented free elections from taking place and had increasingly bad relations with the United States. Diaz once remarked 'Poor Mexico: so far from God, so close to the United States.' As Diaz aged and devoted less attention to Mexico's problems, a series of challengers rose to either succeed or replace him. In 1910 Francisco Madero, a wealthy landowner from northern Mexico, used vague promises of land reform to generate popular support. He looked ready to win the 1910 election. When Diaz tried to prevent him from winning by putting him in jail, Madero's stature only grew. Soon the crisis turned into a civil war,

with Madero's forces emerging successful. In 1911, Madero rode into Mexico City at the head of a triumphant army. The violence, however, continued.

American Intervention

After thousands had died in the Mexican Civil War, a new leader emerged. General Victoriano Huerta took power after arresting Diaz and Madero. The latter was assassinated in February 1913, likely on Huerta's orders. The new American President, Woodrow Wilson, was shocked by the violence and intervened. The president sent American forces to Veracruz and Tampico as America began to take a much more active interest in Mexican affairs. Wilson supported the new government of Venustiano Carranza, angering one of Carranza's rivals, Pancho Villa. In response, Villa raided the American town of Columbus, New Mexico, in March 1916, killing 18 Americans and presenting Wilson with a major crisis.

Wilson responded by ordering what soon became known as the 'punitive expedition,' a force of approximately 5000 soldiers under the command of General John Pershing. The expedition failed to find Villa. More importantly, the situation in Mexico

threatened to grow more dangerous because both Germany and Japan had links to various factions in the ongoing Mexican crisis.

The Zimmermann Telegram

The outbreak of the European war temporarily averted German eyes from Mexico, but as the German government inched closer to war with the United States, it made a fatal mistake. Counting on Mexican anger with America, the Germans took a gamble. In early 1917 German Foreign Minister Arthur Zimmermann sent a telegram to the Mexicans offering them the territory it had lost in the 1846–48 war with the United States in exchange for its support. The Mexican government quickly distanced itself from the idea, but it reawakened in American minds the spectre of more problems on their southern border. It also threatened the American south and west, two regions that had until then remained largely isolationist. The telegram also invited Mexico to open discussions with Japan about a triple alliance against the United States. The telegram was a clumsy misstep that infuriated the Americans without producing any real benefits for Germany.

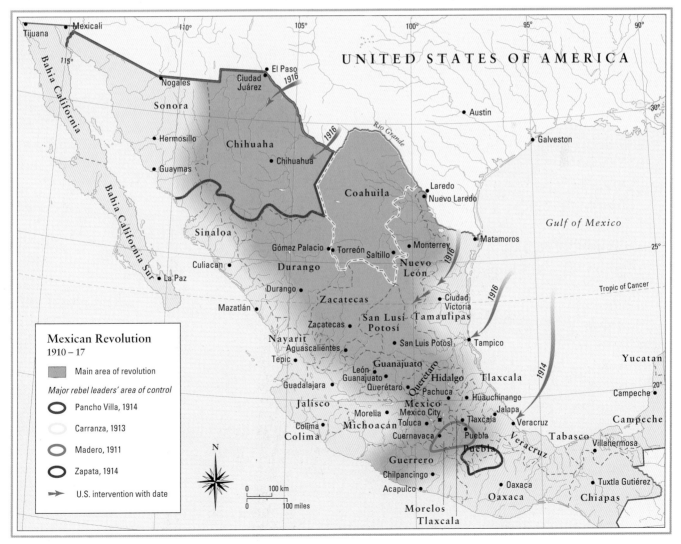

Mexican Revolution 1910 – 17

- ▨ Main area of revolution

Major rebel leaders' area of control
- ⬭ Pancho Villa, 1914
- ⬭ Carranza, 1913
- ⬭ Madero, 1911
- ⬭ Zapata, 1914
- ➤ U.S. intervention with date

The Handley Page O/400 was a much improved development of the O/100 and was the most effective British heavy bomber of World War I.

SEA & AIR WARFARE

World War I began barely a decade after the development of powered flight. Airplanes allowed for the photographing and observation of the front lines, providing key intelligence. Fighter pilots emerged for protection, with several of them becoming world famous as 'aces'. By the end of the war, the belligerents had built powerful, multi-engine bombers that could target major cities. This new kind of war appealed to those who thought that airpower would lead to shorter wars by forcing the other side to surrender rather than face the destruction of their civilian populations, industry and homelands. Blockades and submarine warfare also impacted civilians by cutting off seaborne supplies of food and medicine. Both forms of warfare were founded on the assumption that civilians were legitimate targets in a total war.

An airship overflies a British convoy
The heavily industrialized nature of the belligerents meant that World War I saw massive technological change. Airpower and submarines made the conflict a war in three dimensions.

German air 'ace'
German air ace (defined as a pilot with five 'kills') Ernst Udet with his with Fokker DVII biplane. By 1916 aviation had become an essential cornerstone of virtually all military operations.

Air reconnaissance
Photo reconnaissance units like this American one allowed armies to assess the success of their artillery and plan deep operations behind enemy lines. Mobile labs developed the pictures quickly.

German UC-1 class minelayer submarine
Submarines like this German minelayer wreaked havoc with surface fleets. Their speed and secrecy revolutionized naval warfare and challenged the existing laws of warfare, forcing navies to adapt.

Block ships
One attempt to stop submarines from easily operating involved the British sinking old ships (here, the *Thetis*, *Intrepid*, and *Iphigenia*) in the entrance to the Bruges Canal in Belgium in 1918. It was a clever idea, but not very effective.

British torpedo boat destroyers
British torpedo boat destroyers like these specialized in finding and sinking submarines. Note the 'dazzle' paint jobs on the hulls, designed to make it harder for submarines to spot them.

World Battle Fleets and Major Naval Bases 1914

The years before World War I witnessed a revolution in naval ship building with all of the great powers – even the largely landlocked Austro-Hungarian Empire – acquiring the new Dreadnought-style battleships. These expensive ships were exponentially more powerful than the ships before them.

Navies had many missions in 1914. In peacetime, they included protecting coastlines, securing overseas trade, projecting power over long distances and transporting military and civilian goods worldwide. In time of war, navies could engage in fleet-against-fleet battles, raid an enemy's commerce ships and deploy land forces almost anywhere they could reach. Fleets could also engage in blockades, the process of denying an enemy state vital supplies such as food, fuel and raw materials. Each of these missions required different types of ships. Fighting another fleet required large vessels such as battleships and battle cruisers, but these ships were too slow to chase commerce vessels. That mission necessitated destroyers, which were smaller and therefore fast enough to hunt down commerce ships. Navies had also begun to develop submarines, which could move underneath the water and thus approach coastlines or other ships without being detected. They represented a potential revolution in naval operations and strategy.

In order to complete their missions, navies needed a worldwide network of supply, ports and repair facilities. Before World War I ships converted from using coal to oil to power their engines. Because oil is heavy to transport, ships had to limit the amount they carried. They therefore needed reliable supplies of refined oil as they transited the globe. Geography also conditioned what navies could accomplish. Certain choke points such as the Dover Strait, Gibraltar, the Dardanelles, Suez and Panama controlled commerce in their regions. Although states could not deny them to other states in peacetime, they could block them during war.

Royal Navy

The Royal Navy was arguably the most powerful military force in the world in 1914. Britain had clearly and definitively won the prewar naval arms race, as even the Germans recognized. Britain also owned the world's largest empire, which controlled many of the world's most important geographic choke points. The Royal Navy only faced two major challenges. It had no real answer to the problem of submarines, a weapon the British saw largely as defensive but the Germans intended to use offensively. Second, the German fleet always had the option of remaining in its ports rather than come out and fight a battle it knew it might not win, thus largely neutralizing Britain's greatest advantage.

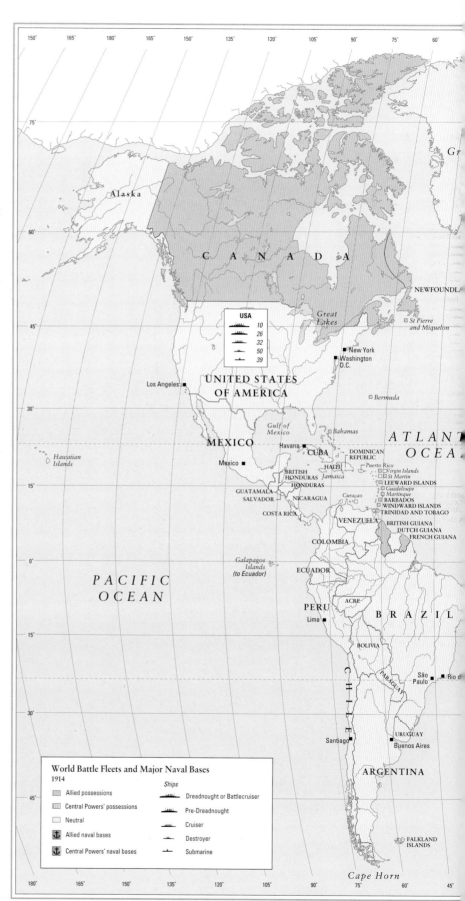

World Battle Fleets and Major Naval Bases 1914

Ships

- Allied possessions
- Central Powers' possessions
- Neutral
- Allied naval bases
- Central Powers' naval bases

- Dreadnought or Battlecruiser
- Pre-Dreadnought
- Cruiser
- Destroyer
- Submarine

USA
- 10
- 26
- 32
- 50
- 39

ARCTIC OCEAN

Germany
	19
	30
	49
	152
	30

ICELAND

NORWAY

SWEDEN

FINLAND

St Petersburg

Russia
	5
	7
	13
	107
	36

■ Moscow

Great Britian
	34
	35
	108
	233
	78

DENMARK

BRITAIN NETH. GERMAN
Berlin ■ EMPIRE

London ■ BEL.

France
	14
	9
	25
	81
	63

Páris ■

FRANCE SWITZ.

POLAND

AUSTRO-
HUNGARIAN
Vienna ■ EMPIRE
Budapest ■

Austria
	3
	12
	7
	18
	14

Ottoman Emp.
	1
	3
	2
	8
	0

RUSSIAN
EMPIRE

ITALY SERBIA
Rome ■ MON.
ALB.
ROMANIA
BULGARIA
Black Sea

SPAIN

Constantinople

Caspian
Sea

MONGOLIA
(Autonomous 1912)

CHINA

Beijing ■

Port Arthur

Weihaiwei KOREA

Tsingtao

JAPAN

Tokyo ■

Japan
	6
	2
	24
	54
	15

PORTUGAL
Lisbon ■ ■ Madrid

Athens ■
GREECE

OTTOMAN EMPIRE

Nanjing ■

Shanghai ■

GIBRALTAR TUNIS
Ceuta Melilla

Malta

PERSIA
Tehran ■

Italy
	1
	17
	11
	33
	20

CYPRUS

Madeira

MOROCCO ALGERIA

IFNI

DE ORO

EGYPT

Cairo ■

BEDOUINS

AFGHANISTAN

TIBET

Delhi ■

NEPAL

BHUTAN

Taiwan

PACIFIC
OCEAN

KUWAIT

BAHRAIN
TRUCIAL
OMAN
Gwadar
(to Oman)

Arabian
Peninsula OMAN

Diu
Bombay ■

Damão

Chandernagore

INDIA

Burma

Hong Kong

Guangzhouwan

Arabian
Sea Goa

Bay of
Bengal

Yanaon

SIAM FRENCH
INDO-CHINA

Manila ■

□ Guam

GAMBIA
GUESE
GUINEA

SIERRA LEONE

FRENCH
WEST AFRICA

ANGLO-
EGYPTIAN
SUDAN

ERITREA

Aden

Socotra

Mahé

Madras ■
Pondicherry
Karikal

CEYLON

Bangkok ■

Saigon ■

PHILIPPINE
ISLANDS

BRITISH
NORTH
BORNEO

NIGERIA

GOLD
COAST

TOGO

KAMERUN

FRENCH
SOMALILAND

Addis Ababa ■
ABYSSINIA

BRITISH
SOMALILAND

MALDIVE
ISLANDS

MALAYA BRUNEI
SARAWAK

Singapore

Borneo

KAISER
WILHELM'S
LAND

LIBERIA

Fernando Po

SAO TOMÉ
AND PRINCIPE

RIO
MUNI

FRENCH
CONGO

BELGIAN
CONGO

LADO

BRITISH
EAST
AFRICA

Lake
Victoria

ITALIAN
SOMALILAND

DUTCH EAST INDIES

Sumatra

Batavia ■

Java

New
Guinea

PAPUA

Solomon
Islands

□ Ascension
Island

GERMAN
EAST
AFRICA Zanzibar

Seychelles

Chagos
Islands

Amirante
Islands

Comoro Islands

PORTUGUESE
TIMOR

□ Cocos
Islands

Christmas
Island

Santa Cruz
Islands

ANGOLA

NORTHERN
RHODESIA NYASALAND

INDIAN
OCEAN

New
Caledonia

ST HELENA □

GERMAN
SOUTHWEST
AFRICA

SOUTHERN
RHODESIA

PORTUGUESE
EAST AFRICA

MADAGASCAR

■ Mauritius

Réunion

AUSTRALIA

WALVIS BAY
(to Cape Colony)

BECHUANA-
LAND

UNION
OF
SOUTH
AFRICA

Cape Town

Cape of
Good Hope

Sydney ■

NEW
ZEALAND

SOUTHERN OCEAN

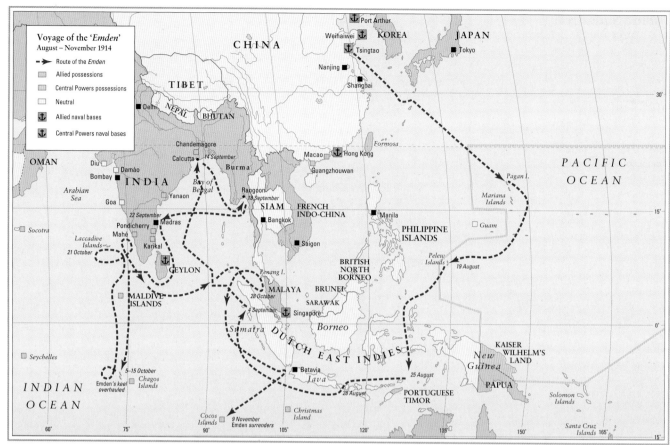

Voyage of the 'Emden'
August – November 1914

- ➤ Route of the Emden
- Allied possessions
- Central Powers possessions
- Neutral
- ⚓ Allied naval bases
- ⚓ Central Powers naval bases

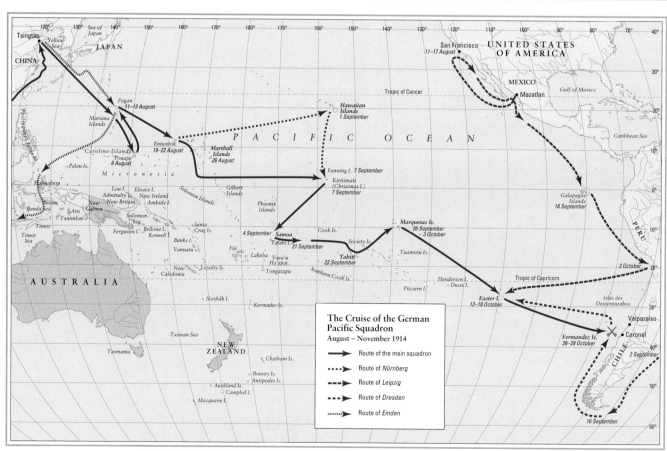

The Cruise of the German Pacific Squadron
August – November 1914

- → Route of the main squadron
- ┈➤ Route of Nürnberg
- ⟶ Route of Leipzig
- ⟶ Route of Dresden
- ⟶ Route of Emden

Pacific Squadron Late 1914

The German Pacific Squadron, consisting of five ships and based at Tsingtao in China, was at sea when the war began. Great Britain's alliance with Japan put the squadron in great danger so it decided to head into the Pacific Ocean rather than risk a major battle at sea.

One of the German ships, the *Emden,* broke away from the others and had great success raiding Allied commerce ships, giving battle only when conditions favoured it. The rest of the squadron sailed to the west coast of Chile where, near the port city of Coronel, it sunk two British ships, causing much panic in London. The Royal Navy had dispatched a powerful force of seven cruisers to hunt down the Germans before they could turn into the Atlantic and head for Europe.

Conditions favoured the better-prepared and better-conditioned British. German ships and their crews had suffered a great deal of wear during their run across the Pacific. British ships acted aggressively, quickly eastablishing the range of their enemy and devastating the Pacific Squadron. British casualties were light, with no ships lost. The Germans, however, lost all of their ships as well as their commander, Maximilian von Spee, who was killed in action. Thereafter, the German surface fleet no longer posed a threat to British commerce in the waters of the southern hemisphere.

Search and Destroy

The *Emden*'s successful raiding missions in the Indian Ocean badly disrupted maritime commerce in the region. The British and their allies eventually dedicated no fewer than 60 ships to finding and sinking the opportunistic *Emden.* Eventually the larger and faster HMAS *Sydney* found it near the Cocos Islands and forced it to ground.

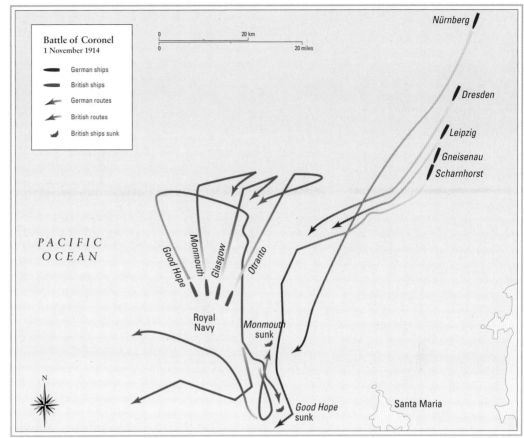

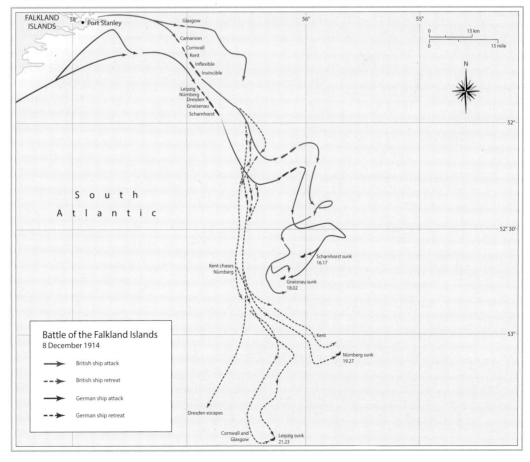

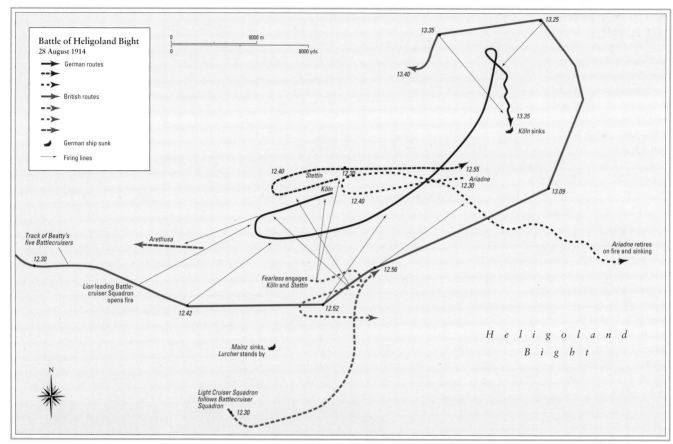

Battle of Heligoland Bight
28 August 1914

➤	German routes
⇢	
⇢	
	British routes
⇢	
⇢	
⇢	
🕊	German ship sunk
→	Firing lines

0 ___ 8000 m
0 ___ 8000 yds

13.25
13.35
13.40
13.35
Köln sinks

12.40   *Stettin*   12.30   12.55
        Köln   *Ariadne*
              12.40   12.30
                              13.09

*Track of Beatty's
five Battlecruisers*
12.30
← *Arethusa*

Ariadne retires
on fire and sinking →

Lion leading Battle-
cruiser Squadron
opens fire

12.42

Fearless engages
Köln and *Stettin*

12.56
12.52

Mainz sinks,
Lurcher stands by

*Light Cruiser Squadron
follows Battlecruiser
Squadron*
12.30

*H e l i g o l a n d
B i g h t*

N

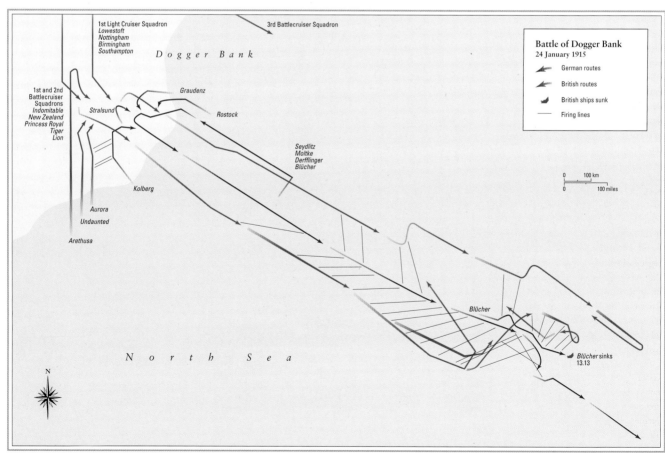

1st Light Cruiser Squadron
*Lowestoft
Nottingham
Birmingham
Southampton*

3rd Battlecruiser Squadron

D o g g e r   B a n k

Battle of Dogger Bank
24 January 1915

➤	German routes
➤	British routes
🕊	British ships sunk
→	Firing lines

1st and 2nd
Battlecruiser
Squadrons
*Indomitable
New Zealand
Princess Royal
Tiger
Lion*

Stralsund

Graudenz

Rostock

*Seydlitz
Moltke
Derfflinger
Blücher*

Kolberg

Aurora

Undaunted

Arethusa

0 ___ 100 km
0 ___ 100 miles

Blücher

Blücher sinks
13.13

N o r t h   S e a

N

North Sea Battles 1914–1916

Two small naval battles in the North Sea early in the war, the Battles of the Heligoland Bight (1914) and the Dogger Bank (1915), showed the difficulty of engaging in major fleet-on-fleet actions.

Prewar naval strategist Julian Corbett had challenged the long-held presumption of admirals who assumed that they could win a major naval battle at the start of a war, thus setting the conditions for future success. Corbett instead argued that an enemy fleet could always take itself 'off the board' by retreating to heavily defended ports.

The North Sea Battles of 1914 and 1915 seemed to prove Corbett right. At Heliogland, aggressive British action sunk three German cruisers and damaged three others. British losses in return were minimal. In the latter battle the British scored a major tactical victory. German ships had sailed into the North Sea to lay mines, but British intelligence had uncovered their movements and intentions, and a fleet was sent to stop them. battle cruisers devastated the German ships and gave the Royal Navy an important victory at sea. Germany lost one of its most important cruisers and suffered more than 950 dead. These battles were important in large measure because they convinced the Germans that the way to win a war at sea lay in the effective use of submarines.

Legacy of Julian Corbett

The two battles seemed to show the dominance of the Royal Navy and its ability to destroy the German Fleet in an open fight. But the Germans reacted as Corbett had predicted, retreating to the safety of their ports. The Kaiser then gave orders for it to stay there unless he personally directed it to do otherwise. The German Fleet thus took itself 'off the board', although it could reenter at any time.

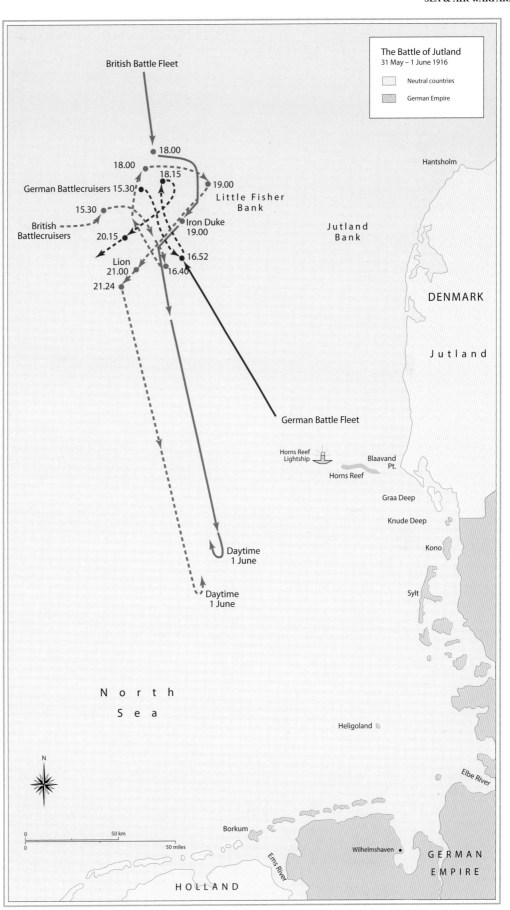

The Battle of Jutland
31 May – 1 June 1916

Neutral countries

German Empire

British Battle Fleet

18.00

18.00

18.15

19.00

German Battlecruisers 15.30

Little Fisher Bank

15.30

Iron Duke 19.00

Jutland Bank

British Battlecruisers

20.15

Lion 21.00

16.52

16.40

21.24

Hantsholm

DENMARK

Jutland

German Battle Fleet

Horns Reef Lightship

Blaavand Pt.

Horns Reef

Graa Deep

Knude Deep

Kono

Daytime 1 June

Sylt

Daytime 1 June

North Sea

Heligoland

N

Elbe River

Borkum

0   50 km
0   50 miles

Wilhelmshaven

GERMAN EMPIRE

Ems River

HOLLAND

Battle of Jutland Phases 1 and 2 31 May 1915

The German Fleet did reenter the North Sea in May 1916. It left in two columns, with the first to act as bait, drawing the Royal Navy into the much more powerful second column.

British naval intelligence had divined the broad outlines of the German plan to attack the Royal Navy with two columns and knew how to stop it. They had set a trap of their own, bringing powerful naval forces into the North Sea. The British thus engaged the Germans on favourable terms. They were all set to win a great victory, but the battle revealed a design flaw on British cruisers that left the ammunition magazines dangerously exposed and vulnerable. That design flaw proved expensive, costing the British three cruisers.

The battle thus proved to be a draw instead of the great victory the British had expected. The Royal Navy failed to trap the German Fleet, thus allowing them to get back to their ports safely. The Germans could also tecnically claim that they had sunk more tons of British ships than the British had sunk of their own, therefore giving them a tactical victory. The British, however, could more easily replace those losses.

Impact of Jutland

The Germans celebrated the Battle of Jutland as a great victory and a sign that they had begun to equal the Royal Navy, but serious strategists knew better. The battle had not broken British dominance of the North Sea and had not done anything to disrupt the British blockade. Thus although the Germans many have won a tactical victory, the British had won the strategic victory. The German surface fleet went back into its ports once more, and largely stayed there for the duration of the war.

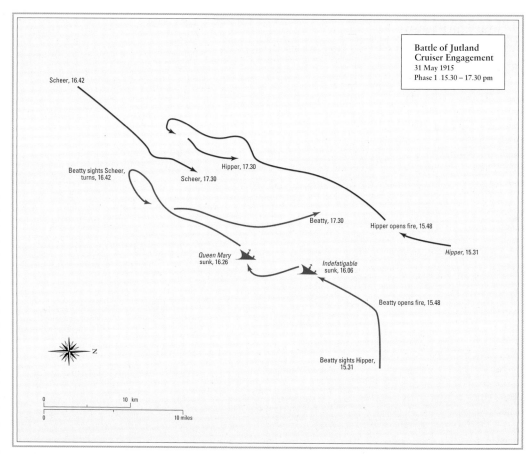

Battle of Jutland
Cruiser Engagement
31 May 1915
Phase 1 15.30 – 17.30 pm

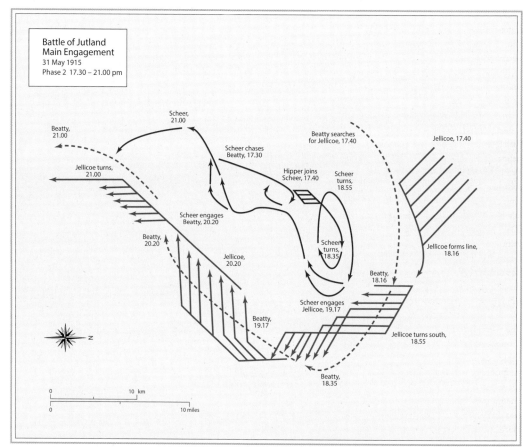

Battle of Jutland
Main Engagement
31 May 1915
Phase 2 17.30 – 21.00 pm

U-boat Campaign September 1916– January 1918

Germany may have lost the surface war, but it could still fight a commerce war by using submarines. They came with drawbacks, but submarines could also give Germany a way to win the war.

Submarines did not fit into centuries of blockade law. Those laws required a ship to give warning and care for the safety of passengers. Submarines, with little space and few defences, could not meet these requirements. Nevertheless, they could be the great equalizer to the dominance of the Royal Navy on the surface. Submarines, or U-boats, could approach a target silently and destroy it from a safe distance with torpedoes.

Due to their limitations, however, U-boats only had the option of sinking a ship or letting it pass. The biggest problems involved ships owned by neutral states carrying cargo to Britain and France. Letting them go meant allowing critical supplies to reach Germany's enemies, but sinking them brought on the ire of the United States.

In May 1915 German U-boats sank the *Lusitania*, a British ship that the Germans believed (rightly) was carrying munitions. In their eyes, the ship was therefore a legitimate target. However, sinking it killed 1198 civilians, including 128 Americans. The incident infuriated the U.S. until the Germans promised to be more circumspect in their targeting, but the debate about the propriety of submarine warfare continued.

The German Debate

Proponents of submarine warfare argued that U-boats were the only weapons that could win the war for Germany and must be used unconditionally. Others worried that sinking more ships and killing more Americans might bring the United States into the war.

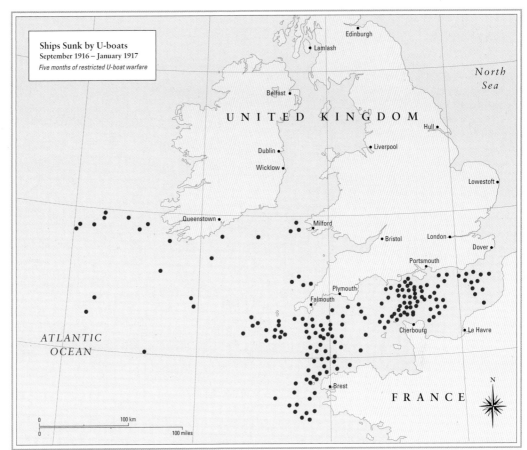

Ships Sunk by U-boats
September 1916 – January 1917
Five months of restricted U-boat warfare

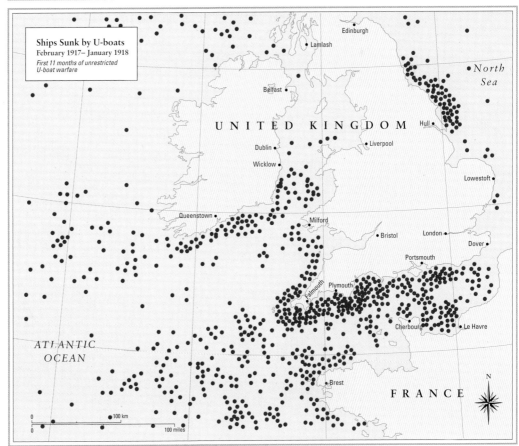

Ships Sunk by U-boats
February 1917– January 1918
First 11 months of unrestricted U-boat warfare

A Typical Convoy Plan 1917

The Allies debated using convoys to protect shipping across the Atlantic. Merchant ships would cross as a group with warships for escorts. Submarines, the theory went, would not surface if they ran the risk of being sunk by enemy destroyers.

Many senior naval strategists objected to convoys as a misuse of naval assets. They argued that convoys only provided submarines with larger target sets and made the warships themselves targets as well. Convoys also had to move, by definition, at the speed of the slowest ship thus negating the advantages of the faster ships. Convoys also tended to overwhelm port facilities when the ships arrived en masse. These problems notwithstanding, the Allies had no choice but to turn to convoys because of the enormous losses the U-boats were inflicting.

The Allies solved the problem of speed by grouping ships together into convoys by speed. Slow ships sailed with other slow ships and fast ships sailed with other fast ships. Warship escorts began to train their men in how to spot U-boats by looking for the wake of their periscopes. Some escort vessels carried observation balloons with men inside scanning the sea with binoculars. Specially designed vessels called 'Q ships' looked like merchantmen, but in fact had carefully disguised anti-submarine guns on board. Often they would lay behind a convoy, offering themselves as prey. Then, when a U-boat surfaced they would reveal their guns and open fire.

The Convoy System's Success

Convoys drastically reduced the losses of merchant ships to U-boats. Although many admirals still resisted devoting their valuable ships to such an unglamorous mission, they could not argue with its results.

A Typical Convoy Plan
May 1917

Merchant

Armed trawler

Warship (Destroyer)

Note: The progress of the convoy is governed by the speed of the slowest ship.

U-boat shadows convoy

Fast warship scouting ahead of the convoy

Ship with balloon 'Lookout'

'Q'-ship, a merchant ship with concealed guns posing as a convoy straggler

U-boat shadows convoy

Ships Sunk by U-boats February–October 1918

Convoys proved to be a dramatic change in the sea war in favour of the Allies. That change was critical to Allied victory because the Americans needed secure sea lanes to move and supply their men across the Atlantic Ocean.

German admirals had assured the Kaiser that they could sink American troop transport ships if the United States entered the war, thereby neutralizing the impact of American belligerence. That promise, although it had helped to convince the Kaiser to resume Unrestricted Submarine Warfare, proved to be terribly wrong. Convoys and better defensive measures in the ships themselves allowed the United States to move men and supplies across the Atlantic virtually unfettered. The U.S. Navy, led by convoy expert Admiral William Sims, could now devote its impressive fleet of destroyers to escort and convoy duty. U-boats were then reduced to targeting ships that sailed without convoy escorts or ships that got separated from their convoys en route. Germany had now lost the war at sea both on the surface and under it.

The increased security of trans-Atlantic convoys had dramatic strategic consequences. Britain and France could now depend on supplies of food, raw materials and fuel from the United States, Canada and South America. The fear that Britain might be starved into submission now faded away.

End of the U-boat Menace

As the escort and convoy systems became increasingly sophisticated, Allied confidence at sea grew. Eventually, the U.S. felt secure enough to dispatch thousands of soldiers across the ocean every day. Sugar, meat and weapons also flowed freely between the new world and the old.

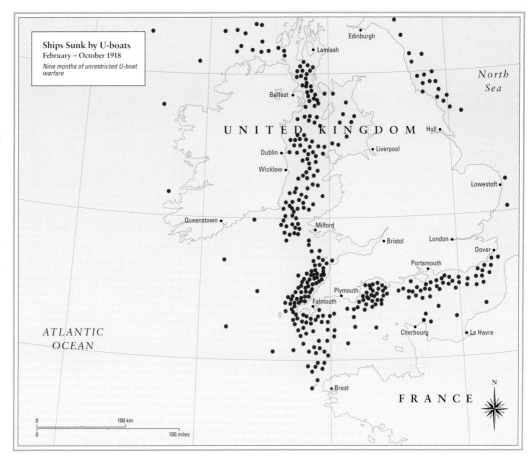

Ships Sunk by U-boats
February – October 1918
Nine months of unrestricted U-boat warfare

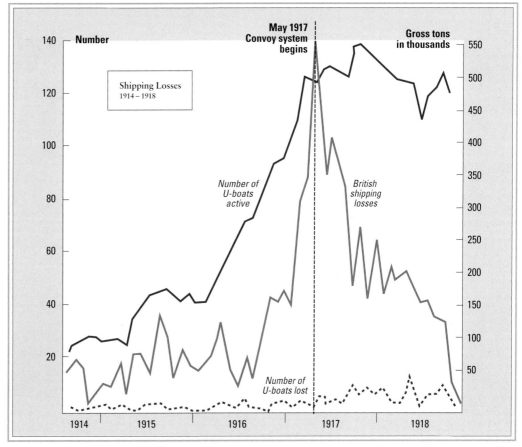

Shipping Losses
1914 – 1918

U-boat Losses
1914–18

Convoys represented a passive solution to the U-boat dilemma. The Allies also developed active ways to hunt and sink the U-boats. With their thin hulls, submarines were particularly vulnerable to enemy fire. The trick was to find ways to attack them even after they dove beneath the waves.

On the surface, submarines presented an inviting target for enemy ships. Piercing the hull of a U-boat in any spot threatened the ability of the submarine to return under water. Once safely submerged, however, submarines were both hard to track and harder to strike. By 1916 the British had developed depth charges, a kind of bomb that exploded when the depth of water exerted a predetermined pressure. The first depth charges carried 140kg (309lb) of TNT.

Destroyers soon developed ways to 'shoot' a number of depth charges set to a variety of pressures, hoping that one or more of them might score a lucky hit. These explosions could damage a U-boat by increasing the pressure of the water on the hull. Thus they did not need to score direct hits. Any charge that exploded within 12m (40ft) could do sufficient damage to disable a U-boat. Any charge that exploded within 4.5m (15ft) would surely destroy its target.

This system depended on a good deal of luck because once the U-boat submerged it was difficult to track. To solve that problem, British engineers designed special cables laid on the surface of sea beds that looked for the magnetic impulses given off by U-boat engines. The British also began work on a technology they called ASDIC, named for the Anti-Submarine Detection Investigation Committee that began the work in 1916. The system, known as SONAR in the United States, relied on sound and radio waves that moved under the water and detected the presence of large objects. Although it was not perfected in time for active use in World War I, it laid the foundation for the systems that was used in World War II.

Aircraft also became integral to the anti-submarine war. They could spot for the tell-tale wake of a periscope in the water and communicate locations to destroyers below. They could also attack the U-boats themselves, dropping smaller depth charges of roughly 50kg (110lb) of TNT.

Sinking U-Boats

With a combination of better spotting, better weapons and more highly trained sailors, the Allies began to target and destroy U-boats. Depth charges alone accounted for the sinking of 28 submarines between 1916 and 1918. These losses had a major impact on the morale of U-boat crews, which grew far less daring in the final year of the war.

U-boat Losses
1914 – 1918
● U-boats

**Submarine Command
Organisation**
1917
Average number of submarines
per base available for operations
■ Ostend, 23
□ Emden, 25
▨ Wilhemshaven, 22
■ Pola, 22
▦ Libau, 9
■ Constantinople, 3

Countries	Number Built	Number Lost
Austria-Hungary	12	3
France	45	10
Germany	225	184
Italy	35	2
Japan	13	—
Russia	44	22
United Kingdom	168	45
United States	40	1

Submarines Deployed 1914 – 18

Submarines 1914–18

A novel weapon, the submarine did not easily conform to the laws of maritime warfare. While all sides had them, the Germans made the most use of them as an offensive weapon. They gave the Germans a means of overcoming the British dominance of the seas.

Submarines promised to revolutionize naval warfare, but they came with limitations as well. They were expensive to run, had limited range and required retraining crews for dangerous undersea conditions. Ironically, even the Germans had initially resisted building them. They also required an attacking power to sink ships rather than board and inspect them as a surface ship could do. Consequently, they became known as the 'ungentlemanly weapon'. Before World War I all powers stated that they would use them only in defence of their home waters. But for Germany, submarines offered a way to remain a sea power even if the German Fleet remained inferior to Britain's. Submarines could approach merchant vessels silently and destroy them without warning. For this reason many German naval strategists saw a potentially war-winning weapon. With enough submarines and crewmen, they believed they could starve Britain into submission.

Threat to Civilians

Because submarines could not guarantee the safety of the people on board merchant ships and liners, submarine warfare killed civilians. Some German strategists were willing to take that risk, while others were afraid that it would bring neutral states like the U.S. into the war. In 1915 and 1916 those arguing for limiting submarine warfare generally won the argument, but as the war went on it became harder for them to argue for keeping submarines from operating at full capacity. Finally, in early 1917, the Germans announced the resumption of Unrestricted Submarine Warfare, even though it knew that the U.S. would likely enter the war on the Allied side.

Allied Blockades of Germany Late 1914

While Germany tried to blockade Britain with U-boats, the British relied on a more traditional 'distant' blockade using ships to intercept on the open seas rather than risk blockading near German ports

The British system annoyed neutrals such as the United States because it interfered with their trading rights and cost them money in lost cargoes. The British, however, blockaded legally according to international law. Because the blockading was done with big surface ships, moreover, the British could assure the safety of passengers.

The British blockade cut deeply into German food supplies, leading to dramatic shortages by 1916. Thus the blockade led to unrest at home and influenced German grand strategy by leading them to take more and more resources from the east in an effort to compensate for their losses. By 1917, however, the German people were reduced to eating turnips, a crop formerly only fed to animals, at almost every meal for weeks or months at a time.

The blockade thus proved very effective and, in the minds of some strategists, played an even larger role in German defeat than the great land battles. By 1918, Germany was on the brink of mass starvation, and because of the low calorie intake of the average German citizen the influenza epidemic struck Germany very hard.

Zeebrugge

In April 1918, the British tried a novel approach to stopping enemy submarines. They targeted a main German U-boat base at Zeebrugge, Belgium. Marines landed ashore to neutralize the land defences while sailors sunk two older ships in the harbour to block it and trap the U-boats inside.

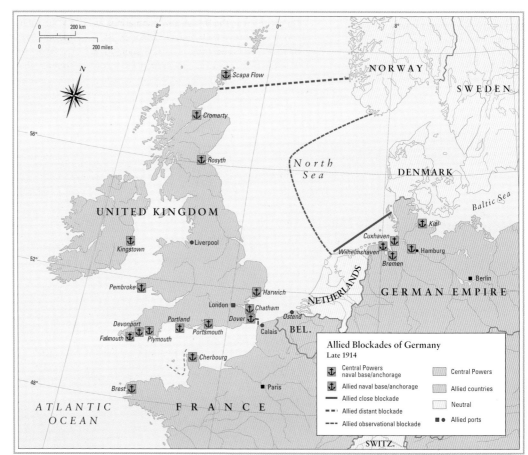

Allied Blockades of Germany
Late 1914

⚓ Central Powers naval base/anchorage
⚓ Allied naval base/anchorage
── Allied close blockade
─ ─ Allied distant blockade
- - - Allied observational blockade

▨ Central Powers
▨ Allied countries
▨ Neutral
■● Allied ports

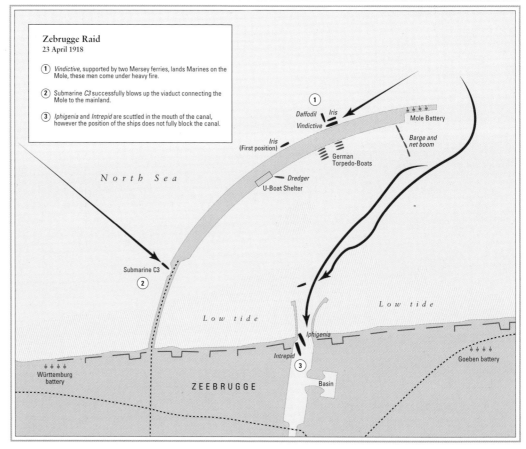

Zebrugge Raid
23 April 1918

1 *Vindictive*, supported by two Mersey ferries, lands Marines on the Mole, these men come under heavy fire.

2 Submarine *C3* successfully blows up the viaduct connecting the Mole to the mainland.

3 *Iphigenia* and *Intrepid* are scuttled in the mouth of the canal, however the position of the ships does not fully block the canal.

British Submarines in the Baltic 1914–18

Before the war, the British saw submarines as a way to improve their coastal defences. As the war developed, they used their submarines in offensive operations, most notably in trying to deny Swedish iron ore to German industry.

The submarines were effective for three years in interdicting German shipping routes in the Baltic. After the exit of Russia from the war, however, the British lost their bases and had to scuttle their ships rather than lose them to Germany.

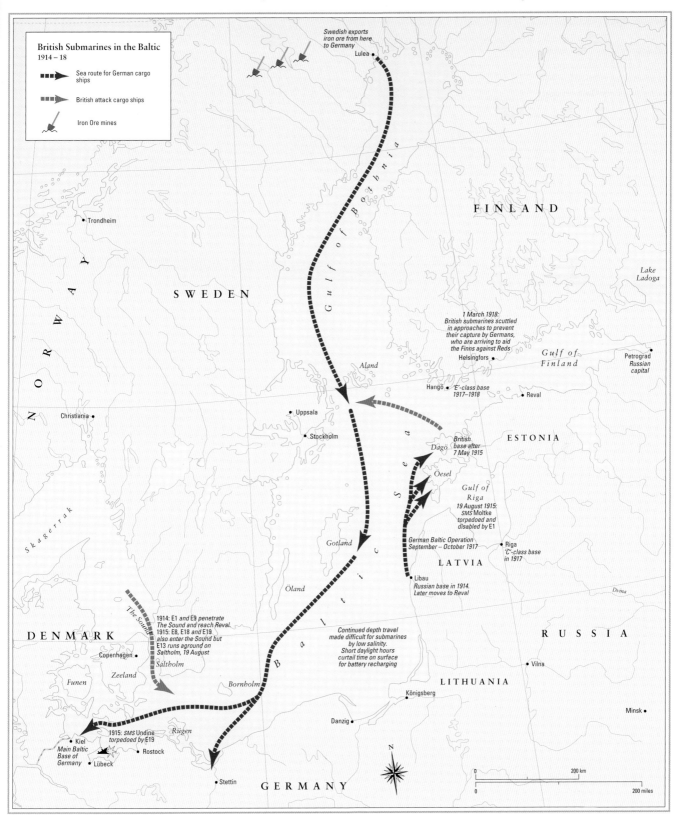

British Submarines in the Baltic
1914 – 18

Sea route for German cargo ships

British attack cargo ships

Iron Ore mines

Swedish exports iron ore from here to Germany

Luleå

FINLAND

Lake Ladoga

SWEDEN

1 March 1918: British submarines scuttled in approaches to prevent their capture by Germans, who are arriving to aid the Finns against Reds

Gulf of Finland

Helsingfors

Petrograd Russian capital

Åland

Hangö   'E'-class base 1917–1918   Reval

Christiania

Uppsala

Stockholm

ESTONIA

Dagö

British base after 7 May 1915

Öesel

Gulf of Riga
19 August 1915: SMS Moltke torpedoed and disabled by E1

Gotland

German Baltic Operation September – October 1917

Riga 'C'-class base in 1917

LATVIA

Öland

Libau
Russian base in 1914. Later moves to Reval

Dvina

Skagerrak

1914: E1 and E9 penetrate The Sound and reach Reval.
1915: E8, E18 and E19 also enter the Sound but E13 runs aground on Saltholm, 19 August

Continued depth travel made difficult for submarines by low salinity. Short daylight hours curtail time on surface for battery recharging

RUSSIA

DENMARK

Copenhagen

Zeeland

Saltholm

Funen

Bornholm

LITHUANIA

Königsberg

Vilna

Minsk

1915: SMS Undine torpedoed by E19

Rügen

Danzig

Kiel
Main Baltic Base of Germany

Lübeck   Rostock

N

Stettin

GERMANY

0   200 km
0   200 miles

163

The Mediterranean 1914–18

The Allies dominated the sea lanes of the Mediterranean basin due to the cooperation of Britain, France and Italy. The three nations also controlled most of the key ports in the theatre.

Dominance of the Mediterranean theatre was critical to the Allies because of the Suez Canal and the need to protect Italy's long, exposed coastlines. Geography helped them immensely, as their ships could neutralize the Austro-Hungarian fleet by blocking the Brindisi Strait between Italy and Albania. They could also bottle up the Ottoman fleet at the Dardanelles and prevent German submarines from entering the Mediterranean at Gibraltar. Allied fleets could also operate with near impunity in support of major land campaigns such as Palestine and Salonica. The Allies controlled the key land components of the theatre such as the islands of Malta and Corsica as well as key deep

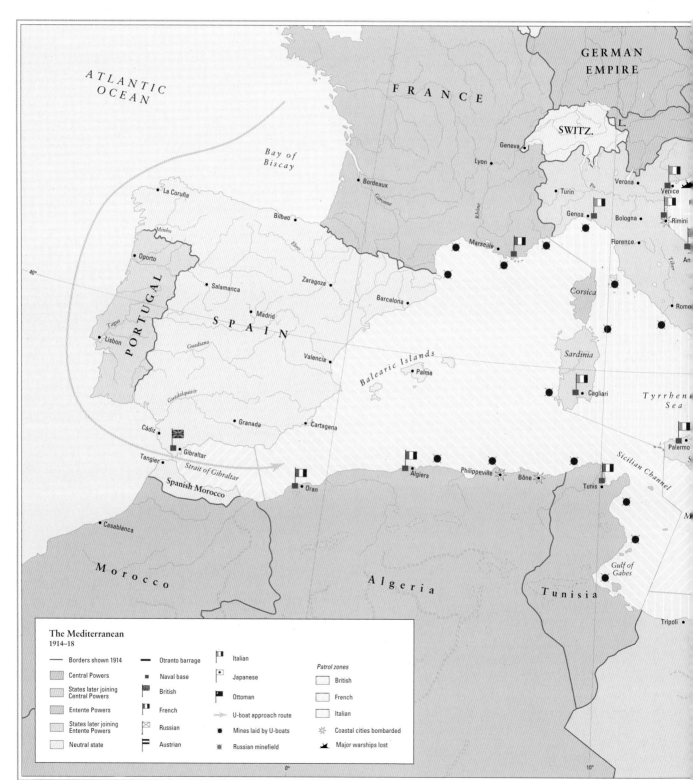

The Mediterranean
1914–18

⎯ Borders shown 1914	⎯ Otranto barrage	▮ Italian
▨ Central Powers	▪ Naval base	⚑ Japanese
▨ States later joining Central Powers	⚑ British	Patrol zones
▨ Entente Powers	⚑ French	British
▨ States later joining Entente Powers	⊠ Russian	French
Neutral state	▬ Austrian	Italian
	⚑ Ottoman	
	⇢ U-boat approach route	✳ Coastal cities bombarded
	● Mines laid by U-boats	⚔ Major warships lost
	◉ Russian minefield	

water harbours like Oran, Naples and Marseille. With the exception of a small stretch of Spanish Morocco, they controlled the entire north coast of Africa between them.

Germany nevertheless scored an early success in the Mediterranean when its sailors evaded French and British patrols and moved two warships into Turkish

waters. Those two ships then entered the Ottoman Empire's Navy and changed the balance of power in the Black Sea. Thereafter, however, the Allies had the advantage. They divided the theatre among them into patrol zones, assuring ease of movement and access to almost any part of the Med. Mines proved to be the Central Powers' only weapon of retort.

Most of the combat in the region occurred in the Adriatic Sea where the Italian Navy had blocked the Austro-Hungarians. In 1918, the Italians sank two Austro-Hungarian Dreadnoughts with fast-moving torpedo boats. For all military intents and purposes, the Mediterranean was an Allied lake for the duration of the war.

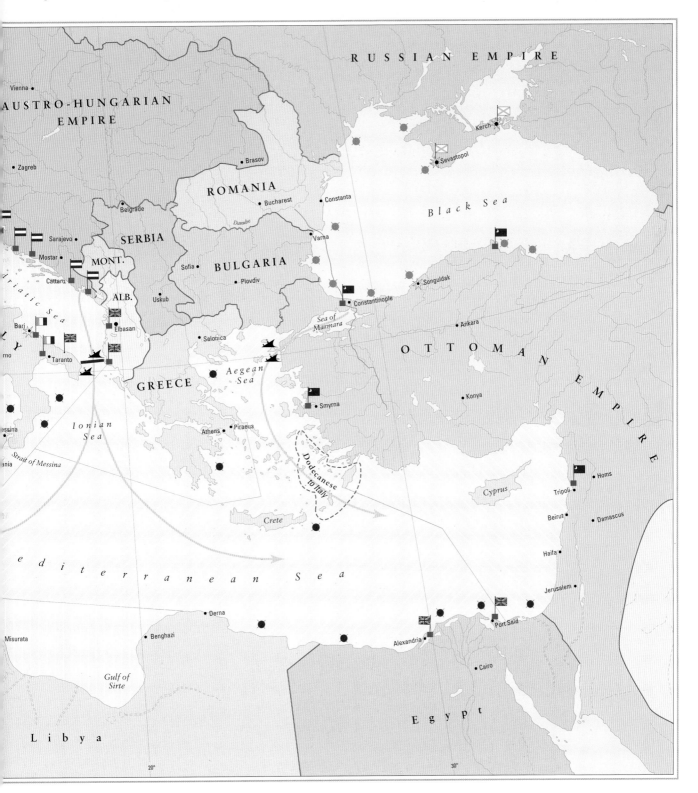

Aircraft on the Western Front
1916–1917

By 1916 no ground attack plan could succeed without control of the skies. War had become three-dimensional and pilots became as important as infantrymen.

The first planes were used to spot enemy movements, make accurate maps and help artillery with accuracy. Pursuit planes were developed both to target enemy observers and keep one's own observers safe. Air combat meant the development of specialized fighter aircraft. All sides developed bombers to attack both military and civilian targets.

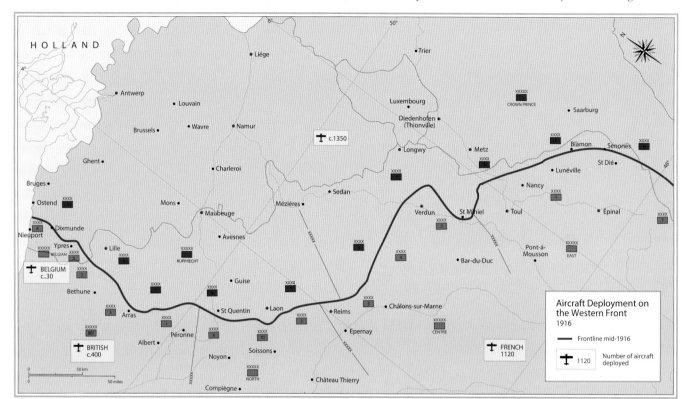

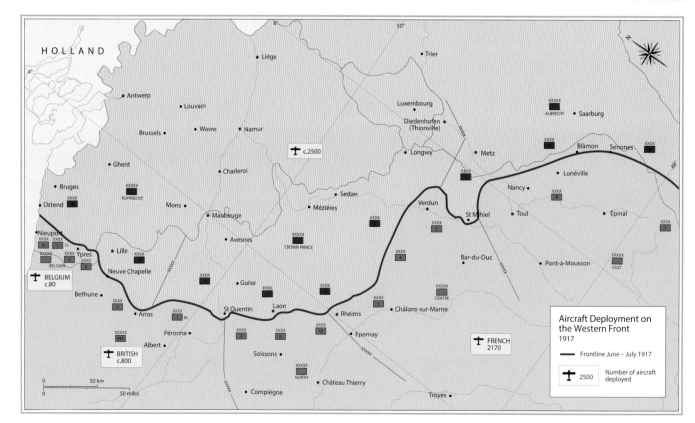

First Air Raids 1915

As the war on the ground intensified, armies began to contemplate new ways to strike at enemy homelands. As early as the first few days of the war the Germans had targeted strategic towns like Liège from the air. As airplanes grew more sophisticated, all sides could develop strategies for flying over the stalemated western front.

In January 1915, the Germans authorized aerial attacks on the British home islands. The government banned German pilots from bombing London itself until May, both out of fear of British retaliation on Berlin and Kaiser Wilhelm's desire not to target his British relatives. The Germans used a Zeppelin to strike at Yarmouth and King's Lynn in Norfolk that month. The damage they did was more psychological than physical, as Britain became vulnerable to a force that the Royal Navy could not stop. The terrifying pulp fiction novels of the pre-war years had conditioned the British people to expect an enemy to target them from the air. Now that premonition had come true and no-one in Britain knew how to stop it. Nor did they know how much worse it could get. In the most horrifying scenario, the Germans could drop gas or incendiaries on the British Isles themselves.

In reality, the Zeppelins proved to be too slow and too susceptible to enemy counter measures. But until the Germans could introduce more powerful airplanes capable of carrying a large payload across the North Sea, the Zeppelins were the instruments of Germany's strategic bombing campaign. They terrified people but the British began to develop ways to defeat them.

London Targets

After a British raid on Germany, the Kaiser decided that London was a legitimate target. In late May two Zeppelins set off from Germany for the British capital, although only one made it past Margate on the Kent coast. Despite this the raid frightened Londoners, but also seemed to prove the limitations of a Zeppelin attack. Although they could carry large loads and fly at high altitudes, they could not easily defend themselves from enemy airplanes.

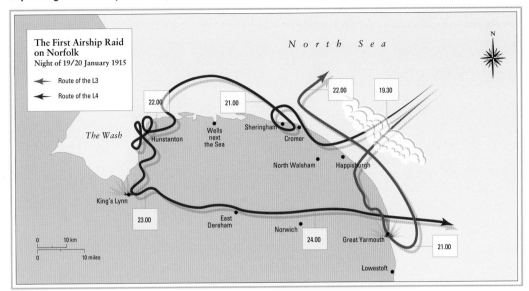

The First Airship Raid on Norfolk
Night of 19/20 January 1915
→ Route of the L3
→ Route of the L4

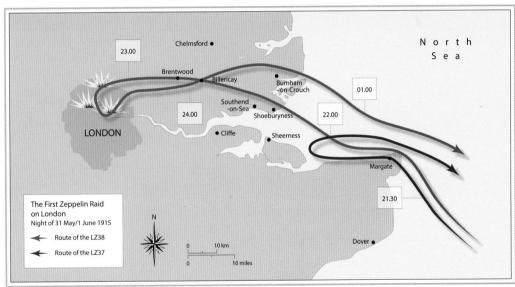

The First Zeppelin Raid on London
Night of 31 May/1 June 1915
→ Route of the LZ38
→ Route of the LZ37

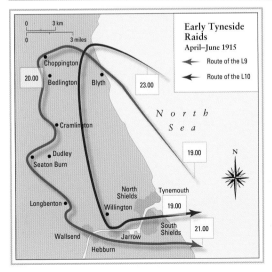

Early Tyneside Raids
April–June 1915
→ Route of the L9
→ Route of the L10

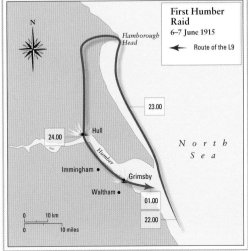

First Humber Raid
6–7 June 1915
→ Route of the L9

The Largest Airship Raid 2–3 September 1916

Despite their limitations, the Zeppelins could cover long distances. They therefore remained the primary airpower weapon of the German forces. In 1916 the Germans made 23 raids with Zeppelins, dropping 127 tonnes (125 tons) of bombs. Although they were inaccurate, they killed almost 300 people and injured 700 more. The Germans nevertheless abandoned Zeppelins in favour of new bomber aircraft that might turn the tide in the air war.

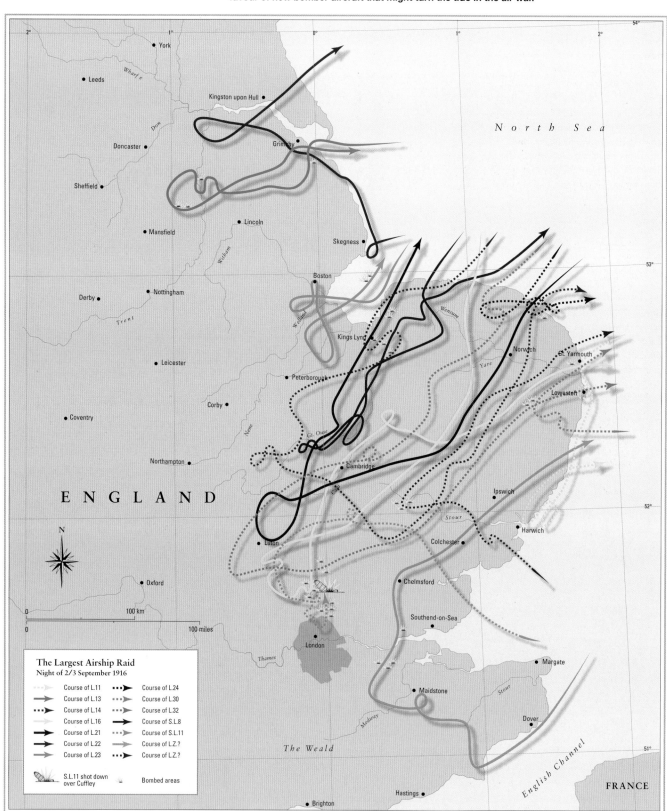

The Largest Airship Raid
Night of 2/3 September 1916

- Course of L.11
- Course of L.13
- Course of L.14
- Course of L.16
- Course of L.21
- Course of L.22
- Course of L.23
- Course of L.24
- Course of L.30
- Course of L.32
- Course of S.L.8
- Course of S.L.11
- Course of L.Z.?
- Course of L.Z.?

S.L.11 shot down over Cuffley

Bombed areas

Bombing of Paris 1914–1918

Despite the greater distances involved, bombing Paris was harder for the Germans than bombing London. Striking Paris, a key industrial and political target, involved flying over the western front and bringing the slow moving Zeppelins within range of planes based at several Allied air fields.

In March 1915 the Germans first used airships to bombard Paris, killing 23 people. Paris enacted defensive measures including barrage balloons that forced the airships to fly higher, thus limiting their already poor accuracy. German airships also faced the risk of having to fly back over enemy territory after they completed their raids. The French soon developed an intricate communications system to warn pilots all across northern France after a Zeppelin had struck Paris. Those pilots could then take to the sky and target them on the most dangerous part of their flights, the return home.

Unable to bomb with any accuracy, the Zeppelin attacks on Paris struck more or less randomly. The air raids did physical and psychological damage to Paris, but many Parisians had personal memories of the great siege of 1870–1871. Living closer to the front lines also gave them a sense of collective danger.

German Bomber Bases
1917

German long-range bomber bases

Front line mid-1917

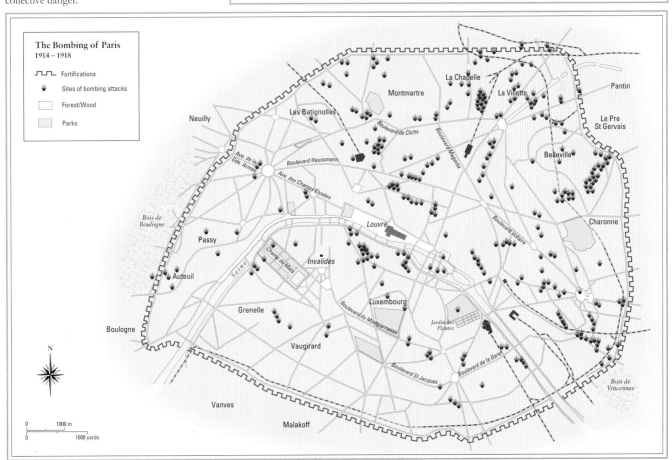

The Bombing of Paris
1914 – 1918

Fortifications

Sites of bombing attacks

Forest/Wood

Parks

Bombing of England 1914–17

German bomber pilots preferred to fly over the relatively safe North Sea towards Britain than over the western front toward Paris. London became the target of more air raids than Paris.

By late 1916, the Germans had developed twin engine Gotha bombers capable of flying at 4572m (15,000ft) and carrying 500kg (1,100lb) of bombs. They had an effective range of 800km (500 miles) and represented an improvement over the Zeppelins in every way. In May 1917, 22 Gothas struck Folkestone, and in June 18 Gothas struck London in broad daylight, killing 162 people. The Germans did not lose a single plane.

In September, the Germans also introduced new Giant bombers. With four engines and an enclosed cabin, they were safer for the crews than Gothas. They could carry four times the payload of a Gotha and crews could work on the engines in flight.

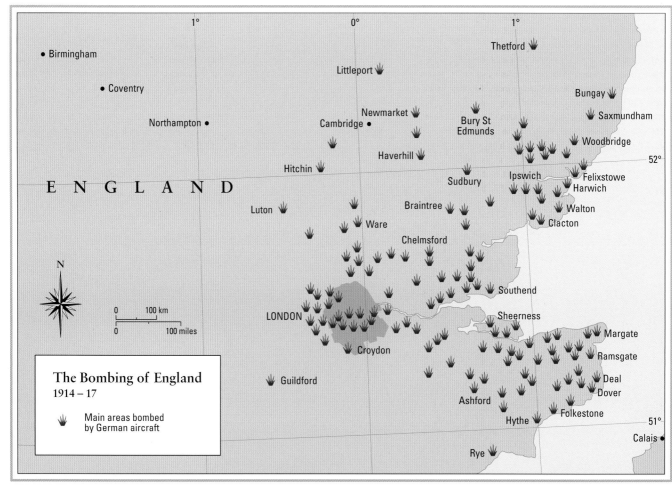

The Bombing of England
1914 – 17

🌿 Main areas bombed by German aircraft

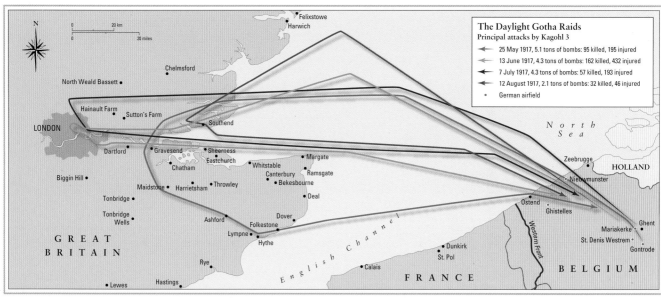

The Daylight Gotha Raids
Principal attacks by Kagohl 3

- 25 May 1917, 5.1 tons of bombs: 95 killed, 195 injured
- 13 June 1917, 4.3 tons of bombs: 162 killed, 432 injured
- 7 July 1917, 4.3 tons of bombs: 57 killed, 193 injured
- 12 August 1917, 2.1 tons of bombs: 32 killed, 46 injured
- German airfield

Air Defence of Britain 1918

Originally, the British had based their air defences inside the Royal Naval Air Service because German Zeppelins had to cross water to attack the United Kingdom. British pilots relied on incendiary bullets to target the airships because they relied on explosive gases for lift. This method produced some successes, but the introduction of the Gotha bomber rendered RNAS tactics less effective. British air defence systems were too rudimentary to meet the new threat. In mid-1916 responsibility for defending Britain from German air attacks moved from the RNAS to the Royal Flying Corps. The new system of defence had both air and land components. In late July, the British activated the London Air Defence Area as part of an integrated air and ground network of anti-aircraft systems.

The new British defence system included a series of airbases in southern England and a massive belt of searchlights about 40km (25 miles) inland used to find German aircraft in the night. Sound detectors also attempted to track aircraft engines by the noises they produced. Police officers, territorial soldiers and volunteers manned local observation posts connected to a centralized communications network that could relay information about German aircraft to waiting pilots at airbases.

British defences grew ever more sophisticated, relying on three primary methods. First, anti-aircraft artillery bands defended broad areas of the southeastern countryside, hoping to strike bombers as they passed overhead. Second, British fighter planes, alerted to the location of approaching aircraft, patrolled key areas near cities and other strategic targets. Finally, a large system of barrage balloons protected London, forcing German planes to fly higher or divert into regions guarded by RFC fighters.

The system worked well enough to encourage German bombers to fly at night because daylight bombing had become too dangerous. Night flying was not only less accurate (and therefore less destructive), it also led to more errors of navigation. Meanwhile, the British made continual improvements in their advance warning networks and dedicated more of the highly effective Sopwith Camel aircrafts to home defence missions. As a result, the Germans lost 61 Gothas – losses deemed too high for the results they produced

Independent Air Arm

Britain became the first power to create an independent air force when the RFC and RNAS merged to form the Royal Air Force in April 1918. By then the German raids had stopped. RAF strategists soon began to debate ways of keeping Britain safe in future wars. Some argued for improving the air defence system built up during the war. Others believed that no system could stop enemy bombers, and argued for building a deterrent force of bombers that could strike Germany.

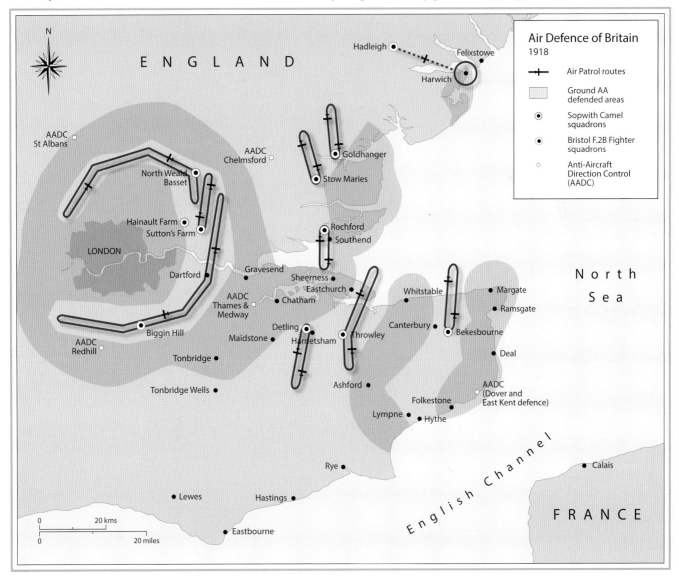

Aircraft on the Western Front, 1918

No technology changed as rapidly from 1914 to 1918 as airplanes. Both sides struggled to adapt to enemy innovations while developing new approaches of their own in the air war.

Technological advances met organizational change in the air war. Air forces developed dedicated squadrons and sophisticated tactics. New planes became more powerful, agile and stable. Air aces learned how to fly the new machines to achieve maximum combat effect. Some aces became heroes, but they suffered high casualty rates.

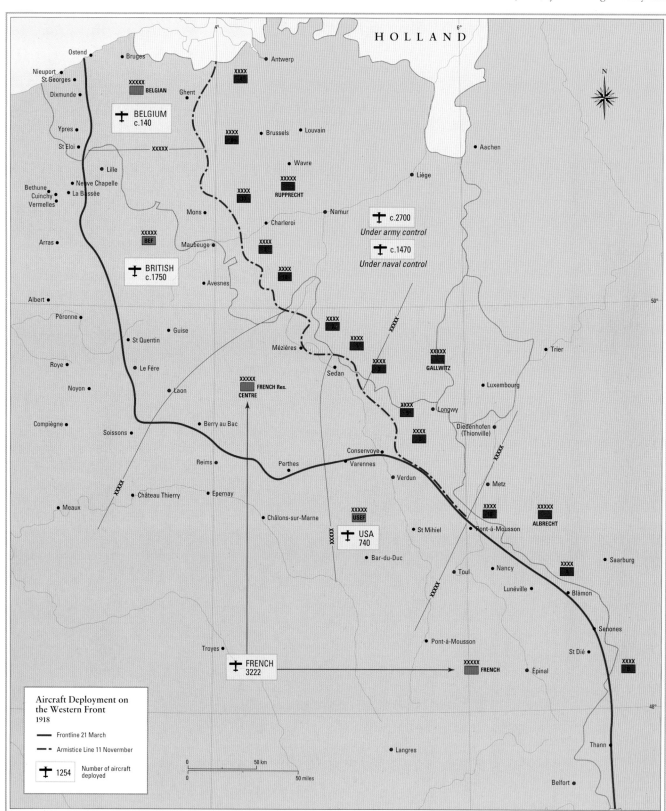

Aircraft Deployment on the Western Front 1918

— Frontline 21 March

-·- Armistice Line 11 Novermber

✝ 1254 Number of aircraft deployed

British Strategic Bombing Offensive 1918

British efforts turned to targets such as German rail lines in France and Belgium. Junctures, marshaling yards and storage areas became obvious targets.

British bombers, primarily those of the RNAS, also struck at German industrial targets, including the sheds, factories and warehouses critical to Zeppelin production. Airfields and troop assembly areas also became targets. By 1918, the British had begun to plan for raids on Berlin, but the mission of supporting the infantry always took priority.

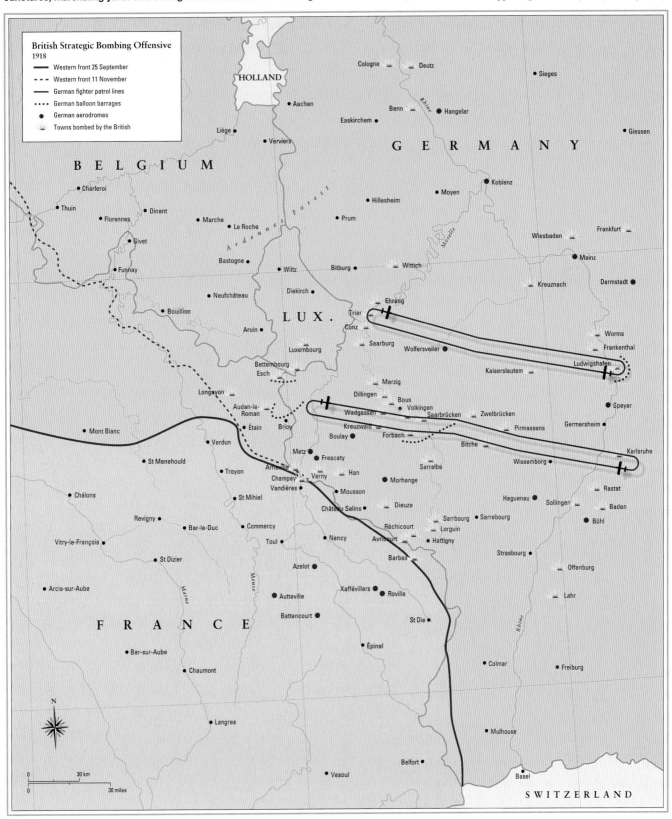

British Strategic Bombing Offensive 1918
- Western front 25 September
- Western front 11 November
- German fighter patrol lines
- German balloon barrages
- German aerodromes
- Towns bombed by the British

Armistice Day, 11th November 1918, is celebrated on Wall Street in New York City.

AFTERMATH

AFTERMATH

Germany's surrender did not stop the global violence and upheaval. The peace treaties that emerged from the Paris Peace Conference (1919–20) redrew the borders of the world, creating as many fresh problems as they sought to solve.

Dissatisfaction with the post-war order sparked imperial violence from Ireland to northern Africa to the Punjab region of India to China. The Russian Revolution of 1917 inspired revolutionaries across the globe to reject capitalism and fight for an entirely new kind of global order.

The American President Woodrow Wilson tried to preserve but reform that order, with decidedly mixed results. Wars across the globe and a devastating influenza pandemic served as reminders that the end of the war would not necessarily bring safety and security.

Middle East mandate
French soldiers enter Lebanon. The secret Sykes-Picot agreement of 1916 gave France control over Syria and Lebanon. The League of Nations ratified that control in 1920 under the Mandate scheme.

Versailles Treaty, 1919
The treaty signing ceremony on 28 June 1919 at Versailles, France. Many of the people in this photo came away disappointed and believed that the order and peace the treaty created would not last.

League of Nations
Delegates at the first session of the Council of the League of Nations in 1920. The League was a dream of American President Woodrow Wilson, but the United States never joined.

Civil unrest
The violence did not end with the signing of the treaties and the end of official hostilities. Here men in bolshevik uniforms inspired by the Russian Revolution fight police in the streets of post-war Germany.

The Unknown Soldier
The body of *Le Soldat inconnu* ('The Unknown Soldier') arrives aboard a gun carriage in Paris on 11 November 1920. Commemorating the losses of this war proved challenging as societies argued over its ultimate meaning.

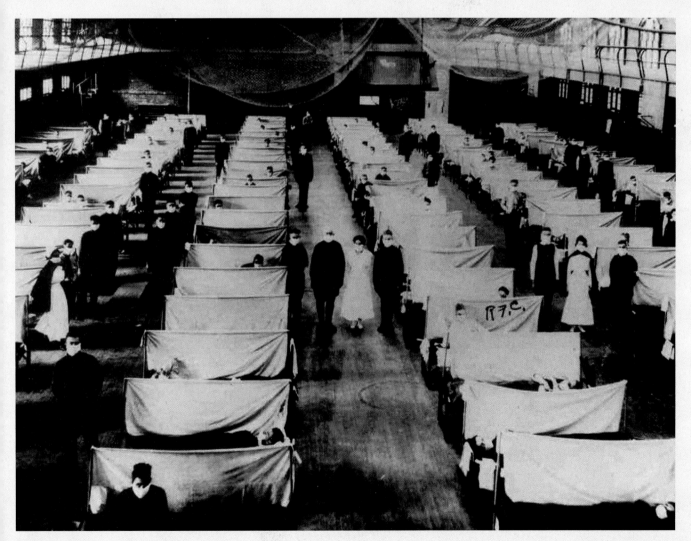

Influenza pandemic
The 1918 influenza pandemic killed as many as 100 million people worldwide. This community converted a warehouse in order to quarantine the sick and hopefully slow the transmission of the disease.

Central Powers on
the Brink
September – October 1918

Central Powers

Allied powers

- - - Front line

→ Final Allied advances

1 German army begins to give ground
in the West.

2 Austrian army giving ground on the
Italian front.

3 Serbian and Allied armies advance
towards Austria-Hungary.

4 Poles prepare to create an
independent state.

5 Slovenians, Croats and Serbs agitate
for independence

6 Czechs and Slovaks agitate for
independence

7 Bulgaria surrenders to the Allies

*Norwegian
Sea*

Arctic Circle

68°

64°

60°

56°

52°

48°

44°

40°

36°

8°   0°   8°   16°   24°   30°   38°   46°   54°

N

0   200 km
0   200 miles

FINLAND
*Independent as a result of
the Treaty of Brest-Litovsk*

• Petrograd

• Helsingfors

N O R W A Y

S W E D E N

• Christiana

• Stockholm

ESTONIA

LIVONIA

R U S S I A

*North
Sea*

Baltic Sea

LITHUANIA

British blockade

DENMARK
• Copenhagen

British blockade

• Hamburg

• Amsterdam

NETHERLANDS

GERMAN EMPIRE

• Berlin

P O L A N D 4

• Kiev

U K R A I N E

• Rostov

• London

• Calais

1

Brussels •
BELGIUM

• Frankfurt

• Prague
6

Cracow •

• Lemberg

April 1918 to Romania

• Paris

Rhine

Vienna •

Crimea

F R A N C E

• Bern
SWITZERLAND

AUSTRO-HUNGARIAN EMPIRE

• Budapest

48°

• Lyon

• Milan
2
• Trieste
5

Danube

3
Belgrade •

• Bucharest

ROMANIA

Black Sea

• Venice

SERBIA

BULGARIA

• Genoa

MONTE
NEGRO

• Sofia
7

• Marseille

Adriatic Sea

I T A L Y

• Rome

A L B A N I A

• Constantinople

• Barcelona

Corsica

• Naples

Sardinia

GREECE

• Salonica

Dardanelles

O T T O M A N   E M P I R E

• Smyrna

Balearic Is.

*Aegean
Sea*

• Athens

Sicily

M e d i t e r r a n e a n

*Italian
occupied*

Crete

Cyprus

• Damascus

Algeria   Tunis

S e a

French North Africa

The Armistice
November 1918

On 11 November 1918 an armistice ended the fighting, but the challenge of peace remained.

The Allies disagreed on the wisdom of an armistice. The U.S. commander, John Pershing, argued for invading Germany and signing the armistice on their soil. The French argued, however, that enough blood had been spilled; an armistice that prevented the Germans from renewing hostilities should be enough to allow Allied diplomats to devise a long-term peace. For their part, the Germans found the terms humiliating, but knew they had to sign because their armies had been defeated.

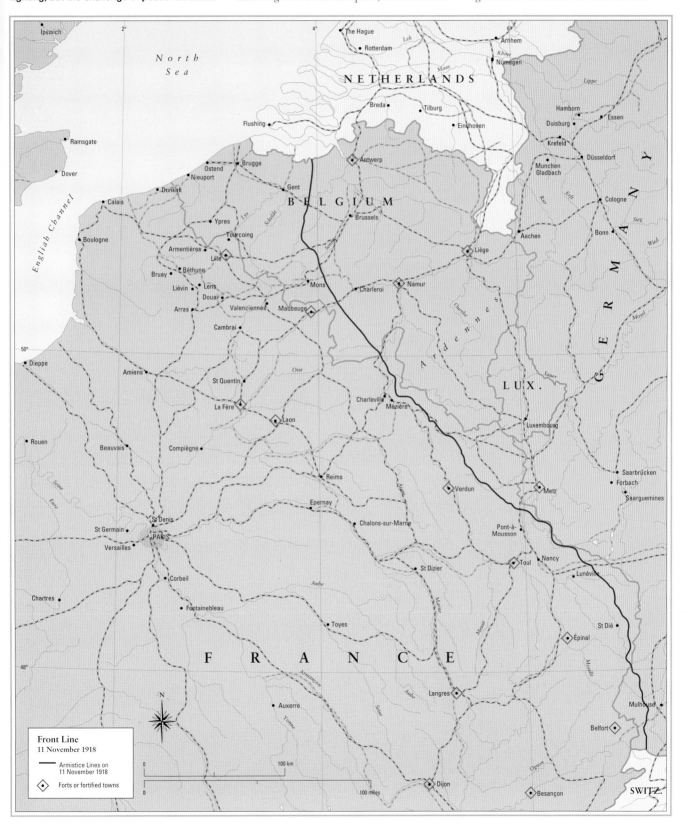

Front Line
11 November 1918

—— Armistice Lines on 11 November 1918

◇ Forts or fortified towns

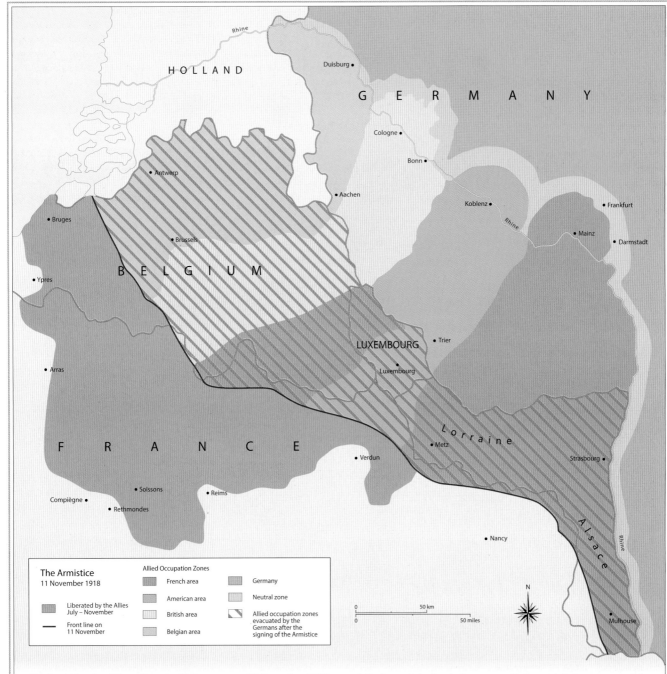

The Armistice
11 November 1918

Allied Occupation Zones

- French area
- American area
- British area
- Belgian area
- Germany
- Neutral zone

Liberated by the Allies
July – November

Front line on
11 November

Allied occupation zones
evacuated by the
Germans after the
signing of the Armistice

0   50 km
0   50 miles

The Armistice Conditions Signed with Germany on 11 November 1918

1. Hostilities to end at 1100 hours on 11 November 1918.

2. Germany to evacuate immediately the occupied areas of Belgium, Luxembourg, France and Alsace-Lorraine, the evacuation to be completed with 15 days. The Allied to occupy areas as they are evacuated.

3. Reparation of all the inhabitants of the above mentioned countries to be completed within 15 days.

4. The surrender by the German army of 2,500 heavy guns, 2,500 field guns, 25,000 machine guns, 3,000 minenwerfer, 1,700 aeroplanes.

5. The evacuation by the German army of the left bank of the Rhine, this area to be occupied by the Allies. Allied garrisons to be established in strategic places in this area, especially the crossings at Mainz, Koblenz and Cologne, where there were to be bridgeheads with a radius of 30 kilometres, (18.5 miles) on the right bank between the Dutch and Swiss borders. The Germans to evacuate these areas within 31 days.

6. No damage to be done to the persons or their property in the areas evacuated by the Germans and all military establishments in the evacuated areas to be left intact.

7. All communications to be left unimpaired, the following handed over to the Allies: 5,000 locomotives (to be delivered within 31 days), 150,000 railway wagons (to be delivered within 31 days), 5,000 lorries (to be delivered within 36 days). The whole of the Alsace-Lorraine railway system (to be handed over within 31 days). All lighters taken over from the Allies to be returned.

8. The German army to reveal within 48 hours the whereabouts of all mines and and devices with delayed-action fuses, as well as any other destructive measures.

9. The Allies to have the right of requisition in occupied areas, and the upkeep of troops in these areas to be charged to the German government.

10. The repatriation of all Allied prisoners-of-war.

11. The sick and wounded in areas evacuated by the Germans to be looked after by personnel left behind by the Germans for this purpose.

Break-up of the Austria-Hungarian Empire 1919–1920

In 1914, the Austro-Hungarian Empire seemed to be on shaky ground, but few people predicted that its dissolution was imminent. Four years of war and the death of Emperor Franz Joseph in 1916, however, proved to be too much for it to handle. By 1918 sections had seceded and others were coveted by the victorious powers. The treaties that came out of the Paris Peace Conference officially ended the Empire in 1919.

The victorious European powers redrew the borders of southeastern Europe with conflicting goals in mind. Some wanted to honour Woodrow Wilson's desire to line up the political borders with ethnic ones, a principle the American president called National Self-Determination. Others wanted to give slices of the Empire to allied states in order to reward them for their assistance during the war. Romania emerged from this process unusually strong. Still others wanted to draw borders that the new states could more easily defend or that contained enough natural resources to make them economically viable. The task proved far too difficult, leaving behind grievances of all kinds. Eight different states took pieces of the former Austro-Hungarian Empire.

The Creation of Yugoslavia

The new borders created potential sources of friction almost everywhere. The great powers hoped, however, that over time and with some outside assistance they would prove to be viable. In the Balkans they hoped to provide stability by creating a single large state for Serbia, Croatia, Bosnia, Herzegovina and Slovenia. Known to many as the 'Versailles state' because of the role of the great powers, it took on the name Yugoslavia in 1929. The new state put many mutually antagonistic ethnic groups in the same region, but the great powers thought that solution was preferable to creating a number of small states that would compete with one another for resources and borders.

The End of Empire – Break-up of the Austria-Hungarian Empire 1919–20

—— Former Austria-Hungary border

European Treaties 1919–20

The Paris Peace Conference produced five treaties that tried to give the world peace after four years of total war.

The conference was dominated by three men. U.S. President Woodrow Wilson was the most idealistic and hoped to encourage cooperation between the powers. French Prime Minister Georges Clemenceau sought security for his country from Germany, which he feared would emerge strong despite defeat. Britain's Prime Minister David Lloyd George wanted stability on the continent. Their goals proved difficult to reconcile and the treaties therefore included a number of compromises.

European Peace Treaties
1919 – 20

⎯⎯ Disputed or unrecognised border

Poland and Czechoslovakia 1919–21

The Treaty of St. Germain in September 1919 forced the new state of Austria to recognize the independence of two new states, Czechoslovakia and Poland. The former was carved out of four traditional regions from the Austro-Hungarian Empire. The latter reappeared on the European map for the first time since 1795 and took territory from the prewar German, Russian and Austro-Hungarian Empires. The two new states fought a short war in 1919 for control of mineral-rich Silesia. In 1920, they divided the region between them.

The creation of Poland destabilized Europe. Both Germany and Russia objected to its mere presence on the map. Nationalists on both sides called it 'the bastard of Versailles' and blamed the great powers for its existence.

Russo–Polish War

Russia and Poland went to war from 1919 to 1921 to determine the border between them, with the west supporting Poland against the Bolshevik USSR. Poland won and set the border on the so-called Riga Line, named for the city where the treaty was signed. Ethnic Poles, while happy to have a state again, disliked the borders the great powers had set. Poland received a strip of land called the Polish Corridor in order to ensure access to the sea, but the League of Nations, not the Polish government, controlled the main port city of Danzig (Gdansk). Germany objected to the corridor, arguing that the land contained large German populations that should not live under Polish rule. The corridor also divided Germany, leaving East Prussia isolated. As many strategists understood, the new borders would be difficult for the Poles to defend. The Germans could put forces on two Polish flanks. Ukraine, too, was angry with the Poles for their taking of land that contained millions of ethnic Ukrainians. The new Poland was therefore born with hostile neighbours on every side and difficult frontiers to secure. The British and the French nevertheless placed great faith in Poland as a counterweight to both Germany and the aggressively expansionist Soviet Union.

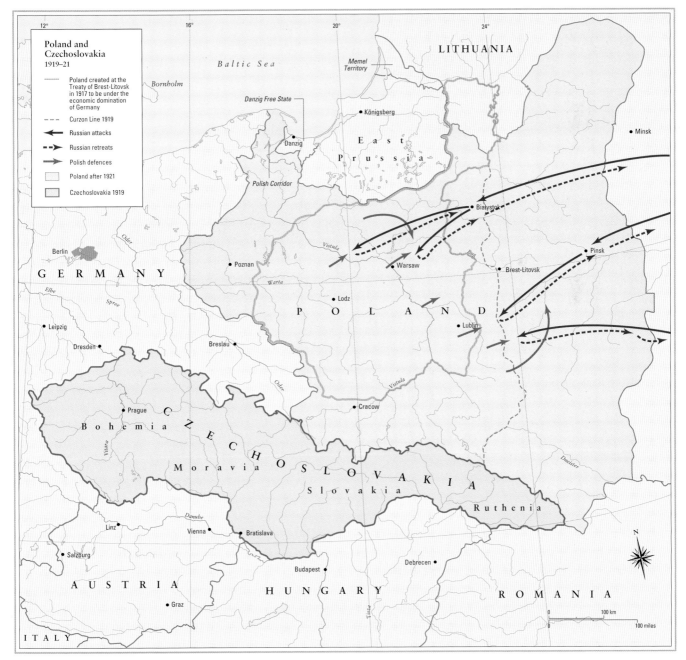

Poland and Czechoslovakia 1919–21

— Poland created at the Treaty of Brest-Litovsk in 1917 to be under the economic domination of Germany
-- Curzon Line 1919
→ Russian attacks
-→ Russian retreats
→ Polish defences
▢ Poland after 1921
▢ Czechoslovakia 1919

Sykes-Picot Plan, May 1916

In 1916, British, Russian and French diplomats signed a secret agreement to divide the Middle East between them after the war.

According to the agreement, Great Britain would receive a dominant role in a wide arc of territory that would link British Egypt to the Persian frontier. France would receive a dominant role in Syria and Lebanon, regions that French nationalists had always coveted. Russia would control Armenia, in part to protect the Christian populations there. Palestine proved to be much more contentious so the great powers placed it in an ambiguous zone of international control.

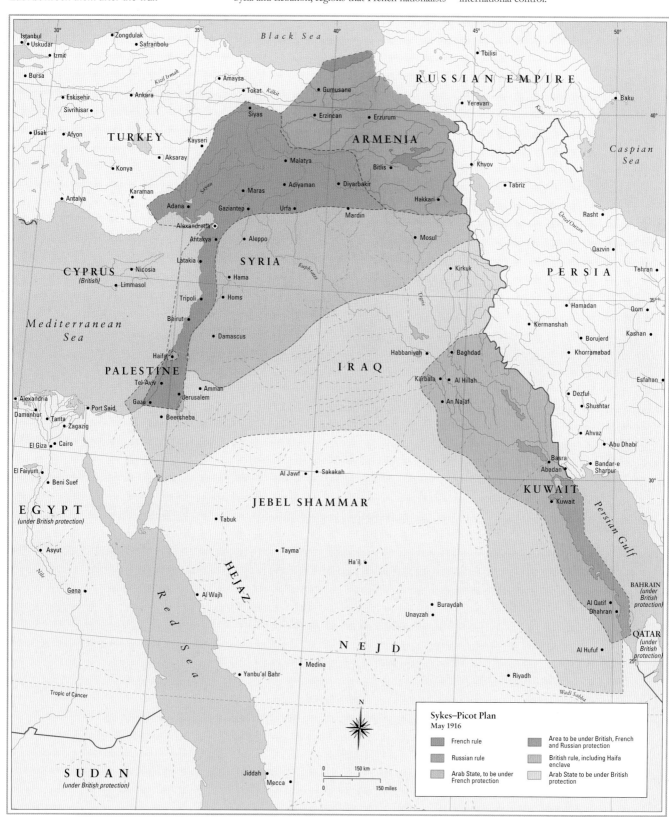

Sykes–Picot Plan
May 1916

- French rule
- Russian rule
- Arab State, to be under French protection
- Area to be under British, French and Russian protection
- British rule, including Haifa enclave
- Arab State to be under British protection

League of Nations Mandate 1921

Rather than annex parts of the Ottoman Empire, the great powers created the Mandate System.

The brainchild of South African Jan Smuts, the Mandate System allowed Britain and France to avoid the charge that they were simply gobbling up pieces of the Middle East. Instead, they received a mandate to govern the regions from the League of Nations. In theory, they were to prepare the region for self-government, but in reality there were few legal restrictions to their behaviour. The system proved unworkable for the Europeans and unpopular in the region.

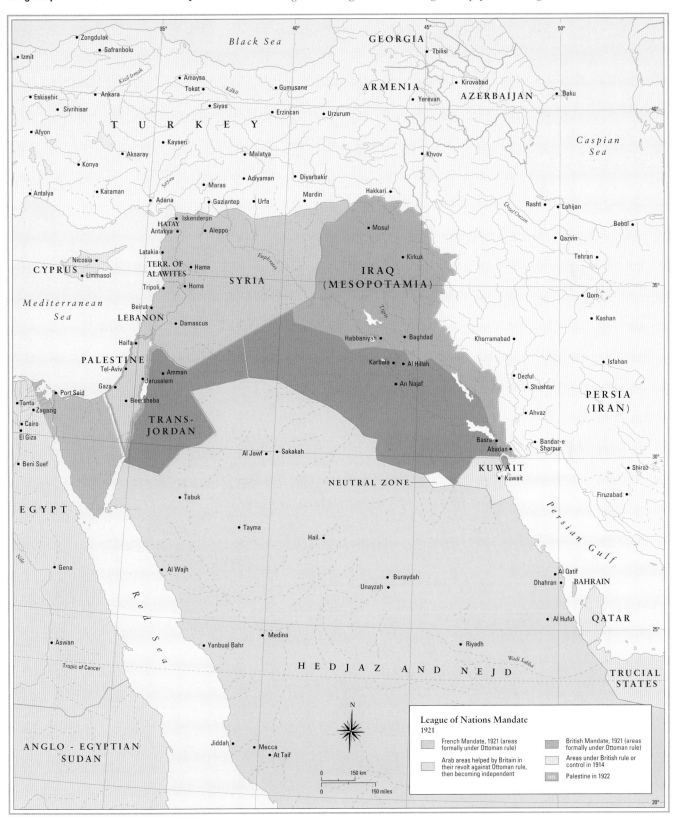

League of Nations Mandate 1921

- French Mandate, 1921 (areas formally under Ottoman rule)
- Arab areas helped by Britain in their revolt against Ottoman rule, then becoming independent
- British Mandate, 1921 (areas formally under Ottoman rule)
- Areas under British rule or control in 1914
- Palestine in 1922

Imperial Manpower Contributions to the War

All of the great powers were empires, and therefore relied on manpower from their colonies. Because the French and British had the largest empires, they were able to make the most effective use of imperial manpower. They also controlled the sea routes, enabling them to move men all over the world.

Each great power subscribed to racialized beliefs about their imperial troops. The British preferred to rely on men from the so-called 'White Dominions,' for the logical reason that such men had closer ties to the mother country. Statistics for enlistment bear this reasoning out, as a disproportionate percentage of volunteers from Australia, New Zealand and Canada had been born in Britain. Similarly, the French depended on white settlers in their North African colonies like Tunisia and, most importantly, Algeria. The British also relied on the so-called 'martial race' theory that preferenced Muslim soldiers from northern India over Hindu soldiers from Bengal. For the French, a heavy reliance on Senegalese soldiers came in part from similar racial ideas. French General Charles Mangin, for example, argued that Africans did not feel pain as intensely as Europeans.

The British preferred where possible to use white troops on the western front. In 1915, they did deploy a number of Indian soldiers in France and Belgium, but they eventually settled on a policy that used Indian troops in the Middle East instead. India's enormous contribution of 1.4 million men is the largest army produced during the war without the use of conscription. To this day historians continue to debate what motivated men from Asia and Africa to volunteer for dangerous military service in Europe. Some were undoubtedly motivated by a connection to the empire, while others may have been more motivated by unemployment or pressure from local leaders.

Chinese Labourers

Chinese leaders found themselves in a difficult position. They believed that the Allies were likely to win the war, but one of the Allies was Japan, the very country making territorial demands on China. The Chinese knew that joining the war would be unpopular, so they decided to offer the French and British the service of tens of thousands of labourers who would go to the western front to free up British and French labourers for military service. The Chinese hoped to use this scheme to gain support for their efforts to keep the Japanese from seizing any of China's territory. They especially wanted the German concession areas in the Shandong peninsula to go to China, not Japan, after the war. The scheme failed, however. The Paris Peace Conference rewarded Japan by giving it Shandong in one of the conference's most controversial decisions.

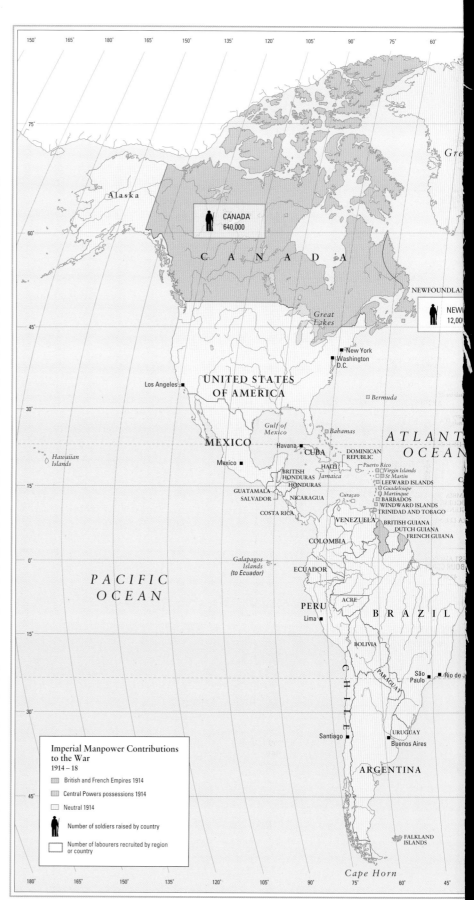

CANADA
640,000

NEW[FOUNDLAND]
12,00[0]

Imperial Manpower Contributions to the War
1914–18

British and French Empires 1914

Central Powers possessions 1914

Neutral 1914

Number of soldiers raised by country

Number of labourers recruited by region or country

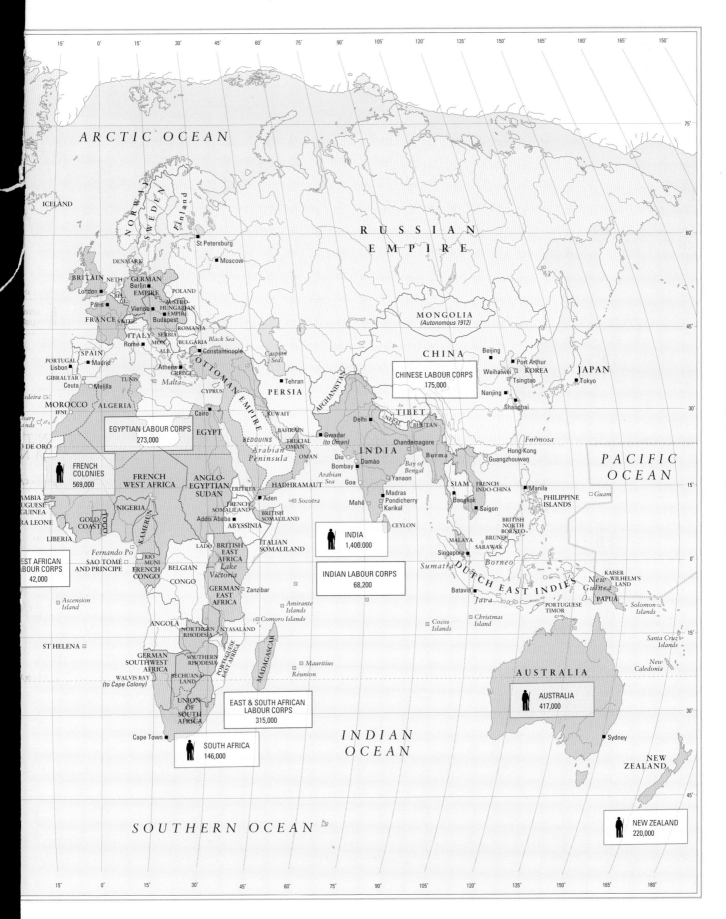

ARCTIC OCEAN

ICELAND

NORWAY

SWEDEN

Finland

St Petersburg

Moscow

DENMARK

BRITAIN   NETH.
London   GER.
          GERMAN
          EMPIRE
          Berlin
BEL.
Paris
FRANCE   SWITZ.
          AUSTRO-
          HUNGARIAN
          EMPIRE
          Vienna
          Budapest
          ROMANIA
ITALY   SERBIA
Rome   MON.   BULGARIA
          ALB.
SPAIN   Athens
Madrid   GREECE
PORTUGAL
Lisbon
GIBRALTAR
Ceuta   Melilla
Madeira
         MOROCCO   ALGERIA
Canary
Islands
IFNI
RIO DE ORO

R U S S I A N
E M P I R E

MONGOLIA
(Autonomous 1912)

CHINA
Beijing
Port Arthur
Weihaiwei   KOREA
Tsingtao
Nanjing
Shanghai

JAPAN
Tokyo

Formosa

PACIFIC
OCEAN

Black Sea

OTTOMAN EMPIRE

Constantinople

Caspian
Sea

Malta

CYPRUS

PERSIA

AFGHANISTAN

Tehran

CHINESE LABOUR CORPS
175,000

TIBET

Delhi
NEPAL   BHUTAN

Cairo

EGYPTIAN LABOUR CORPS
273,000

EGYPT

KUWAIT

BAHRAIN
TRUCIAL

Gwadar
(to Oman)

Chandernagore

Hong Kong
Guangzhouwan

BEDOUINS

Arabian
Peninsula

OMAN

Diu
Bombay   Damão

INDIA

Burma

FRENCH
COLONIES
569,000

FRENCH
WEST AFRICA

ANGLO-
EGYPTIAN
SUDAN

HADHRAMAUT

ERITREA

Arabian
Sea   Goa

Bay of
Bengal

SIAM   FRENCH
        INDO-CHINA

Madras

GAMBIA
PORTUGUESE
GUINEA
SIERRA LEONE

NIGERIA

GOLD
COAST

TOGO

KAMERUN

LIBERIA

French
SOMALILAND
Addis Ababa

Aden   Socotra

BRITISH
SOMALILAND

ABYSSINIA

Mahé
Pondicherry
Karikal

CEYLON

Bangkok

Saigon

Manila

PHILIPPINE
ISLANDS

Guam

MALAYA

BRITISH
NORTH
BORNEO

BRUNEI

INDIA
1,400,000

SARAWAK

Singapore

Borneo

EAST AFRICAN
LABOUR CORPS
42,000

Fernando Po
SAO TOMÉ
AND PRINCIPE

RIO
MUNI

FRENCH
CONGO

BELGIAN
CONGO

LADO   BRITISH
        EAST
        AFRICA

Lake
Victoria

GERMAN
EAST
AFRICA   Zanzibar

INDIAN LABOUR CORPS
68,200

Sumatra

DUTCH EAST INDIES

KAISER
WILHELM'S
LAND

New
Guinea

PAPUA

Batavia
Java

PORTUGUESE
TIMOR

Solomon
Islands

Ascension
Island

Amirante
Islands

Comoro Islands

Cocos
Islands

Christmas
Island

Santa Cruz
Islands

ST HELENA

ANGOLA

NORTHERN
RHODESIA   NYASALAND

Mauritius
Réunion

New
Caledonia

GERMAN
SOUTHWEST
AFRICA

SOUTHERN
RHODESIA

PORTUGUESE
EAST AFRICA

MADAGASCAR

AUSTRALIA

AUSTRALIA
417,000

WALVIS BAY
(to Cape Colony)   BECHUANA-
                    LAND

UNION
OF
SOUTH
AFRICA

EAST & SOUTH AFRICAN
LABOUR CORPS
315,000

Sydney

Cape Town

SOUTH AFRICA
146,000

INDIAN
OCEAN

NEW
ZEALAND

SOUTHERN OCEAN

NEW ZEALAND
220,000

187

Manpower Table 1914–18

As this table shows, a minor diplomatic crisis in the Balkans eventually dragged in forces from almost every corner of the globe.

The mobilization of soldiers for the war shows some unexpected patterns. India's mobilization of 1,680,000 men was the largest done without government-run conscription. Unfortunately, we know little about these Indian soldiers or those from Africa. New Zealand's percentage of able-bodied men volunteering for war was the highest in the world. These figures pose questions about individual and collective rationales for going to war. They also show how global the war became.

Country	Population	Strength on Entering War		Strength 11/18	TOTAL MOBILISED
		Peace	After Mobilisation		
AUSTRALIA	4,872,000	?	65,000	298,000	416,800
AUSTRIA-HUNGARY	49,900,00	450,000	3,350,000	2,229,500	7,800,000
BELGIUM	7,517,000	47,500	177,000	145,000	267,000
BULGARIA	5,500,000	66,000	850,000	425,000	1,200,000
CANADA	7,400,000	3,000	32,000	364,00	620,000
FRANCE	39,600,000	739,000	3,781,000	2,794,000	8,660,000
GERMANY	67,000,000	880,000	4,500,000	4,200,000	13,400,000
GREECE	4,800,000	?	c.150,000	c.250,000	280,000
INDIA	316,000,000	223,700	—	654,000	1,680,000
ITALY	35,000,000	310,000	875,000	2,274,000	5,903,000
JAPAN	67,200,000	c.240,000	—	272,000	800,000
NEW ZEALAND	1,050,000	30,000	8,430	30,000	128,525
PORTUGAL	6,000,000	32,000	150,000	35,000	200,000
ROMANIA	7,510,000	100,000	564,000	—	?
RUSSIA	167,000,000	1,400,000	5,000,000	—	12,000,000
SERBIA	5,000,000	30,000	460,000	110,500	707,000
SOUTH AFRICA	6,000,000	57,000	50,000	9,000	231,000
TURKEY	21,300,000	235,000	?	930,000	2,600,000
UNITED KINGDOM	46,400,000	247,500	733,500	3,196,000	5,704,400
UNITED STATES	92,000,000	208,000	—	1,982,000	4,355,000

Title: Manpower of the Belligerents 1914–18

Military Casualties and Civilian Deaths 1914–18

No-one in 1914 was prepared for death on this scale. Military planners had expected a short but violent conflict, but the number of wounded men and prisoners of war was many times larger than anyone had anticipated. The sheer scale of death left Europe, and much of the world, deeply traumatized.

The numbers, frightening as they are, nevertheless hide some terrible patterns. For the first time in the history of warfare many of the battlefield dead had no remains to bury, a testament to the awesome power of modern artillery. Thus did states have to create enormous memorials to the missing, such as those at Thiepval on the Somme and the Menin Gate in Ypres. They contain tens of thousands of names. The French tended to create mass graves instead of memorials for the same reason. Many wounded men had also suffered from horrifying and disfiguring wounds. The French called men wounded in the face the gueules cassées, the 'men with the broken jaws'. Others, poisoned by gas, had trouble breathing or seeing. Men who had lost limbs had to learn to walk again or pursue new civilian occupations. They also required expensive and lengthy postwar medical treatment.

Legacies and Dark Years

The loss of so many young men had dramatic psychological and demographic effects across Europe. Because so much of military recruitment was locally based from 1914 to 1918, many communities felt the impact of the war in the loss of nearly all of their young men. The French especially saw a massive decline in birth rates in the 1930s that they attributed to the loss of so many young men. France called those years les années noires, the 'Dark Years'.

Military Casualties and Civilian Deaths 1914–18

Country	Population	Number Served in Forces	Killed/ Missing	Wounded	P.O.W.	Total Killed/ Wounded & Missing	Total Civilian Deaths
AUSTRALIA	4,872,000	416,800	53,560	155,130	3,650	208,690	—
AUSTRIA-HUNGARY	49,900,000	7,800,000	1,016,200 539,630	? 1,943,240	1,691,000 2,118,190	? 2,482,870	? ?
BELGIUM	7,517,000	267,000	38,170	44,690	10,200	82,860	c. 30,000
BULGARIA	5,500,000	1,200,000	77,450	152,400	10,620	229,850	c. 275,000
CANADA	7,400,000	620,000	58,990	149,710	2,820	208,700	—
FRANCE	39,600,000	8,660,000	1,385,300	4,329,200	446,300	5,714,500	c. 40,000
GERMANY	67,000,000	13,400,000	2,037,000	5,687,000	993,800	6,400,000	c. 700,000
GREECE	4,800,000	280,000	c. 5,000	c. 20,000	c. 1,000	c. 25,000	c. 130,000
INDIA	316,000,000	1,680,000	62,060	66,690	11,070	128,750	—
ITALY	35,000,000	5,903,000	462,400	955,000	530,000	1,417,400	?
JAPAN	67,200,000	800,000	?	?	—	1,970	—
NEW ZEALAND	1,050,000	128,525	16,710	41,320	500	58,030	—
PORTUGAL	6,000,000	200,000	7,220	13,751	6,680	c. 40,000	—
ROMANIA	7,510,000	?	219,800	c. 120,000	c. 60,000	455,700	265,000 to 500,000
RUSSIA	167,000,000	12,000,000	c. 1,800,000	c. 4,950,000	c. 2,500,000 to 3,910,000	c. 6,750,000 to 5,310,000	c. 2,000,000
SERBIA	5,000,000	707,000	127,500	133,150	70,000 to 200,000	160,400	c. 600,000
SOUTH AFRICA	6,000,000	231,000	7,120	12,030	1,540	19,150	?
TURKEY	21,300,000	2,600,000	236,000	770,000	145,000	1,006,000	c. 2,000,000
UNITED KINGDOM	46,400,000	5,704,400	702,410	1,662,625	170,389	2,365,035	1,386
UNITED STATES	92,000,000	4,355,000	51,822	230,074	4,434	255,896	—

Index